Grid Computing

The Savvy Manager's Guides
Series Editor, Douglas K. Barry

Grid Computing
Pawel Plaszczak
Richard Wellner, Jr.

Semantics in Business Systems
Dave McComb

Business Intelligence
David Loshin

Web Services and Service-Oriented Architecture
Douglas K. Barry

Grid Computing

The Savvy Manager's Guide

Pawel Plaszczak
Richard Wellner, Jr.

ELSEVIER

AMSTERDAM • BOSTON • HEIDELBERG • LONDON
NEW YORK • OXFORD • PARIS • SAN DIEGO
SAN FRANCISCO • SINGAPORE • SYDNEY • TOKYO

Morgan Kaufmann Publishers is an imprint of Elsevier

MORGAN KAUFMANN PUBLISHERS

Senior Editor	Rick Adams
Publishing Services Manager	Simon Crump
Project Manager	Brandy Lilly
Assistant Editor	Mona Buehler, Rachel Roumeliotis
Cover Design	Francis Bacca
Cover Image	"Teotitlán" by Pawel Plaszczak
Text Design	Julio Esperas
Composition	SPI Publisher Services
Technical Illustration	Dartmouth Publishing, Inc.
Copyeditor	SPI Publisher Services
Proofreader	SPI Publisher Services
Indexer	SPI Publisher Services
Interior printer	The Maple-Vail Book Manufacturing Group
Cover printer	Phoenix Color

Morgan Kaufmann Publishers is an imprint of Elsevier.
500 Sansome Street, Suite 400, San Francisco, CA 94111

This book is printed on acid-free paper.

Library of Congress Cataloging-in-Publication Data

Plaszczak, Pawel.
   Grid computing : the savvy manager's guide / Pawel Plaszczak, Richard Wellner, Jr.
    p. cm.
   Includes bibliographical references and index.
   ISBN 0-12-742503-9 (alk. paper)
  1. Computational grids (Computer systems) I. Wellner, Richard. II. Title.

   QA76.9.C58P65 2005
   004¢.36–dc22

                       2005012671

ISBN-13: 978-0-1274-2503-0
ISBN-10: 0-12-742503-9

For information on all Morgan Kaufmann publications,
visit our Web site at www.mkp.com or www.books.elsevier.com

Printed in the United States of America
05 06 07 08 09 5 4 3 2 1

Contents

Foreword

Like many disruptive technologies before it, such as the Internet and Web, the Grid was initially motivated by the needs of scientists. Originally designed to facilitate access to high-end computational resources such as supercomputers, the Grid quickly expanded to enable sharing of a wide range of resources including storage, networks, and scientific instruments such as microscopes, x-ray sources, and earthquake engineering test facilities. Common to all of these applications was the need to form and maintain distributed virtual communities within which resources could be pooled and applied to common problems.

As the Grid enters its second decade, its applications are extending far beyond these pioneering scientific users. The need to share resources to achieve common goals turns out to be fundamental to commerce as well as science. Whether to support business processes across partners in a supply chain, facilitate collaborative engineering among subcontractors, or enable higher utilization of resources spread across business units, resource sharing provided by Grid technologies is becoming increasingly critical to a wide range of business and commercial activities.

As the Grid crosses the boundary from elite scientific research into mainstream business, the supporting literature needs to change and support the new audience. So far, the Grid has been described primarily in scientific articles. The few books that have been published on the subject have been written in technical language and directed to an academic audience or to developers ready to get down in the trenches.

For these reasons, this is a timely book: the savvy manager needs to know about the Grid; what makes it tick; and how it can be used in his or her organization to decrease costs, improve performance, and enable business processes that would otherwise be intractable. Pawel Plaszczak and Richard Wellner take on the brave task of addressing this need and provide the first ever comprehensive, yet compact work directed to CEOs, IT managers, planners, and decision makers, and those who are interested in deploying and using the Grid paradigm without necessarily programming it. They explain why Grid is important and provide the information needed to evaluate whether a transition to Grid is right for you, and how to plan such a move.

The authors of this book are particularly well qualified to make the case for Grid computing to the business IT manager. Both have been intimately involved in developing and deploying Grid technology and applications for many years. Pawel and Richard have both been major contributors to the open source Globus Toolkit, the most widely used Grid infrastructure to date. In addition to their deep knowledge of the fundamental technology, they have both also been part of the commercial sector, developing applications of Grid technology with major corporations.

In this book, Pawel and Richard provide the background knowledge that the savvy manager needs to understand the potential of the Grid for his or her organization. A rich assortment of case studies illustrates the range of problems that the Grid is being used to solve and will aid the reader in identifying which of their problems are "Grid" problems. These case studies also show how to get started and introduce the steps that should be followed to incorporate the Grid into existing IT infrastructures.

The impact of the Grid is already being felt, as corporations roll out large deployments and ISVs start to Grid-enable their products. However, "you ain't seen nothing yet": the next ten years will be exciting indeed and seem likely to lead to radical changes in the way that we interact with our IT infrastructure. With this book, you, the "savvy manager," can understand how to gain benefits today and how to be prepared for the future. We think that you will find it an interesting and useful read.

Ian Foster and Carl Kesselman

Preface

When we first conceived this book in late 2003, it was rapidly becoming evident that the world of Grid computing was about to change. At that time, there were a number of large software vendors beginning to adopt Grid nomenclature in their proposals. A few began tying their products to Grid idioms, and even a couple were starting to take Grid computing into account when developing new versions of their software and producing product roadmaps for their customers. At that time, however, there was a great deal of confusion regarding the principles of Grid computing, what the value in placing those principles into action would be, and how to execute a Grid strategy. It was with this consternation in mind that we undertook the effort to distill best practices from those already doing Grid computing and to understand the direction that various software companies were headed for their products to take advantage of this new paradigm.

During the course of writing this book, we've seen several companies come to market with new Grid products, the advancement of Grid standards in both major infrastructure areas, the beginnings of standards for vertical markets, and, near and dear to our hearts, the creation of our two Grid companies (Gridwise Technologies and Univa Corporation). It is even clearer today than it was a couple of years ago that Grid technology is gaining traction and can be a powerful problem solver in many different areas.

Motivation

Grid computing is now entering its second decade. We've seen a huge amount of change already, and there is now a large pool of experience to draw from—to stand on the shoulders of giants if you will. As early practitioners in the field, we've seen a lot of the same patterns repeat themselves. Some of them are great, and some of them are intuitive but flawed approaches that have better solutions. The need for a book like this was apparent in nearly every conversation we had with our customers and peers. With this book, many people will be able to short circuit some of these paths and better implement Grid solutions in their organizations.

Audience

When contemplating writing one of the first books on the subject of Grid computing that isn't merely a compilation of various research papers, we first had to determine where best to target our efforts. Given the numerous available toolkits and specifications being written, and the generally rapid state of advancement in the technology side of the business, it became obvious that a book about how to think about these things and how to position them in business would be helpful. This book does that. With that target in mind, we've written for an audience of team leaders with direct responsibility for implementing systems on up through directors and executive team management with a need for understanding the broad patterns in the industry today and the direction things will go in the future.

Organization

Many people are still unfamiliar with the concepts of Grid computing. As such, this book takes a step back from the topic and begins instead with the history of the Grid and builds from more common technologies (such as high performance computing [HPC], distributed computing, Web services, and cluster technologies) to illustrate how over the last decade the ideas of the Grid have been built on the foundation of knowledge created by previous generations of technology.

With this foundation in place, we discuss the various ways in which companies today are using these platforms. We introduce case studies that demonstrate how Grid technology has been adopted by companies in several different vertical markets. We also decode the terminology used in the industry today, showing that even in an industry with two dozen plus terms for various kinds of "grids," there are major themes and concepts. This allows a path for greater enlightenment than rote memorization of buzzwords.

Building further on this knowledge, we next begin our presentation of how to adopt Grid technology into an enterprise. This work is a mix of best practices gleaned from our work and those of others in the industry, a discussion of how these practices were arrived at, and also some advice about what we, as people who have worked in the Grid since before its emergence as a popular methodology, believe folks are missing out on. With these high-level concepts in place, we spend a bit of time talking about the issues that managers have to deal with every day (e.g., security, storage, network planning, execution management) and how these old concerns are dealt with on the Grid.

Finally, we talk about Grid computing from the viewpoint of exploiting it as a competitive advantage. We touch on many of the questions that consistently reappear when talking with people who are doing Grid efforts and give answers consistent with the recurring themes from early adopters. We also spend time talking about how the Grid fits into the sociological framework of enterprise and the kinds of issues that must be considered when selling the concept to both other managers and staff.

By reading this book, a manager will walk away with a very broad Grid computing knowledge base, from its beginnings to implementing systems using it today.

Acknowledgments

Writing this book has been an interesting exploration of the various projects we've seen and worked with during the last several years. We must first thank our families whose support has allowed us to be successful in a demanding field with highly variable hours. Karolina, Helenka, newborn Janek, Beth, Sarah, and Jason indirectly devoted more time, energy, and patience to this book than anyone else.

We have been fortunate to work with a large variety of talented people, all of whom were instrumental in the production of this book: people who agreed to allow us to publicly talk about their projects, those who allowed us to reference their work anonymously, those who provided introductions, and others doing interesting work.

The Grid community is one of tens of thousands of developers from around the world. Many people contributed to this effort; any omissions from the list that follows are inadvertent.

Without the efforts of the Grid community as a whole, this idea would not be nearly as successful as it has been. This is a field where community is a critically important concept to getting work done which advances the craft. We specifically thank Ian Foster, Steve Tuecke, and Carl Kesselman for their foundational work in the field and for the fun we've had working with them in both research and commercial spaces.

All of those listed here were helpful in providing us with information about their institutions, deployed Grid solutions, advice, or technology knowledge in general. Some devoted a significant amount of time to reviewing the manuscript. We want to give warm thanks to them all.

In the parentheses we indicate the subject of our consultations.

- Miha Ahronovitz, Sun Microsystems (Sun N1 Grid Engine)
- Charles Bacon (Globus details)
- Doug Barry, Barry & Associates (Web services, plus advice on writing in general)
- John Breshnahan (data transport)
- Marian Bubak, Cyfronet (the CrossGrid project)
- Randy Butler, NCSA (NEESgrid)
- Lisa Childers (Timeline and Globus information)
- Karl Czajkowski (execution management)
- Charlie Dibsdale, DS&S (Rolls-Royce and DS&S case study)
- David F. Dobel, DS&S (Rolls-Royce and DS&S case study)
- Agnieszka Dyduch-Cichocka, Deloitte (IT risk management)
- Jakub Dziwisz, Gridwise (Grid portals)
- Tomasz Farana, MGI (investment advisory practices)
- Tom Finholt, University of Michigan (NEESgrid)
- Mike Fisher, BT (Web services)
- Ian Foster, Argonne National Laboratory and University of Chicago (reviewed all material)
- Patrick Fuhrmann (storage systems)
- Robert Gaffaney (reviewer)
- Wolfgang Gentzsch, MCNC and formerly Sun (comprehensive guidance on several subjects)
- Scott Gose, Argonne Laboratory and University of Chicago (The Grid Report)
- Andrew Grimshaw, University of Virginia and formerly Avaki (Avaki and Legion)
- Urs Hoelzle, Google (Google)
- Lothlórien Homet, Morgan Kaufmann (useful advice on writing in general)
- Paul Hubbard (embedded systems tutorials and other training)
- Hiroki Inatomi, IDG Japan (The Grid World 2004)
- Tom Jackson, University of York (White Rose Grid, DAME)

- Fred James, Sun Microsystems (use of Sun Grid Engine in Synopsys)
- Carl Kesselman, Information Science Institute in University of Southern California (reviewed all material and provided many constructive remarks)
- Nolin LeChasseur, Platform (Human Factors in Grids)
- Joseph Link (data transfer)
- Satoshi Matsuoka, Tokyo Institute of Technology (the Ninf project)
- Sam Meder (security)
- Rich Miller (business case)
- Robert Niedziela, Sabre (Sabre GDS)
- Jason Novotny, GridSphere (Grid portals)
- Robert Ortega, Wachovia (Wachovia Grid experience)
- Simon Oxlade, DS&S (very thorough and useful corrections of material on Rolls-Royce and DS&S case study)
- Louise Pattison (Rolls-Royce and DS&S case study)
- Laura Pearlman (security and retrofitting applications)
- Timur Perelmutov (storage system discussions)
- Don Petravick (early Grid adopter from Fermilab)
- Ruth Pordes (architect of early Argonne/Fermilab collaboration)
- Bernadeta Raczkiewicz, Gridwise (style corrections)
- Ann Redelfs, GridToday (GridToday04)
- Peggy Rosenthal, Sabre (very helpful comments on Sabre GDS)
- Michael Russel, Gridsphere (Grid portals)
- Borja Satomayor (general information and a great tutorial)
- Satoshi Sekiguchi, AIST (the Ninf project and the Japanese perspective on Grid computing)
- Brad Shea, Wachovia (Wachovia Grid experience)
- Sriram Sitaraman, Synopsys (Synopsys Grid experience)
- Jim Snow, OGI School of Science & Engineering (Google)
- Bill Spencer, NCSA (comprehensive interview on NEESgrid and earthquake science perspective)
- Andy Stubbings, BestSystems (the Japanese Grid activities, The Grid World 2004)

- Michal Turala, IFJ (CrossGrid, and other general advice)
- Alan Walker, Sabre (Sabre GDS)
- Vicky White (early Grid adopter from Fermilab)
- Krzysztof Wilk, Gridwise (general help)
- Scott Yates, MCNC (MCNC Grid use case)

CHAPTER | 1

Introduction

Why do people talk about Grid computing? Why would a designer like to rent computers by the hour? Why would an engineering company send away its confidential data for remote processing? How could an investor trust information from someone he has never heard of? What is common between a Web search engine and an airline ticket reservation? In this chapter we learn by example.

If one could name one feature distinguishing the Eastern and Western historical mentality, it might be an understanding of time and place in history. People of the many great Eastern cultures have perceived time as an endless loop and have sought happiness in finding harmony between the self and the cycles of the nature. Taoism taught its practitioners to surrender to the forces of fate instead of fighting them. Confucianism preferred obeying strict societal rules over innovation. Indian perspective of reincarnation diminished the role of a single life. Egypt regulated its life along the annual cycles of the Nile for thousands of years until the Aswan dam was constructed. Even in early ancient Greece, the meaning of history was diminished by the myth of eternal return. Contrarily, people in Western cultures have always believed in their contemporary epoch being historically unique. Crossing the Red Sea by the Jews in 1600 B.C. was remembered in the memory of generations as an event of dramatic historical consequences. The Romans believed that their conquests would change the world forever, and indeed they were correct. One thousand years later the German emperor Otto III hurriedly tried to reconstruct the Roman Empire before the year 1000, which was commonly believed to bring about the end of the world. Marxists in the early twentieth century, and then technocrats in the 1930s, believed that the Earth was only one step from Utopia, where the dictatorship of the proletariat or the miracles of technology would transform the world into a better place. Western people have always thought the time they lived in was special and that their deeds, achievements, and discoveries would make a difference in the life of the coming generations.

At the turn of the second millennium, when Western and Eastern thinking interacts and contributes to our common heritage, we believe more than ever that we live in a special period of history. The world goes through profound changes at an amazing pace for us, unbelievable for our parents, and surpassing the imaginations of our grandparents. In less than a generation most of the world's powerful dictatorships have been disassembled, the Earth has transformed into the global village, and the revolution of digital media has radically changed the way we work and communicate. At the same time, the delicate balance of the planet's ecosystem has been threatened by devastation and pollution at the highest rate in history, the world was shocked by the horror of terrorism, and we have watched in astonishment how a crisis in Asia immediately affected life in Europe and America as a result of the globalized economy.

Changes in the political sphere are closely linked to economical conditions, and economic conditions are often driven by rapid technological progress. Since the Internet became ubiquitous, the so-called net effect has boosted the spiral of information exchange, innovation, and added technological value. In the virtual sphere, entire new industries come into being and disappear almost overnight. As the economy becomes global, technology evolves into one more ubiquitous, distributed, mobile, and on-demand system. These analoguous trends in economics and technology are two sides of the same process. In an economical and political sphere this process became known as globalization. In technology, some call it Grid computing.

As today's IT industry speaks ever more about Grid computing, the term has become a kind of a buzzword, often misapplied or used with different meanings. Some example definitions from mainstream publications are "large scale resource sharing," "harnessing idle processors to do some work," "vitalizing data resources for easier access," "optimizing utilization of computing resources," or simply "The Next Big Thing." What do these statements have in common? What really is Grid computing? What is the Grid? Why should I be interested, as a businessman, manager, technical leader, engineer, student, or an employee affected by the change? Should my company "plug in"? What are the opportunities and dangers brought by the Grid? How should one prepare the decision, plan, and execute the migration to Grid architectures and Grid-enabling of one's applications?

During the last decade of growth in the IT industry, several forces have arisen as a result of continuing improvement in CPU[1] speeds, network speeds,

---

[1] Central Processing Unit; computer's processor

network pervasiveness, and data capacity. Moore's law[2] has been at work and every desktop machine now has far more power than is needed 99 percent of the time.[3] Our desktops spend the vast majority of their time sitting idle. Networking has improved from a few kilobytes per second to hundreds or thousands of megabytes per second; at the same time it is unusual to find a machine not connected to a corporate network or the Internet. Finally, in the last 20 years disk capacity has increased from a few megabytes to hundreds of gigabytes on desktops and many terabytes on servers.

While these developments have occurred, business pressures have consistently forced companies to seek new and innovative ways to enhance the flow of their operations. A car manufacturer wants to conduct simulations with maximal precision to come up with a competitive design of a new auto model. A bank might desire to process ever larger sets of historical data to better forecast the coming months. A pharmaceutical researcher who has access to remote scientific data can make faster progress in developing a new medicine. Hardware servicing firms may want to constantly monitor remote structures and machinery belonging to their clients. Finally, dislocated teams of software developers want to access collaborative environments enabling them to cooperate on a common source code.

Grid computing, which deals with resource sharing,[4] provides abstraction and technology addressing such issues. These are problems characterized by distribution, resource heterogeneity, large scale, and the need for collaboration, at the same time requiring guaranteed levels of reliability, safety, security, and quality of service.

Implementing Grid solutions presents challenges. Permitting the use of resources that were otherwise tightly controlled demands that proper security measures exist. Large-scale resource sharing demands scalability and interoperability of the participating systems. Methods for service discovery, metering, accounting, and billing need to be in place to enable effective sharing even within the same organization. Policies for access control need to be carefully defined to ensure that resource usage does not exceed the available limits for CPU, storage, licenses, bandwidth, and a number of other technology and contract related metrics.

---

[2] Moore's law states that the amount of computing power available per dollar doubles every 18 to 24 months.

[3] We indeed think so. However, it is natural that some readers will find a number of our statements (like this one) provocative. These readers are invited to log in to the online book companion at www.savvygrid.com and share their opinions.

[4] The notion of a resource will be explained in Chapter 2. For now, an intuitive understanding will suffice for the discussion. A processing unit (CPU) and a storage element (hard drive) are examples of resources.

This savvy manager guide will help you navigate those challenges. It discusses in detail the approach needed to quickly integrate Grid services into your business. In doing so we describe various tools available to help you achieve this goal. The book provides a look at the standard processes that make Grid computing possible. It also describes how Grid services can be built using time-tested software production methods.

In addition to explaining the value of Grid computing to your organization, we also present technical sections with overview of many of the standards, technologies, products, and methodologies used to build the Grid. This book provides referrals to the best places to continue your education and begin the training of your technical staff.

This book is designed to be read in order. The first two chapters describe the origin of the the ideas for the Grid, what it is designed to do, and why a savvy manager should be interested in pursuing it today. Chapter 3 focuses on the opportunities available for those pursuing Grid solutions. In particular, we present the taxonomy of existing and possible Grid installations and describe their building blocks and the representative products offered in this market. In this context, we characterize vendor groups and other groups of interest active in the field, knowledge that is of primary importance for any entrepreneur entering a new business niche.

Chapter 4 describes the various schemes by which you can participate in the Grid or otherwise use Grid technologies. This guide considers the situation of today's market as well as the business opportunities of the near future, as foreseen in the most probable scenario by the community and a number of forward-thinking enterprises. This discussion is continued in Chapter 5, which on a slightly lower level gives a glimpse of several technical issues that need consideration in a typical Grid installation.

In addition to these subjects, Chapter 6 begins to introduce management issues that will be faced when attempting such a profound improvement in an organization. After those issues are understood, the building process continues with information on how to integrate Grid production with agile development techniques. By changing the kind of software being produced from monolithic applications to clearly delineated Grid services, agile mechanisms shine and provide good ways to control this new domain.

Every chapter of the book is supported by examples harvested from the experiences of early adopters. Chapter 1, "Introduction," discusses in detail two well-known systems existing today that share characteristics of the Grid. Chapter 2, "The Basics," speaks on the proto-Grid systems developed in the academia in the 1990s. Chapter 3, "Grid Computing Enters Business," describes representative Grid middleware solutions currently available commercially and presents two exhaustive case studies of nonprofit grid systems. Chapter 4, "Joining the Grid," is supported by three more case studies of early commercial adopters of the technology. The discussion on technical planning in Chapter 5 is supported by several real life examples, while large sections of Chapter 6, "Management Issues," are based on the experience of the Globus and NEESgrid project teams.

Although we describe a number of example projects of building or using grids in a number of business application domains, this book cannot serve as a definite guide for vertical Grid solutions in any of those domains. Vendors and consultants specializing in these markets should be consulted for these purposes. This book provides enough generic background information to allow you to feel confident communicating with vendors, and to help you choose wisely instead of being forced into proprietary solutions.

The entire book is supported by the online companion, available at www.savvygrid.com. The companion contains reference links to most of the online materials we consulted while writing the book. The links are ordered by the table of contents; thus the reader of any single section can easily refer to the online resources. At www.savvygrid.com we also plan to maintain an online book counterpart, complete with the errata, community portal, and new material complementary to the printed edition, ensuring that the reader is kept up to date. There are at least three reasons for us to maintain the online companion. First, the topic is very new. We acknowledge that there may be errors in the printed material, although we took care to minimize such errors with great help from our reviewers. The errata, if any, will appear online. Second, Grid technology is rapidly evolving and new business offerings reach the market every month. In the online companion, we will keep track of the products that appear on the market after this book was printed. Third, there are many definitions of Grid computing and some sections of this book will inevitably raise strong feelings in those with a different understanding of the subject. We address this delicate issue later. Meanwhile, we welcome you to log in to savvygrid.com to voice your opinion.

Problems of Today and Promise of Grid Computing

There are many applications that require access to specialized machines, data, or compute power. Applications that cannot practically be run on single large machines often can be broken down into pieces small enough to run on commodity platforms. It is common for an organization to run processes, which execute the same algorithm on large sets of data. Hewitt and Associates, for example, processed employee benefits packages and found that a small percentage of employees were taking a large percentage of the processing time. By spreading this load across many nodes on a mini-Grid, the company was able to reduce substantially the overall time necessary to process the entire set of employees.

Data transfer can be achieved in large quantities on modern networks. This statement, while true, belies the large amount of work necessary to move a lot of data reliably, which is necessary for effective data caching, replication, and distributed access. These problems can be properly handled in data grids that allow data-intensive applications to function in a location-transparent manner.

The specialized machines often used in research organizations coupled with Grid services allow staff to work from where it is best for them, instead of where it is best for the machines. This advantage is beneficial to the company because less frequent travel saves money for the company and reduces stress on those who would have had to travel. This can increase retention rates and lower costs of hiring new staff. However, in more general terms, Grid enables effective, secure, and cost-effective collaboration within and among organizations. This can enhance productivity and speed up progress, in much the same way that the Internet did in yesterday's economy.

A number of applications have already been deployed in a distributed fashion, which uses proprietary protocols to solve some of these problems. Grid technology allows them to be addressed using open mechanisms, which permit quicker integration and more rapid acceptance. As more companies begin to use Grid standards, more services will be available that a Grid-capable organization can use to implement higher-level applications.

A Vision of the Grid

The main problem with understanding Grid computing today is the confusion on its meaning. We will explore this in detail in the next chapter. But first let's have a glimpse at what Grid technology can deliver in the near future. The examples and the company names are imaginary.

Example 1: Techman Runs Simulations Using On-Demand CPU-hours

Techman is a young engineering company. They have just won a contract to design new machinery for the manufacturing plant Robotix. It is the first time that the company has been awarded a contract of such value, and the investors are glad that the young enterprise is already perceived to be mature enough for such an important project. This is an opportunity not to be missed. Techman cannot afford failure, which may result in its being viewed as a second-string player in the eyes of potential big customers as well as venture capitalists.

Techman is now in a bind; staff skills present no problem, but the required precision of the simulation process would take months of processing on its desktop machines. This is not acceptable as the processing would go beyond the delivery date.

To deliver the contract in time, Techman might invest in extra equipment, but this solution would jeopardize the profitability of the project. Hardware assets rapidly lose value with the amortization period of two to three years. Investment in hardware can be justified if consistent usage is foreseen during this time, but not for the sole purpose of a few weeks of computations.

If the equipment cannot be purchased, the company must negotiate the delivery date, which will inevitably affect relations with the customer. The last, and rather unattractive, option is to cut on the simulation requirements and deliver the project on time, but with an inferior quality design that did not go through a complete modeling and testing schedule. Each of the three scenarios brings considerable risks and stress to the management, not to mention the engineers.

The problem has an interesting solution. Techman's client, Robotix, has several hundred machines that are involved in office transactions during productivity peaks but are idle the remaining time. It would be in the interest of both parties to deploy the spare cycles for the modeling process. However, it can be easily seen that such a solution is not realistic with today's business infrastructure, technology, and management attitude.

The first barrier is the complex technical limitations. The simulation software used by Techman does not scale well. The graphical user interface is tightly integrated with the computational module. Such software is designed to run on a single host and simulations cannot be submitted to a remote machine. Also, a host-centered licensing model poses a limit. On the Robotix side, the infrastructure is different in terms of architectures and operating systems. The entire resource base is behind a firewall, which would disable two-way communication frequently needed during a typical simulation process (after one iteration is complete, the engineers often want to personally adjust the parameters and rerun the simulation). Finally, introduction of the third-party processes poses a threat to stability, safety, and security of core applications running on the

Robotix hardware. Thus, preparing a runtime environment for distributed simulations would require a considerable engineering effort.

The second barrier is institutional and political. The policies and procedures of both companies (related to ownership, security, auditing, accounting, etc.) do not anticipate assigning the resources outside of a traditional workflow. These procedures would need to be revisited, with any attempts at modifications inevitably causing formal and legal problems and resulting in rather lengthy procedures. Several issues need consideration, such as the already mentioned system stability issue or the presence of third-party confidential information on the potentially affected machines.

Last but not least, there is a psychological aspect. The practice of sharing resources is essentially unheard of today. Depending on the technological awareness of the management of both companies, they may refuse such a move, investigate the maturity of the technology, or request a report on similar solutions existing in production today. Thus use of Robotix resources is impossible for Techman. Techman must find another way to deliver the contract, and it does not seem to have many options.

Let us project our story to the near future, where solutions to these problems have been provided by Grid technology.

In this future world Techman is using simulation software compliant to Grid standards and is capable of running on multiple hosts in parallel. Because the infrastructure at the Robotix site comes with Grid-enabled middleware, running the computations on Robotix resources requires minimal integration effort. The middleware also provides the security and safety of the runtime environment to shield Robotix systems from threats and side effects coming from the hosted software. The middleware also provides metering and accounting features so that both parties can audit the resource usage. The simulation code runs in a sandbox and is not able to interfere with local applications. Local administrators can set policies to differentiate application priorities and guarantee that core tasks get enough resources in case of conflicts.

Techman will ask its client Robotix for permission to use its spare compute cycles. Techman will explain that the design will go through superior quality testing and modeling without additional cost. The proposition is a clear win-win scenario with a high likelihood of success.

Beyond capabilities at Robotix, Techman could search for compute cycles elsewhere. With established standards for Grid interfaces, there will be several resource providers capable of running Techman's simulation processes. The price will be considerably less than the cost of hardware purchase and maintenance.

Yet another alternative for Techman is to actually purchase the needed hardware, especially if more design contracts are expected in near future. Even if some of these prospects disappear, Techman could itself become a resource provider for other companies and recover a significant part of the expense.

Note that although none of these scenarios is common today, the world is not far from their implementation. The presence of established, stable, non-proprietary standards and middleware is a major missing piece of the puzzle. In the near future, such alternatives may become a reality for businesses worldwide thanks to Grid technology.

Example 2: HydroTech Offers Secure, Remote Processing of Sensitive Data

HydroTech specializes in analysis and optimization of sewers and industry liquid pipeline infrastructure. It has been around for a long time and is a recognized expert in its field. Its client, Petrolium, is evaluating its new design of the factory pipeline system and would like HydroTech to optimize the design. HydroTech had purchased specialized software for such optimizations, complete with hardware capable of running compute-intensive simulations. HydroTech, as a specialist in the field, also has qualified staff to operate the software. Naturally, the process needs to use data supplied by Petrolium.

Unfortunately, the licensing policy does not allow installing some of the required software on Petrolium machines, where the source data are located. On the other hand, Petrolium is not willing to send the confidential data to HydroTech. HydroTech is, after all, an expert in the field and as such does work for a number of different firms. This includes some who are direct competitors of Petrolium; thus the data may be exposed to a third party. Because of the value of the confidential materials, the risk is too high. Thus although the two parties are willing to cooperate, they are blocked by technical issues.

Let us imagine a technology in which applications and data sets can be abstracted as resources (Figure 1.1). Each resource can be accessed remotely according to its individual policy. Thus HydroTech is able to securely grant rights to its customer to access the optimization software. On the Petrolium side, the secret data has been configured as a Grid resource as well. Its policy says that it can be accessed only by the aforementioned application from the HydroTech machine. It also says that any results or by-product of this operation must be sent back to the Petrolium site and cannot be stored elsewhere. Third-party middleware installed at both parties guarantees the correct execution of these policies.

An engineer from Petrolium personally accesses the remote system and runs the simulation on his secret data. Although it is HydroTech's machines that have been running the simulation, the underlying technology guarantees

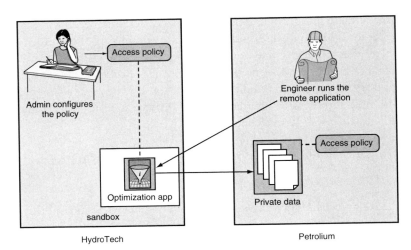

FIGURE 1.1 HydroTech and Petrolium

that the data will be used only for a particular purpose. Specifically, HydroTech can access the data only by means of the designated optimizing application. The technology also guarantees that no leftover data have remained in the system. After the experiment, the customer can audit the job. All transactions have automatically been logged, so that Petrolium can ensure that its data have not been exposed to any security risks. Both sides accomplished their goals without exposing each other to confidential information.

As we will see later, virtualizing assets as abstract resources is one of the key features of Grid technology, which can soon enable scenarios like this one.

Example 3: InvestIT Automatically Acquires Information on Foreign Markets for Niche Customers

InvestIT is a middle size investment adviser who is managing customer financial portfolios. It analyzes financial results of stock companies. The bulk of the technical analysis can be sped up with automatic tools, which process the raw data, and present the results to the adviser in human friendly fashion, which eases the decision making. InvestIT has developed in-house analysis software for this purpose. The software feeds on data available from the stock exchange broker in a standardized form.

A new customer is interested in augmenting her portfolio with foreign IT sector stock from various countries in Europe. She sends in a list of potentially interesting company names and asks for comparative analysis of growth potential and risk. However, the relevant data are not available from the local broker who only signed an agreement with domestic data providers. InvestIT has to first search and determine where to get the data. In some cases the information may be available from other brokerage offices. In other cases, the company needs to deal with institutions abroad. Data from abroad are available in various formats, which the local software is unable to understand. Even when the format follows generic conventions, the data are incompatible because they are prepared for different processing software. Even the descriptions are in foreign languages. Analysis of the list of companies can actually be done faster manually. The price of labor for the contract increases several times, and the customer eventually concludes that InvestIT is not prepared to manage her assets.

As the Grid becomes more commonly available, many of these obstacles will disappear. The financial data providers in this example will expose their resources via Grid standard interfaces. The in-house software from InvestIT would be either integrated with Grid-enabled client middleware, or the InvestIT staff might write code, which speaks Grid protocols. Both of those solutions provide InvestIT with the ability to contact the data provider over secure protocols.

If the provider cannot offer the requested data, there are online directories listing all available providers (Figure 1.2). A query sent to such a directory will initiate a list of providers who are in possession of the information in question. In this example there would be many firms with data about past performance on the European markets. The result of the query also returns other information, such as pricing and the guaranteed quality of service, so that the best offer can be automatically identified. The request is sent to the remote data provider and, as occurred with the local provider, data become immediately available. Soon after, the billing information is also received and processed.

Before processing the data, InvestIT software checks its integrity and ensures that it comes from the trusted source. The certificate chain of trust assures them that the data provider is indeed the company in question, and all the intermediaries have been identified, are known entities, and their quality of service is guaranteed by the well-known financial bodies.

All this happens automatically, only notifying the InvestIT staff in case something is identified as being wrong. Removing this verification task from the financial adviser allows the adviser to focus on the analysis of the results instead of secretarial tasks, market survey, or phone calls.

Implementation of this story will take much less effort than we might think. For instance, note that the foreign companies have already been supplying the data in the format understood in their countries. They will now only need to make this data accessible through interfaces compliant to Grid

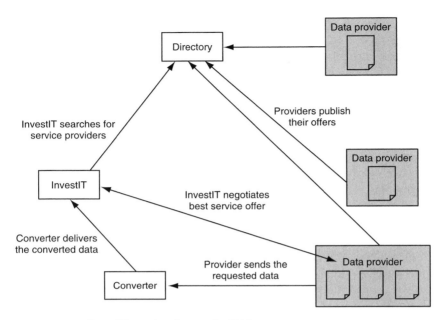

FIGURE 1.2 InvertIT acquires data on the Grid

standards; they do not need to modify their tools and interfaces. They might instead sign an agreement with an online service that is providing conversion services between local formats and standardized Grid interfaces. The query process initiated by InvestIT would in this case only contact that converter service. The converter will automatically poll the data from the foreign provider, convert the data, and present the information to InvestIT in a digestible form. InvestIT does not need to know about the details of the process or even that the process is taking place. It knows only that it is contacting an arbitrary resource to get the stock data it needs. However, once the data arrive, InvestIT can use the accompanying certificate chain to check on the credibility of the data. In particular, InvestIT can find out who the intermediaries were, who guarantees their identities, and who is responsible for any operations performed on the data before its arrival.

The Feel of the Grid Today

Can we experience the Grid today? Surprisingly, most people have already, in a sense, used it. In fact, there are many examples of commercial systems in use today that share the characteristics of the Grid. Before giving the precise definition of what constitutes Grid technology, we will look at some of these systems to have a better feeling of what elements of Grid computing are already present in the business infrastructure today.

Google and the World Wide Web

Established in 1998 by two Stanford researchers, Google soon became the world's most popular Web search engine. To stay on top, Google has to respond to customer needs. This means answering queries within a fraction of a second and with 100 percent uptime. All this needs to be happening in a dynamic environment of a constantly growing World Wide Web. Google needs to scale with the Web. During just the first four years, the Google web-site index has grown from 75 million to 3.5 billion pages.

However, Google not only has remained the uncontested leader among other Web search engines, such as Yahoo!, Inktomi, AllTheWeb, Mooter, Altavista, or Teoma, since 2001, Google has also been profitable. Among the keys to its success is the carefully designed computing infrastructure responsible for the execution of user queries. Ninety percent of the revenue comes from the keyword advertising. Other sources of revenue include Google-hosted customized search services or complete hardware/software products such as Google Search Appliance.

Popularity of the search engine is partly owed to automated search technology based on the patented PageRank scheme, which ensures that the content is relevant, useful, and objective. What also counts is the localized access that Google provides in several countries. However, one of the key success factors is the core principle of maximum simplicity of the user interface. Users only need to enter their search phrase, such as "Krakow train timetable," to receive the complete result set, with the most important pages listed first. Naturally, the site that shows the train connections from Krakow should be at the top, while the local news about the construction ongoing at the Krakow railway station would be somewhat less relevant (although quite possibly also worth looking at). Google should also guess that having limited knowledge of vowels and keyboard keys, the American vacationer typed Krakow when he really meant Kraków. Finally, the fact that the main timetable page is located on a distant server in Poland should not make a difference in locating and listing it on the first position.

Most users will quickly receive satisfactory results and move on to their next task, happily remaining unaware of the massive and sophisticated distributed backend system responsible for the query execution.

Google processes tens of thousands of user queries per second (Figure 1.3). Each query is first received by one of the Web servers, which passes it to

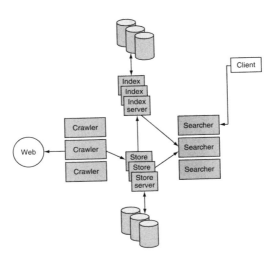

FIGURE 1.3 Google architecture overview

an array of index servers. The index servers maintain a huge index of words and phrases found at websites. Its size dictates distribution of the content over several machines so that the search could run in parallel. In a fraction of a second, the index servers perform a gigantic logical AND operation, returning references to the websites containing the searched phrase. The collection of references is then sent to the store servers, which maintain compressed copies of all pages known to Google. These are used to prepare page snippets, which, in PageRank-rated order, are finally presented to the user in a readable form. This is the result of the user's query.

At the same time, the team of crawler machines is continually combing through the Web, updating the Google database of known pages in the store servers and index servers. Walking down the Web like a spider, the crawler server connects to some remote Web servers, asking for particular pages. Then the page content is analyzed and the content of the Google store and index servers updated. Then the crawler jumps on to a new website, whose address is known from previously collected links. As the result of this ongoing activity, the store servers eventually contain relatively recent, compressed copies of all the pages currently available on the World Wide Web. In the same time, the index servers contain mapping between these pages and the search keywords associated with them. The validity of these huge data sets ensures correctness of the search process described previously.

How large of an infrastructure could ensure operation on such an enormous scale? Google maintains Linux clusters composed of several tens of thousands of machines, but the infrastructure has to scale with the growth of the Web. In 2004 Google expected to spend at least $250 million on capital equipment. It reported leasing 506,000 square feet of space in its headquarters in Mountain View, California, in addition to 24 other worldwide office locations. The system operation is maintained and analyzed by the R&D department, housing one third of Google's 2000 employees.

How does Google resemble Grid computing? The system relies on the interoperability of the Web servers worldwide, based on open, commonly accepted standards such as the HTTP protocol and the HTML-based technologies for building websites. The nature of the Web architecture imposes cooperation of the Web servers with all kind of clients, including search robots. Google makes maximal use of this fact. Web resources worldwide, belonging to various organizations and number of servers are shared with Google. Google is allowed to copy the content and transform it into its local resource: keyword database of the index servers and the cached content database of the store servers. These resources, in turn, are partially shared with human users who send in queries through their browsers. Users can then directly contact the original Web servers of their choice, to request the full content of the documents they are interested in.

Another type of resource indirectly shared by Google is its computing cycles. By performing data caching, ranking, and searching on behalf of the user, Google effectively shares its computing resources, such as storage and computing capabilities, with the end-user. Naturally, this "sharing" is very limited in functionality, but it is the only way to ensure the aforementioned simplicity of the user interface (imagine the alternative Google page where users would have to specify which data sets cached by Google should be searched).

Thus we have a highly distributed system composed of at least three types of entities (Web servers, Google intermediary, and users). They belong to various domains and organizations. Various data resources (Web pages, query result lists) are subject to sharing. Also hardware resources (processor cycles, storage) are shared in a certain way. The system is kept alive thanks to a simple economy ensuring a win-win operation. Website publishers are happy that Google makes them known and brings its content to the user. Some of them are even eager to pay money to ensure stronger ranking of their sites among the search results. Users are obviously happy because the Google engine automates search work that would otherwise not be possible. The one player that makes direct financial profit is Google itself, which, due to its popularity, is able to attract sponsors who pay for displaying its addresses among the search results.

Google and the World Wide Web can be seen as a prototype of Grid computing. The system spans several administrative domains, cooperates in sharing certain types of resources, and communicates with well-known, open protocols. Let us now reverse the question. Why aren't Google and the World Wide Web a full-fledged Grid? Why are we still talking about Grid in the future tense, while Google and the World Wide Web exist now?

First, in the Grid-computing paradigm, the meaning of a resource is broad (we will explore this in Chapter 2). Grid entities share resources such as the processing power, storage, or applications, not just the website data. Google, is a single-purpose system, basically devoted to one application. Tens of thousands of machines in Google data centers are dedicated to the goal of providing effective search results. In this particular case it is perfectly justifiable by continuous demand for this service. However, in most of today's business computing environments, the demand is subject to high fluctuations, and thus dedicated systems become inefficient. Grids of the future are envisioned as being composed of application-neutral platforms, spanning over resources from several providers. Various kinds of applications could be built on top, ensuring optimal resource utilization with minimal hardware cost.

Second, search engines rely on the assumption that the website providers share their resources for free. This may be true in case of generic Web traffic, but will not apply to a broader context, such as that of ASPs (application service providers) or network storage providers. In true Grid environments, resource sharing would be subject to strict economic rules, which in many cases would boil down to financial agreements. There would also be a number of similar issues, such as audit, accounting, metering, security, and reliability, for which the Grid environment would impose constrained regulations. Resource sharing processes would be coordinated by these policies.

As for the World Wide Web, it is often considered a predecessor to the Grid. What the Web offers to humans, the Grid will offer to machines. Today's websites are human-centric. They provide information and mechanisms suitable for people equipped with browsers, but are difficult to read and analyze by automated agents. Google can automatically cache and search through Web pages, but is limited in its ability to automatically deduce their meaning, categorize them, and store in a catalogue. The Google Web catalogue is prepared manually by volunteers of the DMOZ project. The Grid of the future will provide a platform analogical to the Web, but designed for machines that will be able to find resources, communicate, negotiate service conditions, request the service, and obtain results more efficiently than humans can.

Yet another important reason to differentiate between the Web and the Grid is the approach to security. Grid computing aims at secure resource sharing. This means that the communicating parties must first identify each other, after which each can make an autonomous decision, allowing the partner to access the resource. The communication that follows should take place over a secure channel, protected through encryption and integrity checking.

Instead, Google operates on the public network and scans only those servers that allow public access to their data. Also the users of Google can send queries without being identified. There is nothing wrong with this system, as the Web is designed for humans and the option of anonymity is perceived as a great advantage of the information society. Still, mutual identification of the dialoguers is a prerequisite for secure conversation. For this reason, the Web cannot be used for automated, secure resource sharing that is characteristic of the Grid.

Although Google is not part of the Grid now, it could easily leverage itself to such a position in the near future. Its enormous processing capabilities could be exposed through machine-readable standard Grid interfaces. Google could then join the Grid and be perceived by other participants as a Grid resource, providing them with a number of services. A prototype of such functionality is already accessible today through the Google Web API (application programmer interface).

Travelocity, Sabre, and Global Distribution Systems

Let us next consider Travelocity, the most popular travel portal. Travelocity provides online customers with the ability to browse through available airfares and purchase tickets. The online customer specifies his travel requirements such as home airport and destination and date, and within a few seconds the list of price-sorted fares is returned, complete with all additional information such as the airline, number of hops, and total travel time. The customer then selects the optimal connection and after a few more steps his ticket will have been booked, confirmed, and paid for. Short analysis reveals the unimaginably sophisticated procedure that needs to be put in motion to complete this scenario. The distributed system first needs to obtain the necessary information from various airlines, then apply variations of K-shortest path algorithm[5] to find and group the available fare options, and finally execute pricing and booking processes and ensure that both the customer and the specific airline reservation system confirm the agreement.

Travelocity is a wholly owned company of Sabre Holdings, an enterprise that controls about a third of the world's travel reservation market. Most of

---

[5] If the journey requires multiple hops, this algorithm is used to find the most cost- or time-effective connection.

the travel transactions of the world happen in the Global Distribution System (GDS). There are only four such systems in the world, with Sabre being the leader.

What are the origins of the GDS? Systems originally known as computer reservations systems (CRSs) were developed and owned by the airlines in which their booking and pricing took place. Sabre was created by American Airlines to operate its CRS. Even before the Internet was born, various CRSs were interconnected by a network. One of these networks was brought together by SITA, an international organization of airlines. The deregulation of airfares in 1979, rise of Internet TCP/IP connectivity, and the evolution of the market in the 1980s and 1990s induced consolidation of CRS systems and emergence of the handful of strongest CRS players, whose booking infrastructure was from now on known as GDS. At the same time, most airlines sold off their CRS shares, and the distinction between the airlines and reservation providers became clearer. The four strongest GDSs that emerged during this process are Sabre, which owns most of the North American market; Galileo/Apollo, which was developed by United Airlines, BA, Air Italia, KLM, and SAA; Amadeus, which was initially owned by Lufthansa, Iberia, and Air France; and Worldspan, which was associated with Delta and Northwest Airlines. These four dominate today's world fare booking market, with Sabre being the strongest.

Sabre, headquartered in Southlake, Texas, has 6000 employees in 45 countries. The reservation business of Sabre Holdings is based on its three companies. One of them, Sabre Travel Network, operates the GDS providing data from more than 400 airlines, not to mention the hotel companies, car rentals, and cruise and railroad operators. Travel data are supplied to 53,000 travel agencies worldwide, providing them with capabilities of searching through the fares and booking. The second Sabre company, Sabre Airline Solutions, provides products and services for more than 200 airlines. Apart from participating in the Sabre GDS, 90 of these airlines also host their reservation systems at Sabre. The other addition to the puzzle is Travelocity, one of the most popular Internet travel portals, allowing individuals to shop directly with Sabre, without the mediating role of a travel agency. More than two thirds of the Sabre Holdings revenue comes from Sabre Travel Network, while the remaining part is divided between Travelocity and Sabre Airline Solutions.

Figure 1.4 depicts the major components of the sophisticated worldwide ticket booking system developed and maintained by Sabre. Airlines host their own reservation systems, often using comprehensive software solutions such as SabreSonic suite from Sabre Airline Solutions, or competing products from

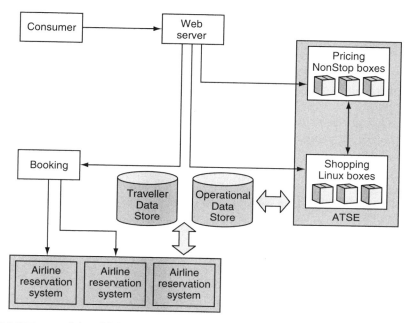

FIGURE 1.4 Sabre GDS

companies such as Sita, Navitaire, or Airkiosk. Their reservation system data contain the routes, schedules, and airfares that can be made available to the public through a variety of channels. The Sabre GDS is one of them. Airlines choosing this option connect to the Sabre systems using Seamless Connectivity protocols, allowing for real-time data synchronization. Airlines then pay Sabre for each flight segment booked. Many airlines, such as American and recently Aeroflot, have simplified their operation by hosting their reservation systems at Sabre. This means that a large chunk of its IT infrastructure, including the reservation database, is being outsourced to Sabre Airline Solutions. Currently Sabre sells hosting services to more than 90 airlines.

It should be noted that this picture has been significantly simplified. For instance, we have omitted other reservation data suppliers such as hotels, car rentals, cruise agencies, and railways. For instance, hotels often host their room availability databases at Utell, a subsidiary of Pegasus, a data supplier for Sabre.

The information from the reservation systems is available for the Sabre GDS engine, which deals with shopping, pricing, and booking. Independent travel agents, participating in the Sabre Travel Network, send in their queries to the GDS and then execute booking. Airlines then pay a booking fee for each segment booked by the travel agent, resulting in a significant stream of revenue for Sabre. Historically, the agent terminals were connected to Sabre systems using pre-Internet technologies such as X.25 protocol. Over the past decade, these have been replaced with TCP/IP, and the graphical front-end is now being offered in addition to the old text-based agent interface. Among the most recent offerings targeted to travel agents is Sabre's Web services suite. There are 22 services in the product, offering full functionality for shopping, booking, and creating passenger name records (PNRs). As the communication protocol the product uses SOAP with an XML dialect standardized by the Open Travel Alliance (OTA) and allows the agencies to gain even better control over the booking tools. We will speak on the benefits of standardized protocols in later chapters.

The massive adoption of the Internet opened the possibility for direct communication between the Sabre GDS and the end customer. For this purpose, the Travelocity portal was launched and marketed as an online travel agency. The portal sends user queries directly to the Sabre GDS engine, giving the user similar capabilities to the travel agent.

It is important to note that in this case, the Internet connectivity acts as a double-edged sword. If one can build a system that allows a traditional GDS to function as a travel agent, one could also take the whole GDS out of the loop and allow the consumer to shop directly at the airline. Indeed, Orbitz, another online travel shop created by five airlines, uses the Supplier Link system that bypasses the whole GDS, minimizing the add-on booking fee costs. Also, most airlines that host their own reservation systems maintain their own independent sales websites. The low-cost airlines such as EasyJet in Europe and Southwest in the United States are associated with the GDS-breakaway movement. To complete the picture, one needs to remember that other GDS systems, Worldspan, Galileo, and Amadeus, own data complementary to that of Sabre. The information between the world's four GDSs flows both ways, so one could, for example, use the front end from Amadeus to book a ticket on an airline hosted by Sabre. For simplification, these channels are absent from the picture (Figure 1.4).

Let us now have a quick look at the internals of the Sabre GDS engine. The system dates from 1960 and is one of the oldest continually deployed IT installations in production. Today, the Sabre GDS consists of three subsystems, one each for shopping and pricing, booking, and fulfillment. Here we are interested in shopping (customer browsing through available connections), pricing, and booking. The system, also known as ATSE (Air Travel Shopping Engine), was long running on IBM mainframes; however, it is currently being remodeled.

Web portals such as Travelocity, which allow individuals to search directly at Sabre, have led to a tremendous increase in the average system load. And, while the transaction volume increased, booking activity did not keep pace. It was determined that initially users would only browse through the options, not necessarily deciding to buy the ticket. The increase of the shop-to-book ratio brought additional load but no extra revenue. For this reason, Sabre decided to dedicate separate resources to the two types of operations. Booking operations, including pricing, are now performed in the master "database of record," sitting on 17 fault-tolerant 16-CPU HP NonStop S86000 servers. Each processor is equipped with 4GB memory. The NonStop kernel ensures reliability of the critical pricing operations.

A separate cluster called the Hybrid farm is dedicated for shopping activity. These include computationally expensive algorithms such as the K-shortest path route search. Because these operations are not critical, they can be performed on cheaper infrastructure.

Hybrid is currently built of 45 four-way HP rx5670 servers, each with 32 GB memory and 64-bit Intel Itanium processors, but it could scale up to hundreds of machines running Linux or Unix. The Hybrid machines run Linux and MySQL AB databases. Data synchronization software from GoldenGate is used to continuously replicate the data from the NonStop boxes to the Linux cluster, which is responsible for the shopping operations.

A customer query received by the Travelocity Web server is first served by the shopping subsystem, which constructs the sorted list of available schedules. It uses data from the Operational Data Store, whose content comes from travel suppliers such as airlines. A small percentage of queries actually results in further interest. In this case, the PNR, containing the customer data, is created in the traveler data warehouse. The pricing subsystem calculates the fare. If the user proceeds with the purchase, the transaction is completed by the booking system, which synchronizes the booking information, together with the new PNR, with the reservation host of the specific airline. As noted before, many of these systems are hosted by Sabre, which simplifies the communication. Eventually, the airline knows about the new passenger. A separate fulfillment subsystem handles ticketing or e-ticketing and payment processing, and the passenger receives her ticket.

What we have described here is a highly distributed computing system, with several domains involved in the process. In the simplest case the service chain consists of the customer, Travelocity, Sabre Airline Solutions, and the airline itself. In more complicated scenarios, there would also be a travel agent between the Sabre GDS and the customer. To complicate the scenario even more, even the Sabre Airline Solutions backend system does not always talk to the airline directly. Often there is a separate hosting company such as Utell, maintaining the particular reservation system. Or, if the airline is hosted by a different GDS such as Amadeus, then Sabre first needs to talk to its system to complete the booking.

A distributed multidomain infrastructure such as this one is characteristic of the Grid. The core notion is the issue of shared resources, which in this example is visible although not immediately obvious, at least in two places. First, let's observe that each customer query starts a time and resource consuming shopping procedure, performed by ATSE on the customer's behalf. Sabre is in fact allowing users to use the computing power of its Linux cluster to perform the queries efficiently. The CPU cycles are a Sabre resource shared with the user.

To understand better where the resource sharing comes into play, one could imagine an alternative architecture, in which the user-side application is responsible for finding the most appropriate schedule by directly contacting several airlines, downloading the fare data and locally computing the K-shortest path algorithm. Then, once the user made her choice, the application would contact Sabre pricing and booking systems. Such a solution is, in principle possible, but it would, in practice, require very fast connectivity and high computing power from the user machine. To save on time, Sabre is allowing the customer or travel agent to outsource the K-shortest path search to the shopping system. This is a good example of resource sharing, the core function of Grid computing.

The backend GDS interface presents us with another example. Some airlines have decided to run their entire reservation systems on Sabre resources. In this case, Sabre is allowing the airline to use its hardware infrastructure, databases, and the local reservation application installation such as the SabreSonic suite. Naturally, the use of resources is limited by the interfaces the application exhibits. Such reservation system hosting is another good example of controlled resource sharing.

Is Sabre GDS, together with its satellite front-end agencies and backend reservation hosts, a Grid system? As we will clearly see in the following chapters, the borderline between what is and what is not Grid can be rather fuzzy. However, most experts would probably state that the Sabre GDS is an advanced distributed system, but not Grid computing. The tightly coupled infrastructure is built for one purpose, and it is impossible to dynamically make it available for a task unrelated to ticket booking. For instance, during low travel seasons, a Grid-based shopping and pricing system could be partly switched to serving compute power to another party, such as a pharmaceutical company. Similarly, the database hosting system, if having spare resources, could serve as a backup database for other Grid participants, not related to the travel industry. Such alternatives should turn very attractive for companies like Sabre as fallback options to situations such as the year 2001 and 2002, when the travel industry collapsed following the 9/11 attacks on the World Trade Center and the Pentagon.

Also, the security solution implemented at Sabre is different from those envisioned for the Grid. The ATSE system lives on a private network; therefore, the security issues inherent for the Grid do not affect it. One element with the public interface is the Travelocity portal; however, its working relies on the assumption that everyone is free to search for travel fares. This is still true for Sabre,[6] but is not valid for several other branches of IT (e.g., banking) where the information is confidential. True, Travelocity does some level of identity checking when it asks the customer for her credit card number. However, this procedure is not suitable for automated agents and is another reason why most experts would not call the Sabre GDS a Grid system.

Finally, the current proprietary system is built to bring the user to shop at Sabre. An alternative common market of travel Grid services of the future (which has been unsuccessfully proposed for decades) could consist of a thin client[7] being able to send a similar query to Travelocity, as well as other booking systems, and then compare the responses. The 2003 shipping of Web services suites that support open OTA interfaces is a step in this direction.

Summary

Grid computing is about sharing resources. The world is gradually transforming itself into a Grid-aware environment. Elements of the Grid are visible in the business infrastructure of today. Sabre has created a sophisticated GDS system that shares information, computing capabilities, and database infrastructure with its numerous partners. Search engines such as Google take advantage of open protocols such as HTTP to analyze the mesh of the World Wide Web and store this information in huge data sets. These are used to perform sophisticated operations on behalf of their users; thus both the data and infrastructure are subject to sharing.

---

[6] Even at Sabre this assumption may not necessarily hold forever. As we mentioned earlier, since the introduction of Travelocity the load at Sabre ATSE rapidly soared. Those who only want to check the prices cost the company more processing time than the actual shoppers.

[7] "Thin client" means client-side software with minimal functionality, while most of the processing takes part on the server side.

Both presented systems involve large-scale cooperation of distributed entities belonging to different organizations that use various resources such as the CPU, the network, and storage. The fact that most people use the system but don't realize its internal complexity brings another strong similarity to the future Grid systems.

In the near future, sharing will be possible on a larger scale and be generally more intrusive in the infrastructure of the companies. To cope with competition, closed systems will have to be rewritten and become open to sharing without sacrifice of functionality or safety. The challenge for Grid computing is to provide technology that will enable safe, reliable, and robust methods of large-scale resource sharing between institutions and domains.

Companies such as Techman, which occasionally need resources for intensive simulations, will be able to find them at the resource provider centers. Other firms will be able to securely grant rights for their partners to access a subset of their resources, as demonstrated in the HydroTech and Petrolium example. Institutions within the same domain of interest, such as InvestIT and its partners interested in stocks, will develop high-level protocols and procedures, allowing for easy and automatic routing of information subject to automatic transformations, monitoring, audit, accounting, and billing.

The road to the Grid infrastructure will require thorough understanding of the technology by the participating institutions. Therefore we have to begin by clarifying the concept of Grid itself, the meaning of which has so far not been agreed on, even within the core expert community. In the next chapter we define more precisely the space of Grid computing within the historical, technological, business, and academic contexts.

CHAPTER 2

The Basics

Where did the ideas for the Grid come from? What is it designed to do? Why do people argue so fiercely about the true meaning of Grid? Why should a savvy manager be interested in pursuing Grid computing today? Finally, why is it important to become Grid-enabled?

This chapter begins with a little bit of history to understand the technology and market trends that lead to Grid computing. The chapter names the basic terms useful for later discussion. In this context, it presents Grid computing, its definition, and an explanation of how it is meaningful for business. The chapter also explains how the Grid differs from a number of technologies that are related but not quite the same. In the context of distributed computing, clusters, or service-oriented architectures, where lies the added value of Grid technology? We will draw a few important borderlines that will be helpful in our further discussion. This chapter also draws the picture of core technical concepts and related standards, which are crucial for the emergence of grids.

At this point, you should gain information that will help you distinguish between the Grid-hype—the "g-" sales term—and the true value of the Grid technology. You should also begin to understand why different groups of people attach orthogonal definitions and meaning to the same word.

This Chapter in Two Paragraphs

At this point, the impatient reader wants to see the mystery revealed and the Grid computing paradigm explained. In short, Grid computing is the technology that enables resource virtualization, on-demand provisioning, and service (or resource) sharing between organizations. Using the utility computing model, Grid computing aims at providing ubiquitous digital market of services. Frameworks providing these virtualized services must adhere to the set of standards ensuring interoperability, which is well described, open, nonproprietary, and commonly accepted in the community.

A short answer can also be given to the key question of this chapter, which is why it is important for companies to become Grid-enabled. Grid computing is the logical next step on the road of the IT market to the ubiquitous connectivity, virtualization, service outsourcing, product commoditization, and globalization. The digital world becomes more distributed, virtualized, and available on-demand. And as a result of the "net effect,"[1] this process is happening sooner than we would expect. Becoming Grid-enabled means getting ready to participate in this global market of services. The secret lies in the word "ubiquitous," meaning that everyone will be participating in the Grid. Those enterprises that participate sooner will gain competitive advantage by pioneering new markets, perfecting the new channels of collaboration, and positioning themselves in the new value chain. Those firms opposing the change will eventually find it more difficult to survive.

Readers who understand the preceding two paragraphs can skip Chapter 2. However, note that to define Grid computing we used terms such as *virtualization, resource, service sharing, on-demand provisioning,* and *utility computing.* Although intuitive understanding of these concepts may be sufficient for some readers, their proper explanation requires a broader context, including some technical and historical setting. This is the purpose of this chapter. We first go back in history, discover the reasoning behind today's distributed technologies, and then revisit the preceding definition of the Grid when we're ready for it. So unless you plan to read this book on a single Detroit-Chicago flight, please forget what you have just learned and go back with us a few decades.

Scientific Roots

To understand the phenomenon of today's inherently distributed Grid solutions, we must identify the scientific beginnings of this trend. The concept of Grid computing had been actively discussed in academia for many years before the commercial world started noticing it. However, the early ideas associated with this term had a slightly different angle from today's perspective.

---

[1] Did you note that the evolution in IT is happening much faster than 10 years ago? This has been dubbed the "net effect," because thanks to the Internet people share ideas faster. It must be mentioned, however, that two and three centuries ago, people were also surprised how things would happen faster than when they were young. And the Internet wasn't there!

Universities and research institutes are traditionally the first hubs for new computing infrastructures. This was the case for both the Internet, piloted in the United States by ARPANET in the 1960s, and the Web, conceived in the European research laboratory CERN. Consequently, the scientific community was the first to discover the benefits of the new technologies and to deploy them for solving their problems.

Science is full of fascinating problems that can be answered much better with the aid of advanced computer technology. Many of these problems share a common feature of being computationally intensive. This means that the more compute power you have, the more precisely you can answer the question. It is even true that some questions cannot be answered at all without sufficient power. Computationally intensive tasks have been a recurring theme in the last 40 years of evolution of computer infrastructure and have often been a driving force in this evolution,

An often-quoted problem of weather prediction is a typical example of a computationally intensive task. A pioneer in weather forecasting, English mathematician, Lewis Fry Richardson, worked out a system for efficient weather prediction during his army service in World War I. He proposed dividing the Earth into cells and measuring the current weather conditions in each cell. The data would then be transformed through the set of hydrodynamic and thermodynamic equations to predict future weather conditions. The completed plan contained an important and startling number, 64,000. This was the number of people who would need to be continuously solving the equations to make the prediction useful.

Even today scientists are unable to precisely predict the temperature, humidity, or precipitation more than a few days in advance. One reason is the so-called butterfly effect.[2] The other concern is that our machines are simply too slow to achieve a certain level of detail in the simulation in a reasonable time frame. These same issues plague virtually any problem that requires simulations of complex systems. Finite element simulations in material science, earthquake modeling, protein folding analysis, or construction of an optimal financial portfolio are all examples of computationally intensive tasks.

The need to solve such problems pushed people to build computers and eventually supercomputers. Large IBM mainframes in the 1960s, followed by the beautiful C-shaped Cray supercomputers in the 1970s and 1980s, dominated computing centers for more than two decades. These machines enabled scientists, for the first time, to solve problems that were otherwise impractical

---

[2] The butterfly effect says that a small change in an initial system condition may result in dramatic changes in the final state.

because of the large volume of computations. Single processor supercomputers were soon eclipsed by architectures abbreviated as SMPs and MPPs[3], containing multiple processors capable of running in parallel.

To effectively use the resources, application programmers needed to explicitly structure their code to allow for parallel execution. Luckily, most computationally intensive tasks were natural candidates for parallelization. Suppose the task is to discover an 8-digit password by trying all possible combinations using a 10-processor machine. The obvious solution is to divide the range of possible answers into ten equal parts, have each processor search its part, and finally combine the results. Such an approach is called *domain decomposition*. The search part can be done in parallel; thus the result will show up almost ten times sooner than it would on a single processor. Tasks of that kind are referred to as embarrassingly parallel problems, because their parallelization is straightforward. Other problems are less trivial to decompose and their speedup will be less than perfect.

With the 1980s came the advent of personal computers available as commodity. People quickly realized that systems composed of a number of interconnected PCs could compete with supercomputers, both in terms of performance and price.[4] Such systems, simply called clusters, first appeared in production in the early 1990s. The high cost of mainframes, both in terms of purchase and maintenance, caused a massive migration of the research centers toward more or less distributed clustered solutions. Also, clusters were scalable while most supercomputers were not. Consequently, the Top 500 Supercomputer Sites, which ranks the world's 500 most powerful machines, listed 7 clusters in 1999 (1.4% of the market). Four years later, in November 2003, 200 of 500 machines on the ranking were clusters (40% of the market). More recently, the percentage has reached 60 percent.[5]

---

[3] Symmetric multiprocessing (SMP) and massively parallel processing (MPP) are the major classes of multiprocessor computer architectures.

[4] In fact, this is a simplified statement. Clusters can happily compete with supercomputers only in certain application domains. For some tightly coupled applications, supercomputers are still a more attractive alternative. The same holds when supercomputers or clusters are being compared to widely distributed desktop computing environments, such as the famous *SETI@home* that harnessed the power of several desktop PCs worldwide. Not all applications can be computed on such a system with time and cost saving.

[5] To check the current number, visit the most recent ranking at top500.org. Even better, visit the book's online companion at savvygrid.com. Throughout the book, we often quote information that comes from various online resources. We will restrain from footnote references like this one, because the Web addresses often change. Instead, whenever you need to refer to the source, visit this book's online companion at savvygrid.com. Updated links to all online reference sites are there.

A clustered architecture is distributed and the first clusters were often homemade. As such, they used different technology than the earlier, well-engineered, tightly coupled solutions. In the early days, because of the absence of operating system vendor support, the open-source Linux emerged as the leading cluster operating system. On this base, cluster management and middleware systems like MOSIX were used. Some of them emulated on a cluster: an environment similar to a virtual machine (Single System Image). Programs written for clusters needed to be aware of the distributed architecture. Message Passing Interface (MPI) and Parallel Virtual Machine (PVM) became the most common programming models. It allowed programming primitives for parallel processing. Each machine came with a hard drive. These separate disk resources were harnessed with distributed filesystems such as NFS (Network File System) or AFS (Andrew File System). The interconnecting network quickly became a performance bottleneck. To counter this problem, Ethernet cables were replaced by Gigabit Ethernet, Myrinet, and other high bandwidth and/or low latency solutions. Many of these add-ons introduced a layer of abstraction, presenting the user with an illusion of a single powerful machine, although physically it was nothing more than a network of commodity computers.

Scientists were now able to submit their computationally intensive jobs to have them executed by hundreds of machines in parallel, thus greatly improving response time. To ensure proper allocation of computing time to numerous jobs from various users, scheduling and queuing systems were installed on clusters. Typically, newly submitted jobs would wait in a queue until the central scheduler allowed them to execute on selected resources. A number of batch scheduling systems were in use in the 1990s (and are still in use today), such as the PBS, Codine (today known as Sun Grid Engine), or LSF. Among the sciences interested in such compute power, the high energy physics community was traditionally most active. Climate modeling, earthquake science, astrophysics, chemistry, and recently biology were also among the users of clusters. Needless to say, the needs were growing proportionally to the available resources, which soon turned out to be inadequate for advanced simulations.

Early Proto-Grids (Meta-Computers)

After the advent of personal computers came ubiquitous connectivity to the Internet. Again, this was first visible at research institutes, which were initially interconnected only to each other. Compute centers, already running parallel tasks now had network connections to other similar centers. For the first time, the consumers of compute power had an interesting option. Instead of building up the local supercomputing and clustered infrastructure, why not cooperate with other institutions, integrate with their resources, and effectively multiply the CPU cycles available for peak demand hours?

In principle, the locally available clusters were nothing more than a bunch of networked machines. Why not simply extend the cluster definition to encompass a few hundred more machines sitting a few hundred miles away? In most cases, this turned out to be impossible for a variety of reasons:

- Clusters typically consisted of identical or similar machines. Two clusters of different architectures were difficult to merge into one system, as were two different supercomputers. Differences in compilers, tools, libraries, or formats of binaries supported by the two operating systems would be an integration obstacle.

- Parameters typical for long network connections turned out unacceptable for cluster technologies (often designed for machines mounted in the same rack, connected by Myrinet). Delay, low throughput, random congestions typical for TCP/IP, and network errors all played a role here.

- There was no compelling technology to overcome the security threats. Loose security procedures fit for internal systems guarded by firewalls were absolutely unacceptable in the open network environment.

- Administrative and political issues added a whole new dimension to the problem. Institutions needed to define conditions on which their resources would be shared. Even if such a policy was defined, with the existing technology there were no technical means for its effective policy control and enforcement.

A number of largely academic solutions were born to overcome these limitations. By this time, the most challenging question was how to effectively connect and harness the geographically dislocated compute power. The word *meta-computing* was used in this context, often referring to academic systems where the knowledge of available compute servers was stored in the central meta-computer. In the 1990s, there were tens of research groups throughout the world who had proposed independent meta-computing solutions. Some of the most prominent ones were Ninf, Netsolve, Unicore, Condor, Globus, and Legion.

Ninf, from Tokyo Institute of Technology, and Netsolve, from University of Tennessee, deployed a client-server computing model. Ninf programming interfaces allowed programmers to submit computationally intensive jobs to powerful machines. A central server then dispatched the requests to machines that were available. Similarly, the German project Unicore (associated with

Pallas GmbH and later Fujitsu) provided job submission and monitoring capabilities in a distributed environment, through a user-friendly graphical interface. Condor, and later Condor-G (University of Wisconsin), was, in principle, similar to many batch scheduling systems. However, it was able to map the scheduling and resource management functions onto a more demanding, distributed environment where machines may have been nonuniform, not dedicated, or not always available. Legion (University of Virginia) provided an object-oriented programming model for resource providers, equipping them with abstraction for resource sharing and remote access, with a strong focus on distributed data. Legion was later commercialized by Avaki.

It was in this environment that the concept of the Grid was originally created. Grid computing was initially understood as a way of building clusters of clusters. For computational applications, such entities would look like a reasonably uniform collection of resources (though it should be noted that the idea of resources as a key abstraction for the Grid hadn't yet been thought of), on which applications would run in a coordinated fashion. Thus, Grid technology created another abstraction layer on top of clustering middleware for higher level software.

The Globus Toolkit from Argonne National Laboratory and ISI at the University of Southern California emerged as the most popular middleware to implement grids. Because Globus still holds the position of the market leader, even readers with few technical skills should become familiar with its fundamentals. Unlike most meta-computing projects, Globus did not provide a complete solution, but rather a system integrator's toolkit—a set of building blocks from which distributed systems could be made. Its architecture fit well into the concept of interconnected clusters. First, the hierarchical directory system, MDS, provided the resource discovery. Users, or higher level tools acting on their behalf, received the list of available resources, complete with their architecture and software details. Then applications, split into parallel jobs, could be submitted to the chosen list of resources. The submission process was automated using DUROC and GRAM, in a similar two-level hierarchical system (Figure 2.1). In addition to GRAM and MDS, Globus also provided a robust data transfer protocol (GridFTP) and security fabric (GSI).

It is worth noting that Globus did not hide the architecture of the underlying components. An opposite approach is taken by the Java Virtual Machine, which offers the same functionality on top of any architecture. This lowers the cooperation boundary between the architectures, but at the same time does not take full advantage of the specifics of the underlying hardware. Instead, Globus provides a uniform API for high-level functions like discovery and job submission, but does not ease building the applications across platforms. Application programmers have to either design for specific archi-

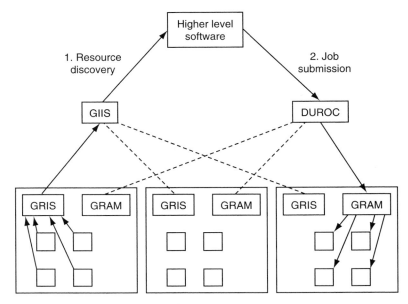

FIGURE 2.1 Globus 2, GRAM, and MDS

tectures available in the system or rely on standards such as POSIX to ensure the application code portability. This burden is compensated by the potential of higher performance and the use of system-specific features.

Globus provided low-level essentials for certain kinds of distributed applications. Many of the aforementioned meta-computing systems later developed Globus-compliant interfaces, allowing for a certain level of compatibility. As mentioned, meta-computing focused on the ability to call a number of distributed machines together to solve a single problem. Naturally, the focus was on the computationally intensive problems that benefited from the combined computing power of many CPUs. For a while meta-computing and Grid computing were considered synonyms. However, it was soon realized that grids must deal with more than harnessing the compute power.

Let us imagine the Grid as a giant computer.[6] The role of its processor could be played by the robust computation apparatus, possibly composed of a set of clusters operated by the Globus Toolkit. But to continue this simple analogy, the processor couldn't do its job without interfacing with devices. The same turned out to be true here. There is a powerful processing engine, but where does the input data come from? It may arrive from another computation center. It may

---

[6] Nothing innovative in this analogy. Remember Sun's slogan "The network is the computer"?

come from a database, or from some scientific apparatus. After the computation completes, what happens to the results? They may need to be further processed, analyzed, streamed to a visualization engine, or simply sent to storage. In each case, different kinds of hardware and software resources will be used, with different interface requirements and processing capabilities. Moreover, these applications typically imply rather large quantities of data; after all, this is the result of calculations performed by a cluster of clusters! It is rather unwise to expect local resources to be able to process this amount of data. It is therefore common to use resources in distant locations.

Thus it is clear that meta-computing (understood as combining the power of multiple CPUs) solved only a fraction of the problem—it built the distributed processor. However, a fully functional distributed operating system needs a range of other modules, such as input/output devices and interfaces.

Noncomputational Resources

To phrase it in terms used in Grid computing, the problem is that these days most of the resources are not of a computational nature; therefore the early Grid architectures could not be applied here. The term *resource*, often applied implicitly to the processing unit, has a much broader meaning. Generally speaking, a resource is any element of the networked infrastructure that is made available for usage with standardized Grid protocols. In general, the system's processing capability is correlated to the number of available resources. Similarly, lack of available resources makes the system useless. A storage system or a database is a Grid resource if it uses standardized interfaces to allow Grid applications to preserve structured data. Networks are also referred to as resources that provide transport bandwidth. All kinds of specialized instruments (sensors, telescopes, industrial infrastructure) can be abstracted as resources, if only they interface the system in question. They are producers of unique data and serve as the devices able to observe or interact with the physical world. It is more exotic, although increasingly common, to speak of software resources. There are several reasons why some applications can be set up only at certain locations. This may be due to the need to cooperate with specific hardware, but often it's simply because of licensing or data confidentiality. This software is a Grid resource when it is made available using Grid protocols. Finally, the system usually needs human intervention so there is a range of resources associated with people. Even people themselves can be described as resources, which is explained later.

Having seen a few examples of resources, let us examine some of their important characteristics. Each resource has a feature set that makes it unique. From the perspective of the Grid, most important are the processing capabilities. Thus a compute node is characterized by CPU speed, number of units, and local memory capability. Network pipes differ by throughput (bandwidth) and delay. A storage element is described by amount of available space and access time.

Resources also differ by other characteristics, not explicitly related to performance. Some examples of distinct resource features are:

- Architecture: depending on the processor architecture, certain programs will or will not compile and run on it
- Quality of Service: for instance, a network may be able to guarantee minimal throughput available to a user within a certain time frame
- Reliability: for instance, hardware such as disk drives are characterized by TTF, average time of activity without failure
- Availability: because of communication failure or the nature of the remote resources, connecting to them may not be possible all of the time
- Capability: application logic is usually able to perform certain algorithms that no other applications can perform

All resources are connected with other parts of the system using well-defined interfaces. These interfaces themselves have important characteristics and are crucial in the system interoperability. They may differ by:

- Supported protocols
- Duplex mode (ability to send and receive simultaneously)
- Synchronous or asynchronous communication
- Support for multiple simultaneous connections
- Client or server characteristics
- Communication module throughput and delay

Two resources will be able to interoperate only if they have compatible interfaces. In many cases this requirement boils down to supporting the same protocol.

In this respect, a network is a special kind of resource. It does not interface with the system in the same sense as do other resources, but it is the means by which communication is transported between the interfaces. Work is being done to expose networks via Grid protocols and thus allow things like bandwidth reservation to be accomplished by Grid-aware front-end software.

Whether people themselves can be abstracted as resources is an interesting question. People usually have crucial roles in the system and they need to interact with it through specially designed interfaces such as visual applications, command line shells, or Web portals. These applications usually interface with other parts of the system using the open protocols. On the other hand, most of them cannot work without human presence in the loop. Thus to a certain extent, people can be treated as resources: Their presence does enhance overall system capabilities, and they do have special interface requirements just as other resources do. A simple thought experiment: Could the Grid-based building fire emergency system work properly without interface to the local fire rescue team?

To summarize: A resource is any element of the networked infrastructure that is integrated with the Grid using open protocols. Resources communicate with each other using their interfaces. Interoperability of the interfaces is among the crucial problems in building the distributed environment.

This extended understanding of a resource changed the original meaning of the Grid. What was initially imagined as the distributed computing unit became a multifunctional distributed engine in which distributed computing was only part of the story. The fabric, such as supplied by the early versions of Globus, was not enough to support this extended functionality. Although the Grid still needed to discover resources, submit jobs, or transport data, it also needed much more. How does one access a database? How does one set up remote applications? How does one operate specialized hardware? Resources associated with such actions were not supported by the existing Grid approach and needed custom in-house communication solutions that were expensive to integrate, difficult to maintain, and not interoperable.

Virtualization

The needs of resource consumers (applications) are being fulfilled by resource providers (infrastructure). In the ideal world, it would be great to buy exactly the "amount" of resources the applications need. However, while the hardware capabilities are generally constant, the application demand fluctuates over time. This results in either suboptimal resource utilization (white space) or the demand unmet (Figure 2.2).

In a typical enterprise, several departments will independently experience this problem. It is likely, however, that peak demands of one group occur in a different time frame from the other groups. By adopting an organized approach to pooling the resources, they could all benefit by acquiring better peak access resource availability, thereby minimizing their chances of demands not being met. Speaking more generally, the utilization of the entire infrastructure is optimized.

One approach to achieving this goal is to introduce a layer of services between applications and resources (Figure 2.3). Services represent the capabilities of the resource layer. In the simplest case, each service can be

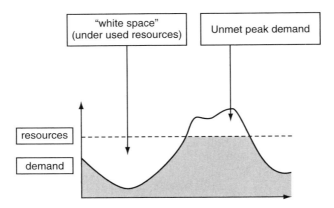

FIGURE 2.2 Resource capabilities versus demand

represented by one resource. However, such one-to-one mapping is not required. For instance, one service could represent an access to combined information from several databases. Another could serve as an access point to the combined processing power of several clusters. Or, one resource with differentiated capabilities could be represented by many services.

Applications contact the services to submit their processing requests, but do not need to know how the execution is being divided between the actual resources. This process of abstracting out the service layer is called virtualization. The benefits of virtualization are:

- Better classification and presentation of capabilities based on the actual needs rather than the physical constraints ("I need 60 processors over half an hour, who cares in how many rooms they sit?")

- More effective utilization of common resources, better white space statistics

- Thinner and better maintainable application layer because the load-balancing logic can be outsourced to the resource layer

- Common access to rare resources with unique capabilities such as specialized applications and hardware

In business terms, IBM technologists speak of virtualization as "a vehicle to become an on demand business without adding complexity to the current business infrastructure environment."

Naturally, with these advantages come dangers. Public access to previously private resources introduces the issues of privacy, confidentiality, ownership, accounting, and access policies. These generally need to be solved at the service layer. These issues are discussed later in the book.

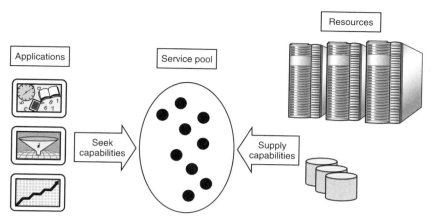

FIGURE 2.3 Virtualization: Introducing service pool between applications and resources

Note on the Term *Virtualization*

The meaning of virtualization has a slightly different connotation among various communities. In operating systems, virtualization is a method of dividing one machine into separate execution environments. In storage systems, virtualization is narrowed to pooling the storage from multiple network storage devices into what appears to be a single storage device. Perhaps both these meanings can be generalized in the broad vision of virtualization presented previously. It is worth keeping in mind these slightly different interpretations when talking to people from different backgrounds.

Scientific Roots: Summary

One of the driving factors for the progress of distributed technologies was the presence of computationally intensive applications. Scientific communities, such as high-energy physicists, who had to habitually solve such problems, constantly searched for more robust architectures such as supercomputers, clusters, and meta-computers. At one time, people realized that the meta-computing architectures carried a broader potential than just larger compute power. This was only one type of resource, but meta-computers could also provision and harness other types of resources, such as storage, network, or applications. These were all resources that could be shared by distributed communities of researchers. The term *Grid computing* was coined to indicate the nature of architectures that enabled cross-organizational sharing of various types of resources. Resource virtualization emerged as a key concept that would enable effective sharing of resources. Unfortunately, it could be realized only in some niche implementations. There was no generic solution to create a ubiquitous platform virtualizing resources, otherwise known as the Grid.

This chapter has thus far talked about the development of ideas at the dawn of Grid computing in the academic world. At this point let us pause the story and look at some trends that developed over the same time in the commercial community.

Business Perspective
Standing on the Shoulders of Giants

Distributed computing was born 30 years ago when ARPANET was conceived as a way of building robust networks. Early standards such as FTP, NNTP, and SMTP allowed for data to be moved between machines, but provided little in the way of distributed application development. As networks became more prevalent and PCs more widely deployed, programmers wanted to move portions of applications to different machines to take advantage of the resources existing there. This began with Remote Procedure Calls (RPC), allowed programmers to create interfaces to applications. COM/DCOM allowed this within a more robust framework, but only on MS Windows. None of the previous protocols were object oriented, so CORBA was invented to present a view of distributed systems more familiar to the growing legions of C++ and later Java programmers. Soon the analogous mechanism of Java RMI was embedded into the Java language as a native solution providing similar functionality.

While CORBA was, in principle, platform- and language-independent, it proved technically difficult. Also, the proprietary protocols limited adoption of CORBA as a ubiquitous platform. On the other hand, RMI was easier and native for the Java language, which was, in theory, available at most popular platforms. Although Java Virtual Machine specification was open, the fact of Sun's license ownership caused uncertainty for several companies to develop on top of that technology. There were also technical reasons not to use RMI. Legacy systems were written in other languages such as C, and interfacing with Java would inhibit their efficiency.

Thus at the turn of the millennium, communication between remote processes was possible through a number of technologies such as RPC, CORBA, COM/DCOM, and RMI, none of which was broadly accepted by the industry. Those wanting to implement truly cross-platform communication were left to find low-level solutions such as TCP/IP, which provided the common communication channel but any semantic abstraction needed to be built on top from scratch.

A common standard for high-level communication was needed. Web services emerged as a technology simple enough and at the same time extensible enough to suit most needs.

Web Services

A Web service is a clearly defined function that is accessible through the network. For instance, a Web service can provide weather information and stock quote information, and perform computations or database searches. Web services have well-specified interfaces, typically accessed with Simple Object Access Protocol (SOAP). The difference between a Web page and a Web service is that the former provides human-readable information, while the latter provides data in the XML format suitable to feed into automatic processes. Thus it is easy to construct distributed communities of Web services that involve complex but totally automatic interactions.

Web service technology defines a common communication platform on which interfaces for various functions can be built. The common denominator is the aforementioned SOAP, a text protocol based on XML, providing both human and machine-readable format of data. An XML message is self-descriptive, with content clearly organized into a hierarchy of elements. Although the meaning of message elements can be understood only by the intended recipient, the syntax is clear to anyone who knows a handful of basic XML rules. (In fact, a human reader who understands XML can often guess the intended meaning of the message.) This common syntax layer allows services to outsource the typical communication functions (such as listening, receiving, parsing, or deserializing of incoming traffic) to application servers on which services are hosted. Services stripped off that common functionality are thus lightweight and quick to write, deploy, maintain, and replace.

Web services, unlike the previous RPC-like technologies, have been embraced by the whole IT community, including the key market, thought leaders such as IBM, Microsoft, Sun, and HP. Web services are based on a set of open standards, provided by renowned nonprofit institutions and market consortia such as W3C, OASIS, and WS-I.

Service-Oriented Architecture

A system composed of a number of interacting services is referred to as Service-Oriented Architecture (SOA). Typically, an SOA consists of a distributed set of entities (services) that exchange communicates using XML and SOAP. These services can live on separate machines. The aforementioned hosting approach is often used, in which case the application servers (hosting environments) would be installed on all machines, while services would be deployed on top. This approach improves maintainability and eases the installation of new services (installation is so trivial that the noun *deployment* is used instead). SOAs are loosely coupled, with services being highly independent from each other. Thanks to the hosted, distributed service approach, actions such as replacement, upgrades, and maintenance in general are easier in SOAs than in tightly coupled, monolithic solutions.

Today's Web Services Are not Enough

Web services and SOAP have been accepted as the communication platform of choice by the key market players, which has led to massive market adoption of the technology. However, when more people began building on Web services, they all faced similar problems. Barebones Web services lacked security, reliability, and performance. Also, interoperability was hampered between various independent implementations. Finally, most WS implementations would benefit from a common set of higher level functions.

While most of QoS requirements were gradually perfected by new generations of performant and reliable application servers, as well as the new Web service standards such as WS-Security, the need for higher level functionality persisted.

The nature of SOA (distributed, loosely coupled service federation) implied the next logical step of evolution of distributed architectures: One should be able to create an SOA across several departments of the organization, or even spanning resources of several organizations. In principle, this is possible today, but it breaks the security model deployed in most enterprises. Web services, which from one side interface local resources and from the other remain accessible for external entities, are a potential security threat.[7] Also, the question of accounting the remote user for resource usage remains open. These problems could be mitigated if the place, role, and capabilities of each service were better defined, constrained, sandboxed,[8] and embedded in

---

[7] This problem cannot be fixed by the security standards, such as the aforementioned WS-Security group, because these standards work on a different level. These standards focus on forming secure communication channel between the two parties, but cannot block the parties from harming each other! In the Grid environment of common resource sharing, there must also be safeguards against intentional or accidental damage to the local resource by a remote user.

[8] Sandboxing means isolation of a certain functionality, often in order to disallow interactions with the hosting system.

the accompanying high-abstraction environment. In such a context, the service should be accompanied by a number of standard functions, typically provided by the hosting environment, allowing better control of its activities. For instance, the service should be subject to a standard way of deployment, monitoring, and logging of actions, as well as resource usage metering and audit procedures. As will be shown later, this requirement is being approached by the Open Grid Service Architecture (OGSA).

Some architects of IT systems also saw more fundamental deficiencies of Web services. As Web services are static entities, they don't give enough flexibility to those developers who would like to create on-demand systems. They would like to dynamically create and destroy entities that represent virtual resources. Then they would like to set properties to these entities, and other participants of the system should be able to inquire about these properties in a standard way.

If this discussion is getting too abstract, let's take the following example. A customer of an online Web hosting provider would like to rent an entire machine to set up a new Web domain. The provider needs a system that is on-demand and automatically creates such virtual machines. Their properties are the amount of virtual disk space, the names of the associated Web domains, and type of installed software available for the customers. With such a system, the provider could fully automate their service, easily and automatically monitor what is being rented out, and charge appropriately for it.

Could one develop a Web service that would assume the role of such a virtual host? With today's WS standards, the answer is no. A Web service cannot be created on demand, and it has no standard way for representing properties. Also, a Web service has no features of persistence, while the aforementioned customer would certainly like her domain to persist until her next visit. Of course, most of these features can be implemented in-house. However, it would be so much nicer if Web services supported such functionality "out of the box." As we shall see later, one attempt to overcome these deficiencies is the Web Service Resource Framework (WSRF) standard that defines so-called Grid services.

The Prospect of Utility Computing

The problems and limitations just described prevent the realization of utility computing, also known as on-demand computing. As explained earlier, today the IT infrastructure is organized by the concept of a physical resource. Such systems are coarse-grained, static, change-resistant, and not optimized for utilization outside the department which purchased them. Forward-thinking enterprises leave this scheme behind and push toward a service-based utility computing paradigm. In this model, resources will be available on a pay-per-use basis, just like electricity, telephone, or running water today. In the utility computing world, one receives the resources in the quantity and quality he or she needs, and pays only for that amount. For example, one does not need to buy and install specialized software to perform a single simulation. Also, one does not need to know or be concerned about the complexity of the infra-structure that provides these capabilities. Resources will be available for con-sumption on-demand, and their provisioning will be taken care by the underlying system.

The push toward utility computing led to creation of Web services, but more abstraction was needed to create a high-level service communication platform. In fact, what was needed was a technology enabling cross-organiza-tional virtualization of the resources. At this point, the largely business-driven Web service community realized that the same problem was being approached by the scientific meta-computing and Grid computing researchers.

Business Meets Academia

At the dawn of the third millennium, the scientific Grid computing commu-nity was already a long way from its meta-computing origins. With the com-prehensive understanding of how resources can correspond to services, the vision of virtualization and on-demand computing were among the ambitious goals. But the technology was far from fulfilling the dream. First, to realize the service layer, a common technology for service communication was necessary. The technology should provide a protocol fabric generic enough for any resource to be abstracted as a service. At the same time, it should allow flexi-ble extension mechanisms, so that each service could build up its own specific abstractions on top of it.

Globus Toolkit 2.x was the leading implementation technology of the time. However, what had been supplied by Globus was a vivid contradiction to these requirements. The three services, GRAM, GridFTP, and MDS, each had their own protocol. They had nothing in common with each other and so there was no foundation on which to build the new services.

In the absence of a suitable technology of its own device, the scientific Grid community began to look at the standards available elsewhere. SOAP and Web services seemed interesting as the first approximation for implementing the vision. Naturally, bare-bones Web services could not answer all questions. They were not designed for on-demand computing. They could not provide optimal performance, and the available implementations were immature. However, the duo of XML and SOAP provided generic, simple, and extensible fabric on which Grid services could be built. The SOA architecture fit the vision of the Grid service layer. Finally, the standard WSDL scheme for defining interfaces gave background for dynamic discovery of services.

At the same time, the business community started to notice the enormous business value in the Grid computing movement. This trend was led by large market players such as IBM who endorsed Web services standards. The idea of resource virtualization, if brought into reality, could enable more effective separation of service providers and consumers in the networked world, opening a niche for those businesses prepared to provide resources. On-demand computing, on the other hand, would provide dynamic service provisioning, cutting the cost of maintaining infrastructure. Resource virtualization and on-demand computing framed within virtual organizations enhanced with higher level services would open the market for real-time ubiquitous resource trading.

The Web service and Grid computing communities were heading in the same direction and had a lot to offer to each other by coming from different backgrounds. The natural consequence of this was an intense dialogue, followed by assimilation of ideas and blending of the trends. At the end of the day, it seemed that Web services, utility computing, and Grid computing communities used different languages to describe a similar vision.

This dialogue rapidly intensified in March 2001 with the inaugural Amsterdam meeting of the Global Grid Forum (GGF). Since then the GGF has met three times a year in various locations around the world.

The need for interoperability was the main driving force behind the GGF. The first step to effectively interconnect the scattered resources was to create protocol level standards. The creation of standards was also championed by vendors who often withheld their investment until a commonly accepted communication technology emerged.

The main body of the GGF is formed by several working groups, most of which are working on certain standards in their respective niche. The working groups are classified in a handful of areas. Currently these are:

- Architecture
- Data
- Security
- Scheduling and Resource Management
- Information System and Performance
- Applications and Programming Models Environments
- Peer-to-Peer

There are more than two dozen working groups and almost as many research groups, the latter of which do not produce standards but rather prepare ground for them.

Many argued that in the absence of real Grid applications, such a massive standardization effort is premature. Indeed, it is worth considering how far one should go before implementing proof-of-concept systems. It is clear, however, that at least the core protocols must be standardized for the first applications to appear. The Grid, by its nature, cannot exist without open, well-known, and commonly accepted communication layer standards covering not only the low-level interfaces, but various higher level aspects of distributed provisioning, which we will discuss later in the chapter.

WS-Resource Framework

In January 2004, a group of researchers associated with the Globus group and IBM proposed a new set of standards collectively referred to as the WS-Resource Framework (WSRF). WSRF proposed a standard way of associating resources with Web services. Extra abstraction was added to Web services, which made the virtualization and on-demand computing easier.

WSRF endorses the SOA, with IT resources accessible through Web services, described in WSDL, and communicating in SOAP. These Web services are gateways through which resources can be accessed by other participants in the Grid network. A resource associated with a Web service is called a WS-Resource. Such associations are possible in a one-to-many or many-to-many fashion: One Web service can be associated with several WS-Resource entities, or one resource may be accessible through more than one service.

Unlike the static services, WS-Resources are dynamic. They can be created and destroyed on demand. Such a dynamic nature implies the notion of changeable state. The state and properties of the resources are represented by "stateful" entities (i.e., such that are associated with state) called WS-ResourceProperties hidden behind the services. Actors of the Grid can discover, inspect, and modify these state properties by contacting the respective Web service.

Since WS-Resources cannot be contacted, other than through their associated services, they do not have an explicit address. They can be identified by using a convention called the implied resource pattern, in which the address of the respective Web service is given (endpoint reference) followed by the relative identifier of the particular resource. These two form a WS-Resource qualified endpoint reference, uniquely identifying the resource.

Note on the Term *Grid Service*

WSRF narrowed the meaning of Grid service to those services that conform to WSRF specification. However, a broader, natural meaning of a Grid service is also in use. As defined in Foster's "Physiology of the Grid,"[9] Grid service is any service used in the Grid environment that conforms to specific interface conventions accepted as standard throughout this grid. We will use this broader meaning throughout the rest of this book. Assuming that grids are coherent in their architecture, in most cases we will make no difference between *Grid service* and *service*.

The Meaning of WSRF

Note that the elements of the WSRF description fit very well our earlier virtualization discussion (Figure 2.3). In the standard terminology, we now talk of WS-Resources instead of just resources. It is a natural consequence of virtualization that resources should have properties as well as the ability for dynamic addition or removal from the accessible resource pool.

The aim of WSRF is thus to define the foundation of the virtualized service layer and its relation to the resource layer. By defining extensions to the "vanilla" Web services, WSRF makes a step toward on-demand computing, dynamic service provisioning, and flexible resource management suitable for virtual organizations.

By building on top of Web services, the WSRF standards are not exclusively oriented on the Grid computing community. Contrarily, the standard is meant for broad adoption in the Web services community. Thus to some extent, we anticipate merging of Grid computing and Web services groups. Grids will become technologically similar to Web services. The Web services community, by picking the chosen elements of the WSRF standard set, will enhance their solutions toward dynamic service provisioning and their systems eventually will resemble grids.

From now on, to stress the fact that grids operate at a virtual service layer, we will frequently use the word *service* instead of *resource*. It is more convenient to talk about services. This abstraction allows for greater flexibility in discussion, shielding us from the complexity and physical constraints inherent to the underlying resources. Users of computing resources must operate at the

---

[9] The article "The Anatomy of the Grid" (2001) and its follow-up paper "The Physiology of the Grid" (2002) by Ian Foster and his colleagues are considered among the most significant articles on Grid computing. Full online references are available from our online companion.

conceptual level of machines and devices. Users of Grid services only know about CPU-hours and terabytes of storage space.

The common and standardized layer of virtualized services will not only ease processes within an organization but will enable communication between services and underlying resources belonging to different organizations. Service providers who allow access to their capabilities in a standardized way will technically be able to provide similar services to external customers. In contrast, service consumers who use Grid-enabled applications will be able to choose and switch between various service providers, based on their availability, quality of service, or other criteria. Service consumers and providers will use mediation of service brokers who will maintain and manage the service market. The appearance of brokers (and other higher level entities) will in turn speed up the process of service commoditization. It will be easy to become a service provider by subscribing one's services into the pool managed by brokering institutions.

Thus we come to an important characteristic of Grid computing. *Grids enable seamless sharing of services and resources over boundaries and other barriers, which should be transparent for the consumers. Grids, as we envision them today, will spread over administrative domains of organizations, economic limits of companies, and political frontiers.*

The virtualized service layer is a step toward enabling such functionality. However, the careful reader has already noticed that the low-level fabric provided by WSRF is not sufficient to implement the vision. Complex higher level functionality will be necessary to provide a seamless, transparent, manageable, maintainable, reliable, safe, and secure common computing environment. The way to obtain these characteristics is through virtual organizations and higher level standards.

Note: OGSI, the Predecessor to WSRF

Browsing through the standard documents from GGF, one may still encounter references to another standard, OGSI (Open Grid Service Infrastructure). For historical reasons, and also to avoid confusion, we should explain its meaning. OGSI was a GGF standard that appeared in 2002. OGSI was a predecessor to WSRF that was revoked only one year after its introduction. In practice, WSRF is the new incarnation of the ideas stated by OGSI.

Major problems with OGSI were more strategic rather than technological. Because OGSI interweaved the notion of state with the core definition of the Grid service, it made itself hard to accept by the Web service community, which understood Web services as essentially stateless. WSRF, proposed by a team of researchers from IBM, Globus Alliance, and their commercial partners in January 2004, expressed the essential idea of a Grid service in the new form, acceptable both by Grid computing and Web service communities.

Today the value of OGSI is mostly historical. However, it is also the communication standard implemented by the Globus Toolkit 3.x. That version of the toolkit attracted a rather small community of users; however, those few installations still use the OGSI standard.

Virtual Organization

To analyze the Grid environment and the requirements for its administration, management, and security, it is important to note that such an environment will not be uniform. Although on the technology layer the goal is to commoditize resources and provide them with uniform gateway services, on the management layer the entities will be constrained by membership to various categories and further differentiated by access privileges.

In this partitioning of the Grid, the basic unit is called the virtual organization (VO). A VO is a set of Grid entities, such as individuals, applications, services, or resources, that are related to each other by some level of trust. In the most basic example, service providers could only allow access to the members of the same VO. The main difference between a VO and any other organization is the membership criterion. A VO will typically span across several "physical" institutions. Entities will join and leave the VO on the fly, based on their current needs. So the entities in the VO are united by a common goal rather than by membership in certain administrative structures. VOs are generally more dynamic than traditional organizations and can have a very short life. For instance, a single distributed procedure that requires access to services at several locations (such as data mining process involving search in several databases) may involve an on-demand creation of a virtual organization to create the security context before performing the actions.

Another definition of a VO is a group of individuals temporarily united by a common purpose or engaged in a common task. It is sometimes easier to define the VO in terms of people rather than network entities. In the end, the services and processes usually run on behalf of certain people. For instance in the UNIX environment, every process is owned by a user (although it is also true that the term *user* does not necessarily imply a human being).

One grid could potentially host several VOs. An entity may join several of them in the same time, thus VOs can overlap.

To sum up, virtual organizations are domains of trust between entities, such as users, services, and resources, characterized by:

- Distribution
- Scalability
- Transience
- A flexible, dynamic nature
- A weak relationship to the parent organizations forming the grid

VOs are the key concept on which higher level requirements for grids can be built.

Security for Virtual Organizations

In this section we present an overview of security in virtual organizations. In Chapter 5, we shall come back to the subject of Grid security and explain its key functions in more detail using a simple example. Readers who wish to know more about terms such as *authentication, authorization,* and *secure conversation* can refer to Chapter 5 before reading this section.

Grid entities must interact in a secure manner. Secure communication may include communication channel encryption (preventing others from reading it) and message integrity (ensuring the receiving side that the message has not been tampered with). Mutual trust must be based on the process of authentication, in which entities establish each other's identity. Access to services must be preceded by the process of authorization, in which the credentials of the requestor must be checked. The rules for authorizing are contained in the security policies enforced by local authorities.

Such typical security procedures must now be implemented in the context of dynamic VOs. Grid security architects quote the following major requirements for the VO environment[10]:

- Grids and VOs are built on top of real organizations, which have the ultimate authority over their resources (services), and want to enforce their own security policies. Therefore the Grid mechanisms must cooperate and integrate with the local security systems.

- It must be possible to create and manage dynamic trust domains, in which users and entities enter and leave on the fly, without manual intervention of an administrator.

---

[10] A lot has been written on Grid security. Two articles from the Globus team, "A Security Architecture for Computational Grids" (1998) and "Security for Grid Services" (2003) are good reference lectures on the issues we cover here. Full quotations and links are available from the online companion at www.savvygrid.com.

- New services could be created dynamically, immediately obtain their new identity and credentials, and be able to interact with other entities.

On a slightly lower level, the OGSA standard (explained later) lists the particular security primitives that should be supported by grids:

- Single sign-on (type a password only once and use it throughout the session)
- Digital rights and key management
- Intrusion detection and protection
- Secure interaction across firewalls (currently firewalls are obstacles for most Grid solutions)
- Authentication, authorization, and accounting
- Encryption
- Support for a certification scheme

These requirements are partly addressed by the Grid Security Infrastructure (GSI), developed within the Globus project. GSI is a security toolbox for the Grid environment. It is a certificate-based security scheme that builds on PKI (public key infrastructure). With this approach, a trusted party within the Grid, the Certificate Authority (CA), issues X.509 certificates to Grid users. Such certificate acts like an ID card, guaranteeing the user's identity. During the communication, users and entities can authenticate each other (i.e., check each other's identity) by reading each other's certificates.

GSI introduces the concept of a proxy certificate. Users can issue such certificates to an entity, such as a process or a service, acting on his behalf. A proxy certificate has a subset of the user's credentials necessary to perform the job.

Proxy certificates allow delegation through impersonation. They also enable single sign-on, because a proxy, once created, can act on the user's behalf. By using proxies, users can also build simple trust domains by issuing proxies to several entities. Such proxies will trust each other if their identity derives from the same source.

Communication channel security (encryption, integrity) in GSI has been traditionally implemented using the Secure Socket Layer (SSL) protocol. With the introduction of SOAP, this changed to WS-security standards (WS-Secure Conversation, WS-Trust, XML-Signature, and XML-Encryption). GSI thus provides mutual authentication and authorization of users and services, communication channel encryption and integrity, single sign-on, and delegation. Proxy certificates enable dynamic creation of entities and simple trust domains.

GSI does not solve the problem of more sophisticated trust domains with differentiated levels of trust. Also, the flat authorization mechanisms are not suitable for all situations. More advanced tools like SAML servers, or Community Authorization Service (CAS) can be used there. The possibility of integration with local security mechanisms is an open issue. Various communities work on gateways between GSI and their own systems, such as Kerberos.

Although currently technology that can fulfill all the security requirements of the virtual organizations is not available, in practice what is provided by frameworks such as GSI should be sufficient as the following examples of virtual organizations working today, often in support of the international scientific projects, confirm.

The Case for Open Grid Service Architecture

Businesses today are challenged to serve an ever widening group of people both within and without their organization. It is no longer sufficient to install a database, stand up a file server, and provision a few machines to run the latest ERP application. The IT organization must do all these things but in a manner that allows for more efficient use of resources, an ability to partner with external organizations in a controlled fashion, and not add any additional burden to their user communities.

The key concept in the Grid environment is the virtualized service layer, in which resources are represented by federated groups of services. Users and applications outsource various functions to these services. Grid applications are often very thin, with the majority of content delegated to the service layer. The separation between the service tier and the application tier is actually an artificial concept to help our understanding. In fact, applications themselves often have Grid service interfaces, so they can be used by other applications. Thus these two tiers will in fact be implemented as multilayer constructs, with several levels of services. Services, applications, and users federate into virtual organizations, which provide them with a higher degree of security and trust.

Applications equipped with Grid service interfaces and an ability to join the VOs are thus equipped to act in the Grid environment. Even so, they are still not effective without higher level standards. Let us look at a simple example. Suppose a company has built a financial analysis engine to calculate the trends of the U.S. stock market in various scenarios of global economic indicators. The application initially consisted of the user interface connected to the computation engine (Figure 2.4A). It was later Grid-enabled. The new refactored system consists of a visual user interface module, Grid adaptation layer, a scheduler service, and the compute engine (Figure 2.4B). User sets the

initial parameters for the simulation. The Grid adapter prepares the job definition for the computation engine. For instance, it may compile the parameterized compute definition into byte code format understood by the compute
engines. Then the adapter contacts the scheduler Grid service and submits the
prepared job. The scheduler identifies the best-suited, least-loaded system and
sends the job; and the system performs the simulation, using the backend
cluster of machines, and notifies the client when the operation is completed.
The client's Grid adapter downloads the simulation results, and the user interface presents them as an animated diagram.

The new system is more sophisticated, but is also more flexible for deployment in a Grid environment. First of all, it does not depend strongly on the
local compute engine. When the cluster goes off for maintenance, it should be

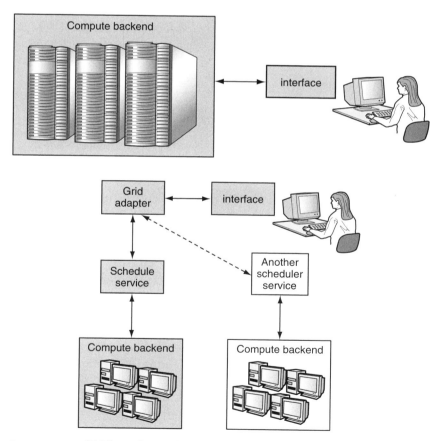

FIGURE 2.4 (A) The applicaiton before Grid-enabling (B) The Grid-enabled application

possible to quickly reconfigure the application to use the spare cycles of a similar system from another department of the company. Naturally the backup cluster needs to be compliant with the scheduling interface that has been used so far. However, at least the financial application does not need to be installed; the staging of executables to the new environment is done dynamically.

Thus the system will work fine as long as it uses services that support the scheduler of the choice. But imagine that the company receives an attractive offer from an online service provider that enables them to access more powerful machines. In the new environment, financial scenarios would be performed with better precision, which would give the company an obvious competitive advantage in the market. The service provider also uses a Grid computing paradigm, with resources being accessible through Grid services. However, it uses another scheduler backend (Figure 2.4B) to which a custom Grid service interface was built. Unfortunately, the Grid adapter in the financial application is able to stage out jobs and receive results, but understands only the options of the local scheduler service. Thus, the two "Grid-enabled" systems, although built on Grid services, are incompatible and cannot take advantage of any form of cooperation unless some additional adaptation layer is created.

This simple case makes it clear that to enable global service sharing and trading, the standardization efforts must reach a much higher level than was possible with Web services. Not only the general communication framework, such as SOAP, must be standardized, but also several classes of interfaces must be categorized by their semantics. Grid applications would then have semantic understanding of standardized interfaces of services (in our example, a scheduler) that suit their needs. Since all service providers would provide uniform scheduler interfaces, switching between providers would require only a configuration change, and in many cases could be done automatically in run time without even attracting the user's attention.

Within the array of services provided in a typical Grid, a vast amount will have standardized interfaces. This concerns first of all services representing commoditized functionality that would often be requested by applications. Submitting computing jobs is one type of such function. Other examples include discovering services, accessing storage, transforming data, authenticating users, consulting the local security policy, or logging the activity.

OGSA is an attempt to standardize and categorize the various higher level services that are considered crucial for grids. The idea for OGSA was first proposed by Foster, Kesselman, Nick and Tuecke in the article "Physiology of the Grid." Currently OGSA is the flagship GGF standard.

OGSA is the vision of architecture for Grid systems and applications, the ones "concerned with the integration, virtualization and management of services within distributed, heterogeneous, dynamic "virtual organizations.'"[11] The standard defines functional requirements for the Grid infrastructure to support such applications.

OGSA assumes that such applications are built on top of service layers composed of Grid services adhering to the WSRF specification. Thus they are all SOAP Web services, augmented by an ability to send notifications and manage WS-resources. For the purpose of interoperability, OGSA is specifying, grouping, and cataloguing higher level Grid services. It also describes the ways the services may interact and be grouped, orchestrated, and cooperatively deployed for common actions.

OGSA attempts to isolate the key Grid functions and encapsulate them as Grid services. The term *service* is used extensively. Each clearly identified piece of functionality is isolated and represented as a Grid service. Apart from categorizing such services, OGSA also defines functional requirements for the Grid infrastructure, Because OGSA is the best known attempt to standardize the Grid, we will take a closer look at the service categories and the mechanisms the standard proposes.

OGSA Services: Overview

Here we present an overview of the types of services proposed by OGSA. Because the specs are in draft form, this list is by no means complete. Its purpose is to signal the types of common problems and solutions addressed by OGSA. Readers interested in more detail should refer to the standard itself.

It is not required that any of the services named next be present in the environment. However, many of them carry some important functionality without which a functioning Grid is hard to imagine. Public grids will need to implement these functions, either as OGSA-compliant services or in some other proprietary way.

Virtual Organization

Specific services will dynamically create and destroy a VO, as well as manage its members and policies.

Composition, Grouping, Orchestration, Workflow

These exotic terms designate a group of services that deal with coordination of other services that cooperate on a common task. This includes defining

---

[11] Quote from the OGSA standard, version 1.0

workflows and addressing their scheduling, execution, and monitoring. Workflows may model business processes as well as perform computational tasks. Readers familiar with the subject will note a synergy with BPEL4WS standard (Business Process Execution Language for Web Services).

Transactions

Transaction services represent transactions and transaction management. Because of the heterogeneous and distributed nature of the Grid, various solutions may be suitable for different environments such as financial application domain or data centers.

Metering, Accounting, and Billing

Effective service sharing and trading between commercial institutions need to be based on commonly accepted Grid economy. Metering services measure the service consumption by the applications and users. Rating services apply the pricing information to this consumption and translate the usage from Grid service terms into financial terms. Accounting service applies it to the user account and manages the invoicing. Finally, payment is received by the billing service. Data generated by the metering and rating procedures may also be cached for the purpose of audit.

Installation, Deployment, Provisioning

Specialized services handle deployment of new services and their provision to users, so that various types of service capabilities can be delivered to the consumer in uniform fashion.

Application Contents

Grid applications are expected to be broken into at least three tiers: application, service, and resource. The application developers write very little code; their main task is assembling the off-the-shelf services to perform tasks in a coordinated fashion. The highest application tier is composed of very little code and a lot of meta-data that defines how the jobs should be performed by the underlying services. This meta-data defines the logical structure of the application and the desired runtime configuration of resources. It describes deployment parameters for the execution units. It may also contain configuration files for various entities engaged in the application runtime, such as hosting environments. In OGSA, such meta-data is called the application content. OGSA is proposing a model for uniform application content storage and management, in which application contents service plays a central role.

Information and Monitoring

In a dynamic on-demand environment it cannot be assumed that applications have static, permanent knowledge of the available services and resources. Rather, at some reasonable time before executing particular tasks, the available services need to be interactively discovered, reserved, and subsequently provided to the application. The discovery process is based on the information system, which monitors the services available in the Grid and stores the service meta-data in a system of registries.[12] In the simplest model, service providers constantly publish their data to the registry, and service consumers query the registry to find out what is available. Various enhancements to this model are possible, such as organizing registries into a hierarchical directory, push information flow (subscription), or differentiated confidentiality levels in the published information. Apart from a service discovery, the information system would also be used by the real-time monitoring services, as well as the optimizing frameworks that constantly collect and store the information on the state of services for later off-line analysis.

Logging

Distributed logging framework is similar to the information system. Rather than the meta-data describing the state of services, it is concerned about the diagnostic information produced by the applications. The logged data would be streamed to the receiver. OGSA proposes common infrastructure for handling and delivery of logs in the Grid environment. Clients of this framework include various diagnostic tools, real-time monitoring, debugging, problem determination, and performance optimization tools.

Messaging

OGSA frameworks will provide the hosted services with extended communication mechanisms suitable for various information flow models. Services can notify each other in real time about the events that occur during their execution. Such notifications would normally be coupled with the subscription mechanism, in which the receiver would signal an interest in the topic.

Security

We have already described the security requirements in the Grid environment. In an OGSA context, part of this functionality may be implemented as services.

---

[12] Most meta-computing systems named earlier in this chapter had a similar information framework. Ninf had meta-server, and Globus Toolkit 2.0 had LDAP directory (MDS).

Actions such as trust establishment, authentication, or authorization can each be performed by a specialized service. Isolating responsible functions such as authentication in a service can simplify the overall system design and maintenance, as, for example, when security patches need to be applied. Another example of a security service is a bridging service, which may be necessary in secure communication between administrative domains, to translate between the security credentials belonging to various domains using incompatible security technology.

Policy

The policy framework will enforce regulations of service behavior. Policies will specify the rules for services in the areas such as security and resource allocation. Policies may have various relations to each other. For instance, the organization structure may be represented by a hierarchy of policies imposed by different levels of administration. Policies are related to agreements (contracts between the service requestor and the provider, further restricting the rules for job execution).

OGSA proposes a unified approach to policy management. Policy Service Manager controls access to the policy repository for the policy providers, while another service, Policy Service Agent, is communicating with the policy consumers. The participating services implement the Policy Enforcement Point interface for effective cooperation with the framework.

Data

Data storage systems and database management systems (DBMS) are natural candidates for resource virtualization. They will be represented by gateway services allowing data access. Data caching, replication, and transportation services will take over the function of optimizing data location in relation to the executing environments. Data transport services will provide abstraction over low-level transport protocols. Data transformation services will be available to perform common operations on data sets such as filtering, search, or format conversion.

Program Execution

Program execution environments, such as computational clusters, are typically managed by scheduler services that ensure optimal usage patterns. Among well-known examples of scheduler families are Platform LSF, Sun N1 Grid Engine, and PBS from Altair Engineering. We discuss these products in Chapter 3. Broker services live on top of schedulers. Brokers cooperate with several schedulers and submit jobs to those that match the requested criteria. An example of a broker is Community Scheduler Framework (CSF), present in the Globus Toolkit 4.

Jobs are executed as a result of cooperation of several orchestrated services taking care of job monitoring, execution optimization, data streaming, etc. Their cooperation is subject to contract with the submitter. This contract is negotiated and instantiated as the WS-Agreement, which specifies the execution rules the local environment will adhere to. Some scenarios assume specialized agreements instantiated as separate services, such as Job Agreement, Reservation Agreement, and Data Access Agreement.

Grid Computing Defined and Redefined

The early definition of Grid computing coined by Foster, Kesselman, and Tuecke between 1998 and 2000 spoke of large-scale, coordinated resource sharing in a distributed, dynamic environment, crossing administrative domains.[13] Ambiguity of this definition caused confusion because just about anyone with a distributed system was ready to call it a grid. In 2002, Ian Foster proposed a three-point test to restrict the definition.[14] A system could be called a Grid if it:

- Was decentralized
- Used open protocols
- Delivered nontrivial QoS

This simple definition was indeed helpful in categorizing the products available in the market as "grid" and "non-grid." It also clearly stated for the first time the obvious fact that no closed system can call itself a Grid. The three-point checklist received acceptance in the academic community and is commonly quoted today. However, it was not received with enthusiasm in the commercial sphere. The uncompromising requirement of decentralization, if obeyed strictly, excluded practically all known "grid" systems in operation in the industry. Most case studies and examples presented in this book do not stand the test of Ian's three-point checklist.

Since in this text we are first of all interested in tangible, operational, and profitable commercial systems, we have to acknowledge that the three-point checklist describes some ideal state. Today's Grid technology, especially the one used in industry, has not yet reached such a state. Nevertheless, this fact

---

[13] "The Anatomy of the Grid: Enabling Scalable Virtual Organizations," by Ian Foster, Carl Kesselman and Steve Tuecke, *International J. Supercomputer Applications,* 15(3), 2001.

[14] "What Is the Grid: A Three-Point Checklist" by Ian Foster, *GridToday,* July 20, 2002.

does not prevent people from creating Grid-like systems that work well, fulfill their goal, and bring cost savings to the company. Therefore in this book, instead of drawing strict borders, we need to describe what is happening today, while the industry is on the road to the Grid. Our descriptive "Grid definition" is not very strict. We think that the savvy manager is less interested in drawing borders between Grid and non-Grid systems. Rather, she would like to know what Grid computing can do for businesses, and why it is important to become Grid-enabled.

Grid computing is the materialization of a trend eminent during the last decades not only in the IT industry, but in the worldwide business environment in general. Massive access to the network and increased connectivity leverage digital communication and the Internet as the natural platform for business interactions. At the same time, commoditization of various IT resources makes it possible to virtualize them and make them available for customers over the digital media.

These tendencies, coupled with globalization, speed up the worldwide process of service outsourcing. As a special case, services provided by the IT resources are easier to outsource than anything else. Their substance is digital, they can be provisioned automatically, and geographical location often does not matter.

Grids will provide the distributed digital environment in which outsourcing procedures will be more advanced than in any other area of business. Virtual services such as spare cycles, storage, applications, and data will be provided to users on demand. An often quoted analogy is electrical power—always available in the socket, paid for by usage, without knowledge of the source. In the same way, IT services available on the Grid will be delivered as utility—always there, available in any quantity, and the user need not be concerned about the source or provisioning process.

In the Grid environment, some end-user applications will eventually be limited to thin clients running on minimal hardware. Presence of numerous service providers will induce frequent outsourcing of common underlying functionality.

The major milestone to achieve this vision is common adoption of open standards, such as OGSA. Standardized, open interfaces, protocols, and interoperability mechanisms are the base for construction of wide-scale public grids, which will serve as business platforms, enabling interactions at a higher semantic level than today's Internet. Online, automatic service sharing and trading will be possible. The Grid will open a niche for new kinds of businesses, such as service providers, infrastructure maintainers, brokers, and those offering multiple specialized services. Eventually this process may lead to a construction of the "World Wide Grid"[15] a structure similar to today's Web, but with better semantics of business processes and oriented to machine, rather than human, communication.

One can only speak of the Grid in terms of open, commonly accepted Grid interfaces. For any kind of a useful Grid, standards compliance cannot stop at fabric level protocols, such as Web services, even with extensions like WS-Security or WSRF. Grid environments must be able to leverage the higher level OGSA-specific standards. Without compliance to the complex program execution framework, it will not be possible to offer competing implementations of Grid-enabled cluster management systems. Without conforming to the standard guidelines of policy and application content handling, it will not be possible to attract the community of service providers. Transparent metering and billing procedures are necessary both for providers and end-users. And a well-known security scheme supporting the notion of virtual organizations is necessary to provide a foundation for the interinstitutional service market.

Systems that do not provide these features can never become fully functional public grids, engaging several commercial institutions. It is possible, of course, to build an internal grid system inside a corporation where many of these services would not be necessary. Such a grid, however, would have very limited connectivity with external systems.

To summarize, *Grid computing is the technology that enables resource virtualization, on-demand provisioning, and service (resource) sharing between organizations. Using the utility computing model, Grid computing aims at providing ubiquitous digital market of services. Frameworks providing these virtualized services must adhere to the set of standards ensuring interoperability, which are well described, open, nonproprietary, and commonly accepted in the community.*

Distributed environments that implement such service sharing are called *grids*. In the future, strict adherence to the standards may cause the grids to merge into *the Grid*, just as the Internet was born decades ago from several disconnected networks conforming to the TCP/IP.

Finally, let us address the initial question: Why it is important to become Grid-enabled? In our eyes, the question itself is flawed, which implies a choice between becoming and not becoming Grid-enabled. We do not think that the latter is an option at all. The process of hardware commoditization, resource virtualization, and service outsourcing seems to be an inevitable global market trend. Grid computing is the next step on the road. Grid computing is

---

[15] Also referred to as the Great Global Grid.

becoming popular very quickly not because it is a hot buzzword, but because it solves problems. This will only become more true as time progresses and both low-level standards for communication and industry specific standards for application level usage become more mature.

Note on Spelling of "Grids," "Grid," and "Grid Computing"

Confronting nonuniform spelling in the community (we have seen grid, Grid, and even GRID), we hereby declare our spelling policy. We feel that when speaking of local or enterprise-wide grids, *grid* should be spelled with lower case, which is the most natural form for an ordinary English word. Only when referring to the ubiquitous world-wide system that may exist in the future will we use upper case spelling—*the Grid* (although some prefer to call it the Matrix). This conforms to the intuitive rules of English spelling; we have the Grid and the grids, just like the Sun and the stars, the Internet versus intranets, the Web and websites.

It seems therefore that *Grid computing* should also be spelled with a lowercase. However, the community seems to have already established a consensus here, and almost everyone spells *Grid computing* and *Grid technology* with an uppercase *G*. Since this seems a commonly accepted convention, we will follow it in this book as well. It is logically acceptable, suggesting that the technology has more links with the prospect of the future World Wide Grid than today's enterprise grids. Note that similar spelling customs populate today's computing nomenclature, with a prominent example being "Web services" based on "Web technology."

Disagreement on the Definitions

The abstract nature of the subject of Grid computing, coupled with scarcity of production examples, have recently been causing havoc in the community. In recent years, waves of business-oriented newcomers invaded the Grid computing space, which was previously dominated by academics. Their search for understanding was often a real struggle, because scientists were unable to produce business cases of their academic discipline, or provide practical meaning and value of the Grid science. As a result, attempts were made to define the Grid in more practical terms. The media attempted to influence public opinion to embrace this new discipline. Sometimes their input only contributed to additional hype and confusion, especially when written in the form of sketchy articles for which authorities in the field were not consulted. All this means that there is more than a dozen quoted definitions of what constitutes a Grid. A Google search "What is Grid computing?" returns 827 hits. This brings to mind a story of a group of blind-folded people asked to find out what an elephant was. Each of them encountered another part of the animal—a trunk, a leg, or a tail. Their reports were quite different, and although all were true, they seemed contradictory because none of them covered all aspects of the elephant. In the same way, many of the niche definitions of Grid computing, although at first contradictory, in fact are complementary. They correctly describe the subject from a certain point of view.

Cluster of Clusters

Especially in the academic environment, Grid systems often are based on a group of clusters, interconnected by network and certain middleware. In such an environment, computing jobs can be executed as if one large cluster were available. For this reason, grids are sometimes presented as "clusters of clusters," while Grid computing is explained as a version of clustering technology. Certainly aggregating the power of clusters in a distributed environment is an important aspect of Grid computing. However, as it was previously explained, grids also deal with various kinds of resources such as storage, applications, network, or various system-specific abstractions.

Cycle Scavenging

Readers familiar with early projects such as SETI@home or mersenne.org often perceive Grid computing to "a method of harnessing the power of many computers in a network" by "tapping the unused processor cycles of thousands of desktop computers." This understanding is popular in the press today, perhaps because of its simple, intellectually undemanding message. While we agree that Grid technology may indeed have its role in shaping the future of desktop-powered computing projects, it is unlikely that production-ready, mission critical Grid systems of the future will rely solely on such infrastructure. Again, what we see here is the definition being narrowed to operate on a certain type of resource only.

Grid versus Distributed Computing

To some people, these two terms are potentially equivalent. However, most of networked business infrastructure systems today are a form of distributed computing, while only a few of them form a grid. Distributed computing is an old phrase, intuitively designating all activity where computation is simultaneously happening in more than one place. Distributed computing systems are ubiquitous and relatively easy to construct today. Most of them utilize the underlying resources for a particular purpose, such as running the tightly integrated business applications. Grid technology would decouple these systems and allow for more efficient resource utilization, thanks to the ability of controlled sharing among applications and users. Grid middleware integrated with these resources will allow for easy deployment and on-demand switching between resource-independent applications.

Since distributed computing is a rather vague term, one can think of Grid computing as an advanced form of distributed computing.

Grid versus Web Services

We have already talked about Web services technology. As we have seen, Grid and Web services approaches have much in common as a result of their underlying technology. Currently, SOAP Web services are an interesting vehicle for Grid computing as a uniform form of high-level transport. However, for fully functional grids, more advanced functionality, such as provided by OGSA standard, is necessary. Also, Web services are limited when it comes to the robust connectivity necessary for high throughput data transfer. Thus it is likely that in Grid computing, the use of Web services will be limited to higher layers of Grid systems such as mechanisms for representing virtualized resources.

However, as both these technologies are young, it is difficult to predict their evolution. Technology transfer is inevitable, especially since some of the core Grid standards have recently been transferred from GGF to the W3 Consortium and OASIS. It is entirely possible that Grid systems and Web service systems of the future will be fully compatible and the distinction between the two will fade.

Grid versus Peer-to-Peer (P2P)

Peer-to-peer architectures have won popularity in recent years. Contrary to previously dominating client-server, master-slave, and other centralized system paradigms, entities of P2P systems are not subject to centralized control. Each one can act as a client or as a server. Such systems can perform better in many scenarios because central server is a single point of failure and an unnecessary bottleneck. P2P architectures have attracted a broad audience, mainly to the Internet-wide file share systems such as Gnutella. However, this is only one possible P2P application.

P2P and Grid communities largely overlap, and GGF has also created a P2P working group. P2P paradigm, as well as Grid, explores the concept of wide-scale, distributed resource sharing. Clearly, multiorganizational Grid systems to some extent will match P2P characteristics. We can see this already at the academic multisite grids, where each member organization maintains administration over its services. Each site acts as a server for certain services, and in most cases failure of one such site does not affect the system as a whole (but may affect some specific applications). However, some features of grids will be more easily implemented in a centralized fashion. In many grids, authentication relies on a single Certificate Authority. In others, a single central meta-data repository collects information on available services. To minimize the potential of failure, introducing minimal redundancy here may be a sufficient solution in most cases.

We observe a similar pattern in the Web today. Although the HTTP traffic of the Web is organized in a P2P fashion, the DNS[16] information propagation follows a centralized model. To ensure constant functionality, the core DNS servers exist in multiple redundant, geographically dislocated instances.

Other Definitions of Grid Computing

There are almost as many Grid definitions as Grid researchers. We hope that we explained the source of the confusion and how these definitions are complementary, rather than contradictory, to each other. For completeness, let's quote the "Technical Definition of the Grid" from IBM, which we like because it represents a view similar to ours, but using slightly different phrasing:

> Grid is the ability, using a set of open standards and protocols, to gain access to applications and data, processing power, storage capacity and a vast array of other computing resources over the Internet. A Grid is a type of parallel and distributed system that enables the sharing, selection, and aggregation of resources distributed across "multiple" administrative domains based on their (resources) availability, capacity, performance, cost, and users' quality-of-service requirements.

Will There Be the Grid?

The tendency to standardize technology and protocols to commonly accepted form brings us to an interesting question. Will the common adoption of these protocols eventually lead to the worldwide ubiquitous service-sharing platform? Will the processes of the future be able to on-demand provision virtualized resources from another part of the globe, just as today users can download and view websites from virtually anywhere? This is the vision of the Grid: a worldwide ubiquitous service sharing a platform similar to the contemporary Web.

It seems that the drive toward interoperability may eventually lead to the creation of such an environment. Whether this will happen depends strongly on whether the community will be able to maintain collective ownership of

---

[16] Domain Name System (DNS) distributed around the world is necessary for the Web to function.

open protocols and standards. Once the available middleware reaches the level of relative maturity and usability, even a small constellation of interoperable sites may spark an avalanche of new institutions joining in to use the resources offered by the community. This is the P2P phenomenon that we have already observed several times.[17] This is the way the Internet was initiated by a handful of ARPANET servers. In a similar fashion, two decades later the Web was born in CERN to soon become a worldwide network generating unimaginable traffic and revenue. More recently, the scheme was repeated by the appearance and overnight growth of file sharing communities based on protocols such as Gnutella or Kazaa. Again, openness of the existing network encourages new entities to join in, since participation in the community allows access to a number of new resources.

Thus, it is entirely possible that the next decades will transform the Internet into a huge virtual resource repository with mechanisms for sharing, aggregating, and collective usage of services. This vague vision is easier to predict than the level of abstraction that the ubiquitous interoperability will reach.

In the optimistic scenario, the Grid would leverage the level of interoperability on high-level abstractions, allowing creation of an open service market. Users running storage-intensive applications would be automatically provided with a list of storage providers and their application would seamlessly choose among them. Users of Internet telephony, unhappy with their operators, would be able to switch to another provider in a few seconds. Common application-level Grid communication standards would enforce commoditization of resources and uniform interfaces.

In the pessimistic scenario, the disagreement on standards would hamper higher level interoperability, leaving the application layer communication to the proprietary solutions. This would lead to fragmentation of the market and creation of separate Grid islands, with sharing limited to their own realm of services.

In reality, the world will probably settle somewhere between these two scenarios. The advance of interoperability will depend on some combination of free economy market pull, input from research institutions, commitment of nonprofit organizations, and state-imposed control regulations.

---

[17] This phenomenon even has its scientific explanation. It's known as Metcalfe's law, which says that the "value" of the network is proportional to the square of participants. We will revisit this rule in Chapter 6.

CHAPTER 3

Grid Computing Enters Business

Having understood what Grid computing is, it is now time to confront this knowledge with practice. In the short term, most readers would like to know how to profitably deploy the concept of Grid computing in an enterprise. More generally, one should be interested in trends existing in Grid business and industry today, signaling the potential for big investments in certain sectors in the coming years. This will be followed by the maturing of existing solutions and the appearance of new choices.

This chapter begins to explore these subjects. After a short look at the popular taxonomy of existing and future commercial solutions, we discuss the key markets and players in these markets. At the same time, we signal the trends that are bringing better solutions every year and paint a possible landscape of the Grid ecosystem in the near future.

This discussion is continued in the remaining chapters. Chapter 4 discusses possible strategies to become a player in the Grid arena. Chapter 5 further explores these strategies by providing starting points for technical planning. Chapter 6 wraps up the discussion by providing management-level guidance, business case hints, and project management advice.

The Grid computing market evolution is currently entering its most dynamic phase, when its entire potential seems not to be discovered or understood by most, and new solutions are appearing overnight. Thanks to this exciting period of evolution, the reader interested in most recent information on Grid products, vendors, and opportunities is advised to visit the online companion of this book (www.savvygrid.com), where we will maintain a knowledge center about the state-of-the-art Grid market.

How the Market Understands Grids

In the previous chapter we explained that Grid computing is a broad concept, which is partly implemented as commercial solutions, partly available in academic proof-of-concept research systems, and partly still present only in visionaries' heads. Also, as we have already explained, providing a taxonomy of Grid solutions is extremely difficult, as a result of several dimensions that need to be considered. If Grid offerings were to be classified technically and presented on a diagram, one simple metric could account for the size of the infrastructure in terms of CPUs. Another axis could designate hardware heterogeneity supported by each solution, and the third could represent geographical distribution.

The preceding description is one possible taxonomy model, but it fails to represent some important information. For instance, a separate taxonomy could be based on types of (hardware or application) resources that are being "griddified" into services. This information could be compared to the list of open standards implemented by the middleware in question.

Yet another way to classify Grid market is utilitarian. It divides the offerings by the business problems they are solving or, more broadly, by the market sectors they are addressing. Such grouping should also take into account whether the solution is a middleware, a tool, or an end-product.

Since such an approach is the most natural for users, we partly address it later in the chapter when describing the market. To begin the discussion, however, let us present the most generic technical classification of grid installations. This taxonomy is the most popular in today's business Grid computing environment (Figure 3.1). It divides the installations according to the level of cross-organizational distribution. Usually, an increased level of organizational complexity goes along with increased size in terms of hardware and number of CPUs, although this is not always the case. According to this taxonomy, we distinguish between departmental grids, enterprise grids, partner grids, and open grids. Next we summarize differences between these types of grids. This terminology is convenient to remember, as it is commonly used by today's Grid vendors. However, keep in mind that there are no strict borders between the four categories. We shall soon come back to this statement.

Departmental Grids

Departmental grids are installations that are allocated to one institution and usually serve one purpose. They are behind the corporate firewall and therefore have minimal security requirements. Departmental grids are often similar in functionality to compute clusters or compute farms. One possible

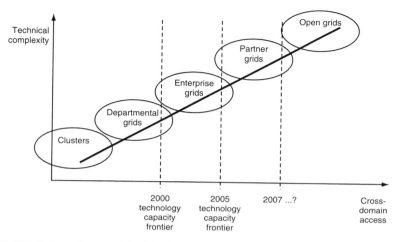

FIGURE 3.1 Commercial grid solutions taxonomy

difference is related to hardware heterogeneity, less common in clusters but possible in departmental grids. In fact, however, vendors in their marketing terminology often do not distinguish between clusters and small grids. This is partly understandable, as many distributed resource management solutions, which form the core of departmental grid systems, have evolved from cluster batch queuing systems and are often still optimized for such use. Departmental grids are usually owned exclusively by one internal user group, who work together closely on a project, set of related projects, or business process. Because of the negligible rate of conflicts, resource sharing is subject to simple rules. Usually there is little need for access policy, time slot plan management, or access monitoring. The purpose of a departmental grid is to centralize and virtualize the resources of the department or project for optimal usage.

Departmental grids can be implemented with a variety of middleware and tools. Apart from commercial offerings, there are a number of open-source solutions that can easily be used here. Many organizations choose to develop the custom, in-house solution based on an open-source middleware. Departmental grids can be easy to set up and, because of their small scale, they may internally use proprietary protocols specific to a particular parallel solution. However, the interfaces exposed externally must use open protocols compliant to the standards in order to anticipate future needs of integration, reconfiguration, and external use. For example, a scheduler compliant to DRMAA standard, or a database implementing OGSA-DAI standard will be easier to integrate with other Grid components than alternative products using proprietary interfaces.[1] A mini-grid and local grid are synonyms for departmental grid.

Before we proceed to the next category, it should also be mentioned that the concepts of departmental and enterprise grid are closely aligned with two classes of software offered by some vendors. Some people believe that the category of departmental grid is rather artificial and largely results from vendors' marketing policies. In defense of the vendors, they can make a good claim that the idea was to provide a nondisruptive evolutionary strategy, introducing Grid terminology early in the process in areas in which customers were already familiar.

Enterprise Grids

Enterprise grids are systems owned by one organizational entity, but used for many purposes. Like departmental grids, enterprise grids usually stay behind the corporate firewall. Restricted external access is possible, but limited to one-way communication (i.e., external users interacting with internal resources). Resources themselves are never being moved out of the firewall.

Enterprise grids are often deployed by corporations who want to pool the resources previously scattered among departments. Initially each department uses a number of CPUs, or even a departmental grid in a "silos" architecture, meaning that the sharing between departments is restricted. After these resources are integrated into an enterprise grid, more optimal usage can be observed. Departments in temporal need of extra cycles can find them elsewhere in the organization instead of purchasing new hardware. This is often possible because the utilization peaks of various departments can vary in time without overlap.

Enterprise grids need mechanisms for conflict resolution, as the demand may sometimes exceed availability. A system of usage policies governs the compute cycle allocation.

Enterprise grids can generally be implemented in two ways. They can either harness resources located in various departments, branches, and offices

---

[1] DRMAA stands for Distributed Resource Management Application API; DAI means Database Access and Integration. Both standards have been developed by the respective Global Grid Forum working groups. Note that OGSA-DAI is distinct from the previously mentioned OGSA. Find references from the online companion at www.savvygrid.com.

of the corporation, or they can manage the resources that are centrally located but serve the entire community. Lately the second, centralized implementation has become increasingly popular.

Enterprise grids must be closely integrated with other systems used in the enterprise. A typical implementation will use a number of integrated products, and usually include an advanced distributed resource management (DRM) system with a system of policy management. A number of solutions are commercially available that enable implementation of enterprise grids. Because of the size of the system, it is important that even the internal interfaces use open protocols, which allow for scalability and reconfiguration without having to resort to a homogeneous solution. Both departmental grids and enterprise grids are sometimes called *internal grids* or *intragrids*.

Partner Grids

Partner grids are installations that go beyond the corporate firewall to allow for sharing the resources of several organizations. Typically the need for partner grids is envisioned in collaborations that involve a number of participants from several entities. Today, a number of scientific projects in Europe, North America, Asia, and the Pacific have created early partner grids, on top of which are created virtual organizations (VOs) for various actions undertaken together. To one of such projects, NEESgrid, we have devoted a separate case study later in this chapter. Since partner grids are in early evolution, the terminology is not set in stone. Some authors would intuitively extend the term *virtual organization* to be synonymous with partner grid, but technically the two terms are not equivalent. A VO might span more than one enterprise and/or partner grid or one partner grid may host several VOs.

Partner grids are more sophisticated in deployment and usage as a result of security, organizational, and even psychological constraints. Exposing resources externally requires standards and policies for security, monitoring, accounting, and audit, which we discussed in Chapter 2. Because many of these standards lack integrated implementations, not many commercial partner grids exist today, although they are envisioned for the near future. Firms that do participate in early partner grids do it for the sake of large scientific projects in which they have a stake, and they are usually very careful with regard to exposing their resources.

Partner grids often have peer-to-peer architectures, as it is unlikely that independent organizations would contribute resources to central management. This arrangement will of course depend on the purpose of the project. One could imagine a cooperative partner grid built for the purpose of generating profit from leasing the harnessed resources to third parties. In such a case, centralized architecture relying on one resource broker may be more customer-friendly. Also, some elements of centralization may always be necessary, such as a central information discovery system. To ensure the minimal level of interoperability, open protocols and interfaces are essential in partner grids.

Few commercial partner grids exist today, although a number of forward-thinking business consortia allocate investment in this direction (see the Rolls-Royce case study). The contemporary scientific partner grids use collections of open- and closed-source tools, the interoperability of which is still rather low but rapidly increasing. It is likely that even when commercial solutions emerge, they will have to exhibit a high level of interoperability with competitive products using open protocols. Because partner grids by nature involve several stakeholders, it may be difficult to force all of them into a single proprietary solution. It is likely that partner grids will always be constructed with the use of a variety of solutions from many commercial and open-source vendors.

Open Grids and the Grid

Open grids, or global grids, are expected to emerge in the future. An open grid means a platform, composed of infrastructure, middleware, and applications, shared by several independent organizations. An open grid would not normally be dedicated to a single project. Contrarily, the participating entities would use the platform to work toward their own independent goals, sometimes working individually and sometimes joining into virtual organizations to achieve common goals. The grid would provide a resource and service base for the projects, as well as a medium for sharing and communication between partners.

Open grids will also be the platforms for a worldwide resource market, access to which will not be limited to participants of particular consortia. Entities disposing of resources would be able to contribute these to one of the grids out there, and have them used by others on a commercial or honorary basis. It is difficult to guess what these structures will look like, but it is possible that there won't be many open grids but only one global Grid, similar in size and distribution to the Internet or the World Wide Web.

The global Grid will be a natural consequence of the parallel existence of several enterprise grids and partner grids communicating by means of the same protocols. On the other hand, organizations using proprietary communication channels for their internal grid solutions will hamper the interoperability with potential partners and contribute to a possible fragmentation of the market and the future ubiquitous Grid platform.

Although the Grid is argued by some to not be here yet, even today we see some signs of the trend leading to the future online resource trading. The potential for outsourcing of the IT services is being used by various application service providers, on-demand storage providers, Web hosting companies, or the virtual CPU provisioning services that appeared lately. The Grid will be used, in a direct or indirect way, not only by institutions but also by end-users; however, these individual consumers will not always be aware of the Grid. They may be using Grid resources just as people use search engines and flight reservation systems today, benefiting from increased performance and accuracy of the application, but remaining unaware of the underlying complexity. Therefore instead of the term *open grid*, some use the term *service grid*, stressing the fact that users will adopt the grid as a utility model.

Taxonomy Summary

As we have already mentioned, there are no clear borders between these four categories of grids, just as there is no clear border between departmental grids and computational clusters. In fact, Grid architectures should in principle be scalable, and therefore one should rather speak of a continuum of possible solutions, starting from small, simple, and concentrated ones, and ending at large installations covering multiple domains and locations. One of the big challenges in being early adopters of any technology is clarification of terms. This taxonomy defines a common ground that can be used to speak in a common language. If two people are using different definitions for the term *enterprise grid*, then the resulting discussion will become fragmented and difficult to drive to consensus.

The taxonomy is therefore mostly useful for the purpose of human communication. It should be thought of as follows: When confronted with a statement "Our company has constructed an enterprise grid," one possible answer would be: "I see, you are thinking of some kind of infrastructure that integrates resources inside your enterprise." However, it may be rather pointless to challenge the speaker by asking: "What makes you think it is an enterprise grid, are you sure it is not a departmental grid?" The discussion to follow would in most cases be a waste of time. Quite possibly, the installation in question indeed has features that place it somewhere on the continuum between the two categories. Still, it is convenient to simply call it by the category where it belongs to a greater extent.

What Is the Market?

Thus far we have presented the taxonomy of existing and future grid installations. It should be noted that the taxonomy does not classify the market products, but rather the end solutions. Each of these grid installations may encompass integrated products from many vendors, as we will see in the case studies.

Now it is the time to look at the market and see where these installations are needed most and what problems they may be solving. The situation at some of the markets characterized here has recently become sophisticated, with new entrants challenging the position of incumbents and niche products becoming highly specialized. These overview sections can provide only a basic introduction. This book, which is centered on a horizontal discussion on Grid computing, cannot serve as a definite reference for those intending to specialize in one of the vertical markets.

The Educational and Public Research Market

The science and educational sector has long been serving as early adopters and the main engine powering grid innovation, and today they still are among the key consumers of Grid technologies. It's important to understand that this environment is not uniform and consists of at least two classes of grid users, with very different attitudes. One is associated with computer science research institutes, faculties, and departments. In this environment, as a result of its specific culture, the high technical abilities, and the do-it-yourself approach, the use of open source and homemade solutions is more popular than the adoption of commercial offerings. Also, this academic group generally considers itself as providers rather than consumers of Grid technology.

The second market associated with the public research sector is composed of sciences that are users, rather than producers, of the IT technology. Contrary to common belief, their applications are often mission-critical. Just as commercial applications must operate correctly in order to allow the enterprise to function, the public sector also has applications which are critical to the functioning of the organization. The typical examples here would include the NASA space programs or the high-energy physics community associated with large experimental facilities such as CERN near Geneva or Fermilab in Chicago, which are characterized by enormous size and cost. High-energy physics has been an early customer for Grid computing, years before the first commercial applications appeared. Other branches of science that frequently use Grid computing include all of those requiring computationally intensive simulations or data mining tasks, such as chemistry, medical sciences, and engineering. Scientists in this second educational market need the technology delivered in an easy, usable form that allows them to devote their time to the actual research, and not the tools. They are frequent customers for cluster and grid solutions. In some regions, they are the only customers.

Engineering and Manufacturing

Industrial and technological sectors of the economy are a large emerging market with proven potential for grids. In the automotive industry, truck and car design requires fast and optimized resources to accelerate time to market. Different groups of design engineers use grids for cross-platform design and implementing the workflow among cooperating departments. Those enterprises implementing such strategies today envision a much broader impact of the technology in the near future when partner grids will enable the sharing of such workflows among institutions.

The manufacturing sector in general makes extensive use of computational simulations. Typical functionalities provided by the grids in these areas include computational fluid dynamics, computer-aided design, finite element analysis, and crash simulations. The electronic design automation sector uses computational grids for chip design, simulation, and testing procedures. These often require collaborative processes involving engineers around the world. It is expected that the grids will support such efforts and speed up the development time.

Life Sciences

In recent decades, bioinformatics and biochemistry appeared as the disciplines forcing the use of computing technologies for medicine. These are largely data-intensive applications naturally suitable for Grid computing and understood as the technology providing vast data processing capability. Grids are used today by data mining procedures in genomic research and drug design applications. These often belong to the category of "embarrassingly parallel" problems, thus being the ideal candidates for Grid computing. The array of jobs produced by some bioinformatics applications can be executed in the Grid environment without much customization. At the same time, these problems simply cannot be solved without sufficient compute power. Thus, the grids in this area do not just provide better solution; often this is the only available solution. We will briefly cover an example of the use of the Grid for bioinformatics in the MCNC case study.

Financial Sector

Financial markets are currently the new adopter for the grids, with every major vendor having a number of associated success stories. Some vendors even specialize in niche financial Grid solutions. Retail banks such as Wachovia or Credit Suisse First Boston are the famous early adopters of Grid technology. Analytical applications, risk management procedures, Monte Carlo simulations, and trade floor support are examples of applications suitable for Grid-enabling by balancing the load on a local cluster or an enterprise grid. For instance, some investment advisors who deployed a Grid computing model were able to introduce new quality in customer treatment by reducing the time of analytical support to the investment portfolio planning from minutes to seconds. This enabled the advisor to provide answers before the end of the conversation with a customer. Financial markets also benefit from the technology. Predictive and analytical algorithms support the stock trader's need to match highest accuracy with maximally quick response time. Server farms managed by Grid middleware provide an adequate compute power appearing to be the optimal trade floor computational support platform. Similar types of applications, although in a different market context, are also being run on the Grid by the insurance industry for asset liability modeling and risk management.

The Future Market

Once the potential of the Grid has been demonstrated, more markets realize the previously dormant need for intensive computing. Among the recent newcomers to the field are the sectors of oil and gas research, telecommunications, government, entertainment, and retail trade.

Note that the preceding overview describes the market as it is today, when the technology capacity stops at the enterprise grids. Grid applications of today are usually data or compute intensive and use grids simply as if they were large computers. In the near future, we should see the emergence of partner grids, enabling the sharing of various kinds of virtual resources. The focus on Grid computing will shift to collaborative environments, federating services, and exchanging transactions. At that point, it would be difficult to name industries that would not need Grid technology.

How Can Market Segmentation Hamper Open Grids?

Commercial open grids are commonly thought to belong to the realm of the future. The term *open grid* has almost become a myth, perpetuated by the lack of stable commercial offerings supporting the notion of the open grid.

That vendors today are still struggling with the subject, however, does not necessarily mean that open grids are not achievable within a short time frame. We can even risk a more controversial statement. The presence of commercial open grid offerings is far less important for the Grid computing movement than the presence of similar solutions from academia and the open-source community. Interoperability is the key factor in this area of engineering. Open grids need to be standard-compliant at a high level of abstraction. To be successful, any commercial middleware needs to exhibit such a level of inter-operability, or else its installations will be able to communicate only with other nodes from the same vendor. Therefore open-source projects that typically aim at providing complete implementations of standard protocols may be more attractive for the community than commercial offerings, which typically focus on providing extra functionality but cannot communicate with similar platforms from other vendors. To survive on the Grid market, middleware vendors will either need to attempt to partition the market into "Grid islands," compatible only within their own small community, or base the differential advantage of their products on features not interfering with interoperability, such as reliability or robustness.

Unfortunately, history shows that the first strategy is usually more appealing as long as the vendors have reasons to hope to control the majority of the market. It can already be seen that some vendors leverage their position in other technology sectors to gain momentum in the Grid arena. A year after Oracle announced its Oracle10g, a study by Evans Data showed that 37 percent of database developers planned to implement a "Grid computing" architecture. In January 2003, IBM embedded "grid" load-balancing features into the WebSphere application server. In this context it should not be surprising that at the same time, Apple announced similar capabilities to be integrated with its MacOS X operating system. Xgrid, currently offered in the Technology Preview version, turns a group of Macs into a cluster capable to balance its load.

There are also concerns that there may be efforts to segment the market by special interest groups. Some observers see the Enterprise Grid Alliance (EGA) as such a wedge in the community by creating standards that stand in opposition to those created by the GGF. This is just one example of the general issue. If multiple standards bodies create similar classes of standard, then it becomes much more difficult to create the Grid in such a way that it benefits a global audience. As with all large-scale computing efforts, segmentation will always be a challenge that the Grid must face. It is in no small part the responsibility of the readers of this book to push their solution providers toward specifications and standards that will allow the Grid to prosper in a manner similar to the Web.

➤ **CASE STUDY:** The MCNC Enterprise Grid

MCNC Grid Computing & Networking Services is an independent, private, nonprofit institution located in the Research Triangle Park in North Carolina, whose mission includes the testing, development, and deployment of emerging information technologies in the state. Since the mid-1980s, MCNC has operated a statewide IP network for more than 180 institutions, including North Carolina's public and private universities and colleges, called North Carolina Research and Education Network (NCREN). Partly because of the network provider role, MCNC eventually became the supercomputing center for North Carolina universities, including the three largest research universities: the University of North Carolina at Chapel Hill, North Carolina State University, and Duke University. Having this infrastructure base, MCNC investigated a move to the Grid space, which in its case required evolution from a network provider to a Grid resource provider. A powerful network is an excellent foundation for a powerful grid. Also, becoming a provisioning center for Grid resources is in line with the MCNC mission to invest in technology that benefits North Carolina's economic development.

In 2001, MCNC cooperated with the three universities associated with the Research Triangle Park (University of North Carolina at Chapel Hill, North Carolina State University, and Duke University) as well as major vendors (Cisco, IBM, and Sun) to launch a pilot Grid program, with the goal of acquiring experience by using and implementing Grid software. The North Carolina BioGrid was designed as a test bed for life science research on the Grid. On this platform, incorporating resources from the N.C. universities and MCNC, bioinformatics applications could be developed and tested. The test bed allowed access to a variety of Grid software available for use, testing, and integration, including Avaki, Globus Toolkit, LSF, Sun Grid Engine, CHEF/OGCE, and MyProxy.

The BioGrid was an evaluation environment, where the participants could discover the benefits provided by the technology and work out their model for cooperation. However, it was not a production environment, in the sense that the relation between providers and customers was not based on a financial agreement. The test bed currently involves resources from the University of North Carolina at Chapel Hill, North Carolina State University, Duke University, and MCNC. Participants of the N.C. BioGrid project included a number of small bioinformatics and cheminformatics companies, including startups, clustered in or near the Research Triangle Park.

By 2003, MCNC gained enough experience in building and maintaining Grid resources, the next step was to launch the production-phase enterprise grid. A similar software stack was now to be run in the production environment. Site access was being provided by Globus 2.4. Avaki was managing the data grid. Platform LSF and Sun Grid Engine were the main schedulers, and CHEF from University of Michigan was used as the user interface. In addition to the standard Grid Security Infrastructure (GSI) security provided by Globus, MyProxy server was used to manage user security credentials.[2]

By 2004, the MCNC enterprise grid provided users with computing site hosting, data center and archiving services, and permission security services. Hardware infrastructure currently counts more than 200 nodes, mostly in 16-node clusters provided by IBM, Sun, and SGI.

Unlike its predecessor BioGrid, the Enterprise Grid is not limited to life sciences. The service has drawn the attention of commercial users, including some of the large corporations that also have their offices in the Research Triangle Park. These firms calculated that on-demand paid access to the MCNC Grid resources would be more cost-effective than building and maintaining their own infrastructure.

In accordance with the taxonomy we use in this book, the MCNC enterprise grid exists completely within the MCNC firewalls. However, it is only the first step of a long-term plan that will eventually complete with the creation of a statewide production grid infrastructure. In the next phase, Grid-enabled cluster nodes will be pushed out beyond the BioGrid partners to universities in Greensboro, Charlotte, Wilmington, and other cities. The current enterprise grid will become a kernel of a much wider system, with resources estimated as thousands of CPUs.

For those interested in setting up an on-demand Grid computing infrastructure themselves, it may be interesting to know what it took for the MCNC to position itself as a Grid resource provider. We will now look in a bit more detail at various aspects of the functioning of the described system. We begin with a description of the provided service and continue with an overview of the customer base. We then cover the project funding and pricing plans and end with a discussion of resource acquisition and the importance of location.

Service

The bioinformatics companies in the small business sector are interested in the periodic use of compute cycles. The volume of computations is variable

---

[2] SF, Sun Grid Engine, Avaki, CHEF, GSI and MyProxy are all examples of various classes of Grid products. These and other products are further explained later in this chapter.

and does not justify equipment purchase. MCNC provides two models for compute power leasing. One includes per-CPU hour pricing, while the other warrants dedicated access to a number of CPUs.

Most computations needed by these companies can be performed by typical software used in bioinformatics and genome research such as BLAST. These are computationally intensive data mining operations, which can easily be broken into parallel execution by domain decomposition. Often, the same operation must be performed on large amounts of data representing the genome. In such a case the data set can be divided into pieces, and each chunk can be processed in parallel as a separate job on a separate processor. Such an array of jobs from BLAST are perfect natural candidates to be executed on the Grid. They can be handled by one of the popular cluster resource managers (LSF, Sun N1 Grid Engine) after little or no customization.

Besides the computer cycles, the MCNC grid provides data center and archiving services, as well as access control and security services. Inadequate security is often quoted as the psychological entry barrier to Grid architectures. In the case of MCNC enterprise grid, this was not the main problem. In practical terms, the level of security is being defined in terms of time and trouble met by a potential intruder to break into the system. In this context, there are no unbreakable systems, but the level of security needs to be adequate to the importance of the data, applications, and systems protected. External customers communicate with MCNC systems through Secure Shell (SSH) services. Future service offerings are being constructed with the OGCE portal, using secure GSI-encrypted channels. MyProxy server is used to store and manage user proxy certificates. Companies using the MCNC system decided that these levels of security are adequate for the type of operations they are performing. Data spoofing can be effective only if a significant percentage of information has been intercepted, which may not be practical with large amounts of data. By contrast, the risk of hackers tampering with results can easily be minimized by checking of the result integrity through various redundant strategies.

Customers

Today a vast majority of the MCNC grid customers are academic institutions, who use about 99 percent of the provided resources. Those institutions became customers of MCNC because of a shift in funding regulations. The funding, which previously went straight to the MCNC compute center in order to maintain the supercomputing infrastructure for the local academia, is now being partially distributed to the universities, who are encouraged to spend money for leasing MCNC resources. Thus a provider-customer relationship was formed. The transition required effort on the part of MCNC, who now had to compete with other service providers. Also, universities could use the funding to purchase their own computers instead of cooperating with MCNC. The package the center proposed had to be highly competitive from now on, not only for alternative resource providers, but also with regard to the internal capacities of clients. This encouraged business thinking and customer-oriented planning.

In this work, however, we are more interested in commercial customers of MCNC, who today consume only a small percentage of their resources. The art of attracting such customers to Grid solutions requires special attention. As we will explore further in Chapter 6, business customers are rarely interested in the Grid "as such." Rather, they are interested in finding the way out of particular problems they are experiencing, and grids are interesting only as long as they provide these solutions. However, because of the specifics of the emerging sectors, potential customers are often unaware of the potential offered by the new technology. According to Wolfgang Gentzsch, managing director of MCNC, business relationships must be preceded by the long process of building Grid awareness in the community of potential customers. For those who don't even understand the benefits, the entry barrier must be lowered to the minimum. MCNC has done this several times. The first wave of commercial customers (bioinformatics startups) was attracted through the externally funded BioGrid program, where the participants learned how Grid resource sharing can work in practice. When BioGrid ended, these companies were among the first to express interest in the enterprise grid, this time on commercial conditions.

Currently, MCNC is offering an alternative program to attract a new business audience to the enterprise grid. Startup companies interested in access will receive a free "grid appliance," a server box with the preinstalled Grid software stack worth approximately $10,000. The appliance can be used to connect to the MCNC enterprise grid (naturally, one could as well connect with a home PC, but the appliance minimizes sophisticated setup activities). Together with the appliance, MCNC is considering a business model that provides companies a 3-year grid access package. In the first year, access and resources are free. During the second year, companies pay a small percentage of the actual cost. Only in the third year, depending on their performance and success, will they start paying per use.

Financials

Although MCNC is a nonprofit organization, it is able to largely maintain itself from various past technological investments. From the beginning, it was the center's strategy to invest in emerging technologies. MCNC created a venture investment fund, which helped to incubate several startups in the 1990s. Some of them were later sold and the revenue was allocated for new investments. As an example, $30 million acquired from the selling of Cronos Integrated Microsystems was used for building the North Carolina networking infrastructure through a grant to another local non-profit for extending broadband Internet service to rural areas of the state. Now the center's network services bring about $12 million annually; another $2.5 million is anticipated in the next few years from new data center services.

The Grid computing initiative has been allocated a new investment of $6.7 million over the next 3 years. An aggressive action plan estimates that the investment breaks even after this period. Currently, the business users of the MCNC compute power pay $1 per hour per node in an hourly pricing plan, or reduced rates in the exclusive access plan. Similar options are available for the storage services. The customer base is expected to grow as a result of the attractive 3-year plan mentioned earlier, which lowers the entry barrier. With wide interest of MCNC service, it is hoped that this stream of revenue will steadily increase. However, as is the case with emerging technologies in general, the investment is charged with a high-risk factor. The kind of paid services that people will be most interested in is not yet clear.

Resources

As the institution was a precursor in Grid computing, the process of becoming a technology provider was rather difficult. It took several years for the center to establish a critical mass of skills and infrastructure. MCNC first had to become the network provider. Then it could establish itself as a supercomputing center, centralizing the resources for three universities. This move resulted in the concentration of the supercomputing infrastructure, but also in building a skilled technical team of 50 engineers and scientists. The possession of these two key resources (people and network/computing infrastructure) enabled MCNC to evolve into a Grid resource provisioning center. However, it is precisely these two types of resources that are particularly problematic to maintain because of their volatile nature.

Processors, compute nodes, and data storage are often amortized and replaced every 2 years. Therefore investment in a state-of-the-art computing infrastructure can be justified only if you foresee its immediate usage. For this reason, institutions that already have resources deployed (supercomputing centers, telcos, large corporations with transaction processing centers) will find it easier to become Grid resource providers.

In contrast, skilled people are often easier to acquire than to keep. The loss of a few employees can be devastating to a technical company by the disappearance of skills base that took years to build. MCNC was successful in attracting a large group of experts in high-performance computing and Grid technologies. Being located in the famous technological hub of the Research Triangle Park and the proximity of university knowledge centers helped a great deal. This fact, coupled with a friendly human resources policy, helped to stabilize staff resources, with an average turnover time of 6 years, which is quite good by U.S. standards.

Location

In the context of Grid technologies, the question of localizing the business is an interesting one. It would seem that, as a result of the ubiquitous nature and connectivity of the Grid, location would be less important. This may well become partly true in the coming decades, when skills and infrastructure become available globally. As we have just discussed, however, in the case of MCNC, the location played an important role with respect to the availability of technical staff.

A separate, although related, question needs to be posed with regard to the geographical distance between MCNC and its customers. Because the MCNC mission is to strengthen the presence of emerging technologies in North Carolina, how is this going to be achieved by building a grid, which is by nature ubiquitous? After all, if grids are about location-independent resource sharing, customers from Japan or Poland should be able to connect in the same way as local customers from North Carolina. How is MCNC going to achieve its mission goals? Is the access going to be restricted only for those North Carolinians who would be treated with preferential terms?

In fact, it is understood that the North Carolina Grid infrastructure and the expertise that is being built should bring benefit for North Carolina, but at the same time it must address the whole world. The infrastructure will inevitably strengthen the Research Triangle Park's reputation as the skills and technology center. In the same fashion, as the presence of the three universities contributed to the foundation MCNC, the center expects to attract technology companies interested in grids to move their offices to North Carolina where they could benefit from thought exchange. Providing free and discounted grid services to start-up companies at incubators throughout the state will help to accelerate the interest. In this fashion, the investment is, first of all, expected to positively influence the state's economy.

At the same time, it is difficult to track and impossible to predict how exactly customers use MCNC's resources. International companies present in the Research Triangle Park have a worldwide presence with offices, customers, and partner connections in many countries. Business processes run using MCNC grid resources could easily become part of workflows including many geographically separate stakeholders. Thus MCNC grid projects will certainly impact the worldwide economy, science, and technology. The same will be true for any open grid built in the future.

Who Is Who: The Ecosystem of the Grid

After the market overview, let us have a closer look at those who provide solutions to the market (Figure 3.2). Considering how young the market is, the system of relationships is surprisingly complicated. In fact, this should not come as a surprise, as immense growth is predicted to the Grid market. Also, this new market has something in common with several "old" industries such as the HPC (high performance computing) industry, Linux clusters, distributed applications, and Web services. Many institutions that have had a stake in the old industry are now trying to put their foot in the new field as soon as possible. In this section we describe the various corporations and organiza-

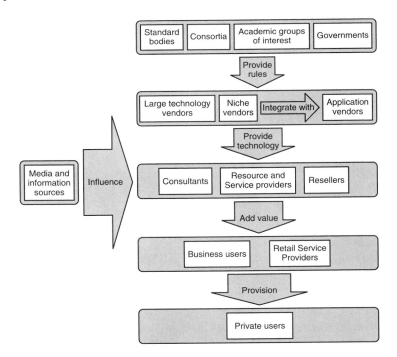

FIGURE 3.2 Grid ecosystem value chain

tions involved with the creation of the modern Grid. Because products, standards, and requirements change quickly, we specifically do not pretend to present a matrix that will allow managers to quickly check off vendors and products in a quest to identify a solution. The closest that can be done there is to suggest that interested managers do their homework using this section as a guide to help kickstart the process.

Standard Bodies and Consortia

Open standards are the key enabling factor of the Grid. The role of the consortia is to build and maintain such standards, with participation of representatives of industry and academia, to ensure that the standards are commonly accepted. Since 2001, the GGF has been the most prominent organization in Grid computing. The GGF, which used to focus only on producing standards, now includes a comprehensive conference that includes vendor exhibitions, business plenary sessions, and case studies sessions. In Chapter 2 we spoke in more detail about the GGF working groups.

The role of EGA is to work on short-term goals that are in line with the incorporation of Grid technology in commercial enterprises.

W3C and OASIS are the standard bodies responsible for Web services (WS) standards, including the WS-Resource Framework (WSRF) collection. The mission of the WS-I group is to foster interoperability among various Web service platforms.

Some pre-WS Grid standards are still maintained by the Internet Engineering Task Force. This is the case with the GridFTP protocol and the GSI Proxy certificates.

Currently there is a visible level of uncertainty as regards the standards community. After the merger of the Grid and Web services communities, the roles and the relations of these bodies to each other became confusing and sometimes questioned. The Open Grid Service Infrastructure standard, which was considered one of the key products of the GGF, has been replaced by the WSRF standards collection and transferred to W3C.[3] The creation of WSRF itself was largely driven by the Globus and IBM teams. At the same time, the OGSA standards, which remained in the GGF, needed to undergo revisions because from that moment it relied on a different underlying technology, managed by a remote standard entity.

The identity crisis in GGF became more visible with the creation of the EGA, which included several industrial members of GGF and is meant to

---

[3] World Wide Web Consortium, responsible for the Web standards.

drive industrial adoption of grids. As pointed out by the former GGF chair Charlie Catlett, 40 percent of GGF members belonged to the industry anyway. The relation between the two organizations remains unclear to several observers; however, closer cooperation is in the interest of almost everyone.

As the industry of the Grid matures, much of the preceding information will become dated, so we urge you to check our online companion at www.savvygrid.com for current information.

Academic Projects and Groups of Interest

Grid computing started in academia and this connection is still very strong. The Globus Alliance associated with Argonne National Laboratory and Information Science Institute at USC, California, is the most frequently recognized "brand" among the academic institutions involved in Grid computing. The Globus Toolkit, the flagship software product of the Alliance, is identified by many with the Grid itself, just as Ian Foster is being called "Mr. Grid Computing." The Globus team, apart from producing the Toolkit, played a major role in the creation of the GGF and the subsequent standards authored by Carl Kesselman, Steve Tuecke, Karl Czajkowski, and other members of the Globus group. In Chapter 2 we named a number of academic middleware "competing" with Globus. The emergence of Globus as the most popular middleware is associated with collaboration of the Globus team with the industry, most notably IBM and Platform Computing. So far, Globus has always remained an entirely open source (unlike Legion or Codine, which after commercialization also maintained closed source versions) but at the same time made sure that their BSD-style license was acceptable for business use.[4] To combat negative perception by the Europeans as a solely American project, in 2003 the Alliance spread internationally and today includes academic institutions in Europe. One year later, in 2004, a commercial offshoot named Univa was created to bring the quality of the Globus Toolkit closer to commercial standards. At the same time, Globus Consortium was created to institutionalize support for Globus Toolkit from large vendors. The Toolkit has a rather small amount of commercial installations. We will return to this topic in the section "Globus Toolkit 4 Grid Service Container" later in this chapter. In Europe, the academic Grid computing movement is strongly

---

[4] BSD is a version of Unix operating system originally developed at the University of California, Berkeley. BSD became popular because of its liberal open-source license.

associated with CERN[5] and the European Union framework programs. The European Data Grid, a Fifth Framework project, was the large collaborative effort for high-energy physics that used the Globus Toolkit as the middleware element. Currently the effort is being continued by a follow-up project called Enabling Grids for E-science in Europe (EGEE), with a broader, horizontal scope of interest. The EGEE is a massive project infrastructure, encompassing a large number of scientific and supercomputing sites throughout Europe. It is aimed at creating a large international Grid infrastructure in Europe based on common middleware.

There are also dozens of less well-known governmental and academic Grid initiatives. Most of the developed countries now have at least one national Grid program. The UK e-Science program, the German D-Grid, Japan's Business Grid Computing, and TeraGrid in the United States comprise part of a long list of such initiatives. Additionally, in 2004 four new major pan-European Grid initiatives—SIMDAT, NEXTGRID, ACOGRIMO, and COREGRID—were funded by the European Union.

When speaking of academic groups of interests, one cannot forget about the projects initially associated with academia, which later became commercial. Most of them maintain strong academic links and have their areas of influence in the GGF. These are Legion (commercialized as Avaki), Codine (now Sun Grid Engine), and Unicore.

In the United States, an interesting, noncommercial institution that escaped the previous classification is MCNC in North Carolina. Although associated with the state of North Carolina, the MCNC is an independent nonprofit organization, which became the grid provider and technology excellence center for a number of research and commercial institutions. MCNC has been covered in a separate case study earlier in this chapter.

Large Vendors

Even those who have never heard of Grid computing could easily guess who are the largest industry players in this game. The usual suspects are IBM, Sun, Hewlett Packard, and Microsoft. IBM has been especially active in supporting Globus, GGF, and other Grid initiatives for several years. IBM's vision of Utility Computing, on-demand business, and commitment to Web services is in line with the Grid technology development. After all, this technology leads to on-demand service provisioning. IBM offers an extensive

---

[5] CERN, the particle physics laboratory located near Geneva with the world's largest particle accelerator is also the birthplace of the Web.

portfolio of solutions where Grid products from their partners are comple-
mented by the IBM products and services. Platform, DataSynapse, Avaki,
and United Devices are the key Grid independent software vendors (ISVs)
participating in this offer. Also, IBM Solutions Grid, with three locations in
the United States and one in the United Kingdom, offers infrastructure and
assistance for vendors in bringing products to Grid standards.

Sun's slogan "the network is the computer," popularized by Sun's CEO
Scott McNealy, has later been rephrased into "the Grid is the computer" after
Sun purchased Gridware, the vendor of Codine. Today Codine's successor,
Sun N1 Grid Engine, which is integrated in the N1 package, is the key Sun's
DRM offering, hovering around 10,000 installations—a market share to
which only Platform's LSF can compare.

HP has been approaching the Grid field through initiatives such as
Adaptive Enterprise. HP has also packaged a "Grid" portfolio of their existing and new products topped with consulting and engineering services. This
includes support for the Globus Toolkit adapted for the HP platform.

Microsoft has been rather absent in the mainstream of the Grid computing
trend, which focuses on large processing powers and platform interoperability.
However, the company plays an active role in creating the GGF and Web service
standards. Microsoft's marketing slogan closest to the Grid trend is the
"Autonomous Computing," though it has never been as aggressively promoted as
by other vendors, who integrated Grid slogans in their main marketing strategy.

The list of major OS vendors cannot be complete without Apple. The
company plays virtually no role in the mainstream Grid community.
However, it has been successfully building "Grid" installations, based on its
Xgrid technology. This niche product is limited to Macintosh architectures
and mostly focused on combining the processing power of several Macs into
a cluster. This is the lowest common denominator of understanding the word
"grid" and has a long way to contribute to the vision presented in this book.

Grid-Specializing Vendors and Niche Vendors

There are several names which are closely associated with the Grid movement.
Platform, the producer of LSF scheduler, has been in the field for the past
decade. Previously targeting stand alone clusters, the LSF suite now provides load
balancing and resource management engine for enterprise Grid installation.

United Devices and DataSynapse also make scheduling engines are more
recent entries to the field. United Devices is associated with the famous
SETI@home initiative and is the producer of GridMP, a job management
engine designed for open environments. DataSynapse's product, GridServer,
is marketed as a Service Scheduler.

Avaki has lately removed Grid from their marketing to announce itself an enterprise information integration (EII) solutions provider. However, the company, founded by Andrew Grimshaw from the University of Virginia, is being remembered in the community as the new incarnation of the Legion, providing a unique data grid solution.

In the Globus market, Univa Corporation[6] was founded by the three fathers of the Grid, Ian Foster, Steve Tuecke and Carl Kesselman. Univa provides a commercial version of the Globus Toolkit and professional services around it. As a statement to the growing importance of Grid computing, the year Univa was founded Network World named them a top ten start-up to watch.

At least a dozen other names of companies are providing Grid-related solutions, including Altair, GridSystems, GridXpert, and Paremus. Many of these offerings, as well as those of Platform, United Devices, and DataSynapse, are some form of Distributed Resource Management, thus reducing the concept of Grid to cycle scavenging. As we mentioned earlier, there are not many products building on more advanced Grid concepts such as virtual organizations.

Note that we have purposely excluded hardware vendors from this discussion. Grid computing is about a rather high-level interoperability and thus Grid-specific hardware is rather hard to imagine (although we could imagine that, when protocol standards become stable, Grid-specific communication could be implemented in hardware stack to increase the speed). In contrast, to construct enterprise grids, you need a variety of equipment, such as is needed in any larger IT infrastructure.

Application Vendors

It is important to distinguish between the generic Grid middleware vendors and the application vendors. The first group provides the resource management fabric. Applications can be Grid-enabled by being integrated with this fabric. Often this integration process is performed case-by-case, on site, and manually. For instance, Threshold Digital reconfigured its image-rendering installation, enabling it to outsource the rendering tasks to the IBM Deep Computing Capacity on Demand center in Poughkeepsie, NY.

However, some application vendors choose to prefabricate integrated Grid solutions and provide the user with ready-to-use solution with some sort of parallel functionality built in. The classic example is Oracle who "Grid-enabled" its database management system. When Oracle10g is installed on a cluster, parallelism, failover, and redundancy features will be provided automatically.

---

[6] Disclosure: Wellner is the Enterprise Architect with this firm.

Many application providers choose to integrate with existing Grid solutions, instead of developing their own from scratch. For instance, in 2004 Algorithmics and DataSynapse have signed an exclusive OEM agreement to provide Data Synapse's on-demand application infrastructure software in Algo Suite 4.4. Another example is SAP, who integrated its offering with Grid middleware from its long-term ally Sun, to announce Sun Infrastructure Solution for N1 Grid for SAP Solutions targeted at those enterprises who need to consolidate equipment in their data centers. SAP has also done technology demonstrations using Globus to manage the provisioning of SAP services.

Vendor Taxonomy According to the 451

The 451 Group in their Grids 2004 report classified vendors with respect to their potential for capturing the market. In the report's terminology, there are three tiers of Grid solutions producers. Tier 1 vendors are those with a strong momentum and potential to capture market share. These are HP, IBM, Microsoft, and Sun. Tier 2 are those middle-sized companies with strong strategies or technology portfolios. Those are Computer Associates, Intel, Oracle, Platform Computing, SGI, and Veritas. Tier 3 are important pure-play Grid vendors that, according to The 451, would need to evolve to capture a significant market position: Altair, Avaki, Axceleon, DataSynapse, Ejasent, Enigmatec, Entropia, GridFrastructure, GridIron, GridSystems, GridXpert, Powerllel, Tsunami Research, The Mind Electric, and United Devices.

Grid Resource Providers

An interesting emerging class of institutions is the Grid resource providers. These companies and consortia providing access to on-demand resources are the first generation of the Grid infrastructure providers of the future. Examples of such initiatives includes the HP Utility Data Center, IBM Deep Computing Capacity on Demand, Sun Fire Capacity on Demand, White Rose Grid consortium, MCNC Grid Computing, and Networking Services or Gateway Grid Computing Services.

We have seen the example of MCNC Grid Computing and Networking Services. They provide users with the Grid software stack on which users can deploy and run their own Grid-enabled applications. Users then pay for the resources they have used, measured in CPU-hours or storage units. White Rose Grid consortium in the United Kingdom, centered in the universities of York, Sheffield, and Leeds, delivers a similar service to a handful of local companies.

In the commercial space, since 2001 HP has offered Utility Data Center services; IBM Deep Computing Capacity On-Demand has been offering servers for hire in two centers, Poughkeepsie, NY, and Montpelier, France. Recently, Sun announced Sun Fire Capacity on Demand (COD) 2.0 program.

Another interesting example of a resource provider is the Gateway Grid Services program started in December 2002. Gateway installed GridMP middleware from United Devices in their retail stores network. However, unlike most enterprise grid customers, Gateway did not use it for its own computations, but sold the computer power. One customer is the American Diabetes Association, who uses the combined power of 7000 Gateway PCs for its research.

These initiatives aren't yet truly on-demand. In most cases, they require intervention of technicians and administrators. Also, what is offered for hire are physical servers, not virtual resources. With virtual computing services, one would buy a number of cycles. Today, one has to hire a number of server racks. For instance, until recently HP UDC offered an entry package of its services for $1 million. Nevertheless, these initiatives demonstrate the huge step forward toward on-demand computing technology that has occurred in recent years.

Consultants

The offer of technical consultants and service companies complements the products available on the market. Grid installation usually requires considerable integration effort; therefore picking the right service company can be as important as choosing the right software solution. Also, a consulting agreement usually precedes the deal with the vendor, as external consultants are often involved in the process of designing the system, building the proof-of-concept, and choosing among vendors. We will return to this process in Chapter 6.

Most vendors cooperate with large service companies such as IBM. Stronger vendors, such as Platform, also have their own service teams available locally in many countries. Other vendors, such as Sun or Altair, are more likely to cooperate with independent service companies that usually specialize in their local market and deliver local integration support. A special class of integration service firms are the resellers, who are usually oriented geographically and represent vendors locally. Resellers often augment the original vendor solution with their own products. For example the NICE, an Italian reseller of Platform, delivers the original vendor products together with a convenient Grid portal, EnginFrame developed by themselves. Most vendors partner with a number of resellers available locally in several countries.

There are few pure-play technical advisors not associated with any Grid technology vendor. Their strength is an unbiased, objective market perspective. Those include Gridwise Technologies[7] (Europe, United States) and BestSystems (Japan). These companies, apart from vendor-independent advice, also provide engineering resources for cross-vendor integration and development tasks.

Apart from technical consultants and service companies, there is a number of analytical firms researching Grid computing. Next to the well-known global analytical institutions such as IDC, Gartner Group, or Forrester Research, there is a number of smaller firms who specialize in the Grid market. Market reports produced by these groups and sometimes distributed at professional events can be a good source of insight for the newcomers in the field. These firms include The 451 Group ("Grids deployed in the Enterprise"), The Economic Strategy Institute ("North Carolina Report"), Grid Technology Partners ("Grid Report 2002"), and The Tabb Group ("Grid computing in Financial Markets").

Media and Other Information Providers

There is a variety of information channels with a varied power of market influence. The Grid-specific ones can be broadly divided into the press, Web portals, and professional events. We will cover this topic in detail in Chapter 6, in the section "Marketing Mix."

The Panorama of Today's Products

We are now entering the most volatile part of this book, in which we present a taste of the Grid market solutions. Because product specifications and features change frequently, we urge you to continue your research in our online companion, where the up-to-date information is posted. This companion can be found at www.savvygrid.com.

For the same reason, here we present only some representative examples of various families of solutions. The list is not, and will never be, complete. However, it may help to understand what classes of software products are important for building grids.

The choice of products is arbitrary. We will later use some of these products as illustrations in grid-building scenarios (Chapter 5). However, this does not mean that we endorse these particular solutions. In each section, before discussing a representative product, we provide a list of competitive offerings belonging to the same category.

---

[7] Disclosure: The authors of this book are partners in Gridwise Technologies.

Distributed Resource Management

The class of products that used to be called scheduling systems are now often referred to as distributed resource management. This addresses the fact that these systems are far more sophisticated, and their use is broader, than when they were used only to dispatch jobs over Beowulf clusters. The aforementioned Platform LSF, Sun N1 Grid Engine, the PBS family, the open-source Condor from the University of Wisconsin, GridMP from United Devices, or GridServer from DataSynapse belong to this group.

SUN N1 Grid Engine Family

In 2000, Sun Microsystems acquired Gridware, a small company based in Germany and the United States with academic traditions and distributed computing offerings. The key products of Gridware, Codine, and GRD (Global Resource Director) were refactored into the DRM toolkit, which is currently the SUN's flagship Grid computing product. At first simply called the (Sun) Grid Engine, or SGE, the latest version is marketed as N1 Grid Engine 6 (N1GE6) to stress that it is an integral part of the N1 line of products. This middleware allows for managing the computing power of the Solaris and Linux machines available in the company by virtualizing them as one computing resource. In consequence, the resource usage is increased and the user access is simplified.

The system is organized in a three-tier fashion similar to the Grid service virtualization scheme presented in Chapter 2. Users grouped in the Access Tier send processing requests to the Grid Engine server (Management Tier). The server dispatches the jobs to the resources aggregated in the lowest Compute Tier, consisting of the available machines. Currently the Grid Engine server does not exhibit a Grid service-compliant interface; thus the client machines must use the proprietary software from SUN. However, the vendor has published the Grid Engine programmer application programmer interface (API) on which custom-built Grid service interfaces are possible. Sun is working with the GGF to standardize this API. This effort is being implemented by the Distributed Resource Management Application API (DRMAA) working group. Also, the code of the Grid Engine has been made available as open source under the Sun Industry Standards License and is accessible online.

The software is available in two distribution lines. The basic version, Grid Engine, is open source and available for free download under the standard Sun Industry Standard License (authorizing free use). It allows for grouping resources and submitting jobs. The full version of the software, N1 Grid Engine, comes with commercial support and additional accounting functionality.

N1 Grid Engine works on Solaris and Linux (2.4 kernel) on SPARC and x86 platforms. Sun N1 Grid Engine 6 (formerly called Sun Grid Engine Enterprise Edition, and before that Sun ONE Grid Engine, Enterprise Edition) works on a number of platforms and operating systems, including most versions of Unix. N1GE6 addresses the need of enterprise grids, where multiple teams and departments with various projects share the common resources. Resources are assigned over specified periods of time (weeks, months, quarters) to each product, project, design team, and user. Units of work are represented as "tickets." Using a share-based policy, departments and users are assigned a certain number of tickets, equivalent of a share of available resources. In circumstances where the resources are fully utilized, the system does not allow users to use more tickets than already assigned.

If there are spare resources available, however, the active users are temporarily allowed to consume a higher number of tickets, in proportion to their default-assigned share. In such a case, users effectively use more resources then their share allows for. Users who are inactive during this time may later be compensated for their inactivity by being allocated extra resources. At the same time, those users who had overused their policy-allocated resources may be penalized by access restrictions. This is regulated by the half-life factor and the compensation factor set forth by the administrator. The administrator can also assign an "Override Policy" to a certain user, granting him an extra quantity of tickets that is not subject to the share-based allocation and penalties.

N1GE6 allows virtualization and single system-image centralized management of resources such as CPU, memory, and I/O. Its advertised benefits are increased utilization and ease of access to resources. It is suitable for compute-intensive industries. The product does not have an open Web service interface, and its integration with a Service-Oriented Architectures (SOA) will require customization. However, the open-source policy of SUN provides a solid foundation for such work. Thanks to the product line maturity, as well as the liberal open-source policy, Sun is proudly able to quote the number of installations of the SGE in the tens of thousands worldwide.

LSF Suite from Platform Computing

With more than a decade of history in commercial Grid solutions, Platform Computing is among the most experienced technology providers in the field. Platform is a privately owned company dedicated to Grid and distributed computing. The Toronto, Canada-based company grew from an academic environment, where its founders first developed the Load Sharing Facility (LSF) middleware. The commercialized LSF became the Platform's first offering, and its success enabled the impressive growth of the firm. Platform now offers a broad range of products and reports more than 1600 customers worldwide.

Today, when the company offers a broad family of products, LSF is still the core system behind most of them. LSF is the DRM that manages batch processing of compute-intensive applications. When installed on a cluster of nodes, it creates job queues and handles the load balancing among the machines. Internally, LSF consists of the Load Information Manager and batch submission system. The cooperation between the master and slave batch submission processes (mbatchd and sbatchd), which is run on all machines, allows for a job-queuing and execution mechanism that is transparent to the user, thus providing virtualization of resources. Applications built on top of LSF use LSFLIB and LSFBLIB API to access the system. Platform LSF also includes an API for its extensible, modular, multiphase scheduling framework.

LSF has failure-resilience capabilities. In the case of a master host failure, the responsibilities are taken over by one of its peers who automatically starts the master daemons.[8] Also, LSF allows for checkpointing of instrumented code of submitted applications. LSF runs on a majority of popular platforms, including those from HP, IBM, MsWindows, SGI, Sun, Apple, and Linux. The enhanced version LSF HPC with advanced scheduling algorithms is run on several Top 500 clusters.

Platform offerings, with rare exceptions, are not available as open-source. However, the company actively cooperates with the open-source community, with the notable example of the Globus Toolkit, the recent versions of which have been augmented by the open-source Community Scheduler Framework (CSF) contributed by Platform. CSF is a collection of Grid services run in the Globus container, acting as a single point of contact to multiple clusters. CSF is capable of advance reservation, execution, and monitoring of jobs submitted to clusters that run LSF or Globus GRAM. CSF can also be used simply as a standard-compliant Grid service interface to LSF.

Platform ActiveCluster is a tool suitable for data mining applications, where sophisticated pattern queries are executed against large volumes of data. It is able to decompose both the domain and the query into pieces, to later split it into an array each-by-each computation and submit it to very large LSF clusters.

---

[8] In Unix terminology, a daemon is a process running in the background. In the case of LSF, the master daemon is the process running on the LSF master host responsible for the core functions.

The LSF family also contains complementary products such as LSF MultiCluster, LSF Licence Scheduler, LSF Reports, and LSF Analytics. All these solutions allow to optimize the use of resources and adapt them for the execution of various business processes.

Service Containers and Hosting Environments

The trend to SOAs and resource virtualization leads toward a smaller granularity of independent, self-contained services that cooperate in federations. Because one machine can host thousands of service instances, manual administration is out of the question. Services must be highly commoditized, with their typical administrative functions conforming to the well-known schemes of the underlying platform. This lower level hosting environment must expose management procedures, ensuring automatic provisioning, hosting, configuring, and monitoring of services. Some hosting environments are referred to as service containers, reflecting that one such environment may, although not necessarily, host multiple services.

Globus Toolkit 4 provides the WSRF-compliant service hosting environment. This container, based on Apache Axis, is often considered for reference implementations of Grid environments. However, a number of related solutions should also be seriously considered for Grid systems, although they do not carry the "Grid" logo.

The open-source Apache Axis provides the base Web service technology for Globus. Axis implements SOAP and provides a simple service container server. Other popular application servers include IBM WebSphere, Orion, open-source servlet container Tomcat, and EJB containers: commercial Sun Java System Application Server and open-source JBoss.

The advantage of Globus over these solutions, apart from the liberal BSD-style open-source license, is the community leadership in WSRF standard compliance. As explained in Chapter 2, even today a certain part of the community considers Globus 2 the de facto standard, ignoring what the GGF invented during the last 3 years.

Unless another major storm occurs in the standards field, we shall soon expect to see many WSRF products competing with Globus. WSRF has already been implemented simultaneously by a number of projects such as WSRF.net from the University of Virginia. Commercial implementations include the IBM Emerging Technologies Toolkit (ETTK), currently available for a free trial period.

Note on Service Containers, Server Containers, and Service Provisioning Systems

Service containers are separate but, in some cases, difficult to differentiate from service provisioning, or application management solutions. Products in this category assist in automatic administering of large numbers of services and applications, which are not necessarily hosted in one service container. For instance, a provisioning system could automatically apply security patches to all installations of the same application present in a cluster or a grid. Other automated functions include deployment, management, provisioning, configuration, and updates. Well-known commercial products with such functionality include the open-source SmartFrog from HP, Sun N1 Grid Service Provisioning System, and IBM Tivoli Provisioning Manager. As an example of academic compute farm management systems, we cite the Quattor system administrator tool suite developed at CERN.

Another group of solutions functionally close to all-software service containers are the server containers implemented at the OS level. Sandboxing a service in a separate virtual operating system instance provides better isolation, easier debugging, fewer side-effects, and improved security. Naturally, this solution is more heavyweight, demanding more resources than typical solutions, and requires more administrative effort. Still, considerable improvement in streamlining these tasks has been reached, most notably the Solaris 10 operating system, where the administrator is provided with the N1 Grid Console Container Manager GUI for the configuration of multiple containers virtualized on a blade server. In the open-source world, initiatives such as User Mode Linux provide similar OS-over-OS hosting.

Globus Toolkit 4 Grid Service Container

Globus Toolkit (GT), which has already been partly described in Chapter 2, is a collection of highly independent software modules. One important component present in the fourth release of the toolkit (GT4) is the WSRF Grid service container.

This Java-implemented server can be used for hosting a number of Web services. Some of these (base services) are provided by the toolkit, but Globus provides programmers with tools and libraries to implement custom services using Java. According to the WSRF principles, the services are static but they can be associated with transient "WS-resources" representing volatile concepts such as database records, transactions, results files, or temporary data. Globus provides tools that should in principle speed up developer's tasks by generating WSDL interfaces, as well as simplifying the deployment, logging, and debugging of services.

Services that are hosted in the container and the WS-resources associated with them are either stand-alone applications or interface lower-level applications. The three "pillars" of Globus Toolkit 2—the GRAM, MDS, and GridFTP—all have their Grid service interfaces; thus at the same time they provide an example how applications can be Grid-compliant (Figure 3.3). The toolkit comes with a set of trivial self-contained services that also demonstrate how entire applications written in Java could be hosted in the container. These include a fileshare service, providing a simple peer-to-peer file sharing. One example of an external application hosted in the Globus container is the NEESgrid's NTCP system that takes part in multisite earthquake simulation management. NTCP, initially developed in the previous version of the toolkit, is being currently ported to GT4. More detail is provided in the NEESgrid case study.

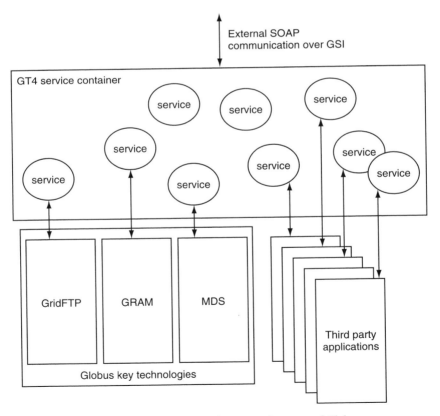

FIGURE 3.3 GT4 service container in relation to other parts of Globus

Globus-hosted Grid services take full advantage of the GSI security that is an integral part of the toolkit. The SOAP communication between services can be easily authenticated, authorized, integrity-checked, and protected. This Grid service GSI security implementation is compliant with the WS-Security standards.

Because we listed the Globus container among other commercial offerings, it should be clearly stated that there has been a huge commercial interest, but not many commercial deployments of previous versions of the toolkit. On the other hand, there are some market signals that the enterprise interest in practical Globus installation may rapidly grow in the coming years. The maturing of standards, a large number of CEOs at the GlobusWorld'05 conference, the formation of a commercial offshoot of Globus and the adoption of advanced testing procedures all suggest that the project may be driving toward providing a commercial, rather than academic, quality software. However, since version 4 is being issued only while this book is going to print, proper assessment of the current situation may be difficult.

Portals and End-User Interfaces to the Grid

Just as the Web portals are designed for the humans who look for organized Web contents, the Grid portals are the human interfaces to the Grid resources. In most cases, the Grid portals are the specialized Web portals. Users of portals can browse through resources, submit computational jobs, track their status, transfer large files, and participate in collaborative environments.

In the portals, as in the other component technologies of Grid computing, the role of standards is important for the interoperability and the ease of integration. Portals do not provide value by themselves, but add value to the backend systems. Therefore the issue of integration is crucial for them.

One strong standards-driven Grid portal solution is the Gridsphere, developed within the GridLab collaboration between Europe and the United States. Gridsphere is a portlet container compliant to the Portlet API (de facto standard developed in the Java Community Process). The Gridsphere team is currently also working toward WSRP (Web Services for Remote Portlets) consumer compliance. The product also supports Java Server Faces.

A parallel effort is the Open Grid Computing Environments collaboration in the United States, in short known as the OGCE consortium, sponsored by the National Science Foundation National Middleware Infrastructure. The OGCE is a large project that develops a collection of Grid portlets. In the OGCE, the access to Grid resources are made available through integrated third-party technologies, such as the Java Commodity Grid Kit (CoG Kit) from Argonne National Laboratory and CHEF from University of Michigan. Another open-source Grid portal effort worth quoting is the GridPort and the associated HotPage from National Partnership for Advanced Computational Infrastructure in the United States.

There are also a number of commercial portal solutions. One example is EnginFrame by Italian company NICE. EnginFrame integrates with commercial DRMs, which NICE resells. In fact, many Grid computing software products today come with a customized Web portal interface.

Apart from the specialized Grid portals, a number of user communities reuse generic Web portal suites and enhance them with Grid functionality. Jetspeed, uPortal, or CHEF are some examples of middleware used here.

Portals are convenient because they are delivered to the user inside the browser. However, this is not the only way to provide the users with interfaces to the Grid. The Java-based Migrating Desktop from the Crossgrid project provides a Windows-like environment for remote users logging onto the Grid. The functionality available to the user is similar to what can be achieved through the browser-based portals.

It should be interesting to track the evolution of the Grid portal market in the coming years. Although a number of advanced solutions have been developed, there are no clear market leaders. In a few years from now we should expect a drastic change in the role of the Grid portals. Many of these interfaces operate on the abstraction of jobs and CPUs. In the mature Grid environments of the future, users should be shielded from these concepts. Instead, the portals could become the containers for advanced application-specific interfaces.

Security Solutions

Although there is intensive work being done on the Grid security front, there has yet been no compelling security architecture for partner grids. Today, as 3 years ago, firewalls are the major obstacle for extra-enterprise expansion of Grid computing. Grids are either being created inside the firewalls (department grids, enterprise grids) or not at all. Virtual private networks or client-server communication tunneled over Secure Socket Layer (SSL) are among the few early steps toward commercial open grid connectivity. On the other hand, a number of advanced security solutions were developed in the academia and were based on the GSI scheme. We have to admit that because of the critical nature of security in grid architectures, these academic solutions have difficulties in paving their road to enterprise usage. We have already covered GSI in Chapter 2 and will pay special attention to some of its derivatives, such as CAS and MyProxy server in Chapter 5.

Data Solutions

Perhaps second only to compute cycle optimization, data solutions present the most obvious and well-understood area of Grid computing. There are several existing standards (e.g., GridFTP, SRM) and most products claiming to do things on the Grid have support for at least a subset of them. Chapter 5 contains a discussion of various aspects of data handling including storage, transport, and dealing with data sensitivity.

Avaki

Among the early meta-computing systems (see Chapter 2), there was Legion, from the University of Virginia. Developed in a group effort led by Professor Andrew Grimshaw, Legion was written in C++ in 1996[9] and was first released in 1997. Since then, this system has attracted the academic community and is an active academic project to this day.

In parallel to this activity, the fathers of Legion created a commercial company that has been selling the commercial-class Grid software. The company, founded in 1999, is named Avaki,[10] like its flagship product. The code of Avaki was based on Legion through the early version 2.6. Later it was rewritten in Java.

The original Legion is a full-fledged object-oriented Grid system, allowing scientists to share a wide variety of resources. Legion provides a location-independent data and resource access layer, so that remote data sources can be accessed the same way as local ones. Moreover, the system allows to seamlessly access other types of resources, such as scientific instruments or applications. Finally, Legion has features of remote execution and parallel processing. In the object-oriented approach, it models Grid resources as "object files," hiding their complexity and the fact of being remote. Although Legion is certainly among the most interesting academic Grid solutions, we should rather focus on Avaki here, for it has had more commercial impact and is being widely used in business and industry.

---

[9] To be precise, prototype-level versions of Legion existed before that date. They were based on the code of the earlier distributed system, Mentat, and were not distributed publicly.

[10] In one of the native languages of French Polynesia, *avaki* means to share or distribute.

Although Avaki shares with Legion its origins and design principles, it is now a separate product. Where Legion serves a wide variety of resources, Avaki focuses on managing the data layer on the Grid. In business terms, the product falls into the category of EII solutions. There are several EII providers in the market, and Avaki is unique because of its usage of Grid technology. Their customers come from various domains such as the pharmaceutical industry, oil and gas, and financial services. However, the Avaki offering is not specific to any of these sectors.

Avaki EII provides provisioning, integration, and access of data and information resources throughout the enterprise. It gives a uniform, integrated look at these resources. Avaki is able to harness various data sources such as files, relational databases, XML,[11] and Web services. The user can access all of them in a uniform fashion, whether local or remote. The fact of physical distribution is hidden and the user often cannot tell the fact of using Grid. In this respect, Avaki is somewhat similar to a distributed filesystem, such as NFS or AFS. However, these systems fail to provide secure and reliable data access across firewalls. Also, NFS deals exclusively with files and directories, while Avaki extends the abstraction to other data sources and formats.

Avaki also provides an integrated view of data and makes it easier to transform, aggregate, and integrate data, assisting users in creating derivative data objects. For instance, if a file contains a spreadsheet, a data object derived from this file can provide methods to conveniently access the spreadsheet data by rows and columns, without the need for explicit file parsing.

The single data access layer hides the underlying complex Grid architecture. This architecture solves the problems of caching for performance and coherence maintenance. In principle, network failures should be invisible to the user. If a connection with a remote data sources is broken, users should be able to continue to operate in a disconnected model. Avaki is managing caching and cache coherence necessary to operate in such mode and later reconnect and synchronize with the remote resources. All this happens under cover; the user does not have to think about the process.

Through its Grid architecture, Avaki provides scalability among projects and potentially even organizations, lowering the burden of unnecessary data redundancy and replication. Avaki is currently the best known commercial product that offers what has been known in the academic world as the Data Grid.

Avaki offers a complex licensing model, based on the components of the system that the user is interested in using. A free distribution is available to chosen academic institutions on direct requests.

---

[11] Extensible Markup Language (XML) is a format for storing information in a text file.

Applications

Grid-enabled applications are those that are able to access resources with the mediation of the Grid middleware layer instead of directly accessing the local operating system. Thus, Grid-enabling means refactoring low-level modules of the application such as local file I/O layer, to make it compliant to Grid protocol standards. One could Grid-enable an application to access data through the common Grid interface, communicate with WSRF Grid services, become accessible through the distributed collaborative environment, or become part in the workflows of secure virtual organizations. However, the most popular way of Grid-enabling is to make applications work faster by integrating them with a DRM solution for parallel execution of its jobs.

Some scientific applications, such as BLAST, which is used for searching of nucleotide and protein databases, are Grid-enabled by nature, and their integration with a scheduling system is straightforward. Other applications require more work. However many application vendors go through the effort of Grid-enabling to provide the user with the integrated solution. This is the case for Algorithmics, producer of Algo Suite, and SAP, the two examples mentioned previously.

Since 2003, IBM has had a special program for ISVs planning to ship Grid applications. If this is integrated with IBM Grid solutions, the company invites the vendor to one of its Solutions Grid centers, where the application can go through integration testing against an array of Grid middleware solutions from IBM and its partners. In 2004, IBM announced that applications from seven vendors (Citrix, Cognos, Enginous Software, Abaqus, Actuate, Fluent, and Sefas) had successfully completed the Grid-enabling program.

Oracle10g is also being marketed as a certain type of Grid-enabled application. The system uses the Grid technology to make the database jobs run in parallel on a cluster of servers. The specifics of database requirements (moderate geographical distribution possibilities) suggest that "cluster-enabling" would be a more adequate term. However, this may only be the first step on the road. As we have seen from several examples, mastering clusters is the prerequisite to proficiency in Grid computing.

➤ **CASE STUDY:** The NEESgrid Cyberinfrastructure

At the turn of the twentieth century, earthquake science in the United States was being done in several independent experimental facilities. Although each of them was making progress and gaining momentum within its own scope of research, it was felt that collaboration between the facilities was not done in the most effective way. When the researchers from two centers needed to share experience, one group would typically send its staff and graduate students to the other laboratory. Once there, the notebooks would be opened up and reviewed. The data were exchanged, but it required the inefficient process with humans in the loop. In a similar way, if researchers from one site wanted to use the experimental facilities located elsewhere, they would typically set off for travel, because their physical presence at the experimental site was necessary. Some groups managed to set up multisite experiments, but each one was a monstrous task, requiring development of specialized software that was not suited for reuse.

Earthquake science today largely relies on physical simulation experiments, characterized as large and expensive. Not many scientific sites can afford such an infrastructure. Scientists working at sites without costly infrastructure have limited opportunities to participate in experiments, but even those who worked where experimental facilities were located could only benefit from the local infrastructure.

To improve this situation, an interoperable infrastructure was needed to enhance collaboration and reduce the stovepipe solutions at each site. Interconnecting experimental facilities, systems, resources, and skills of various sites would result in an organism whose capabilities would by far exceed these of each of those sites working separately. Moreover, if all those systems used common data and meta-data standards, and common protocols and processes, interoperability would be brought to a higher level. Experimental data could be kept at repositories accessible for all to browse. Analytical tools, simulations, and interfaces could be developed to operate on such repositories. Earthquake science could rapidly progress, benefiting from the "net factor" similar to what is today happening in the Internet at large. Therefore the National Science Foundation (NSF) decided to build a common *cyberinfrastructure* integrating several experimental sites for the benefit of the entire earthquake engineering community in the United States. The vision of the NEES project (in full, George E. Brown, Jr. Network for Earthquake Engineering Simulation) was to transform the nation's ability to carry out earthquake engineering research, to obtain information vital to develop improved methods for reducing the nation's vulnerability to catastrophic earthquakes, and to educate new generations of engineers, scientists, and other specialists committed to improving seismic safety.

NEES, started in late 1999, was a Major Research Equipment program at the NSF. Planned as a 15-year initiative, its first 5 years[12] were planned for building the infrastructure, with overall funding of $82.9 million. The system

---

[12] As it was explained to us by Randy Butler from NCSA, for various formal reasons the work did not actually start until 2001. In this context it is important to realize that the entire NEESgrid infrastructure was completed and production-ready in 3 years.

was to become operational in October 2004. Although most of the funding was spent on hardware purchase and upgrade of equipment facilities, $11 million was allocated for the cyberinfrastructure development. This money funded a group of about 20 designers, developers, and engineers participating in the development effort called the NEESgrid.

Technical Overview

The technical goal of NEESgrid was to provide a Grid-based infrastructure to enable the community to access and share resources (experiments) and data, in a secure and dependable fashion and without respect to the geographical location or institution boundaries. This goal is easier to explain using a simple example of an experiment named Multisite Online Simulation Test (MOST), prepared and performed by NEESgrid in 2003. The goal of the experiment was to simulate the behavior of a fragment of a building during an earthquake ground motion. The simulated fragment consisted of a two-bay single-story steel frame (Figure 3.4).

It was required that at least part of the structure should be simulated by a physical model. The difficulty is that due to its material properties, the model often needs to be constructed in a 1-to-1 scale. This particular experiment belongs in a pseudodynamic category, in which the duration of the experiment is not constrained by the actual duration of the simulated event.

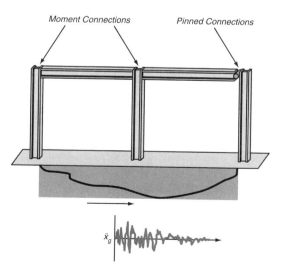

FIGURE 3.4 Simulated structure

This is important because earthquakes often take a fraction of a second, which would be difficult to repeat in the laboratory. Thus, the size constraints of the simulation model are strict, but the time constraints are not. In the MOST experiment, the simulation was designed so that the model was to be split into three parts located in three geographically separated facilities (Figure 3.5). Two columns were simulated by steel beams in a 1-to-1 scale, located at University of Illinois in Urbana-Champaign and University of Colorado, while the center part was simulated computationally. Grid technology was used to compose them into one virtual experiment, by seamlessly connecting the three pieces in a way where each one "thinks" it is part of a larger structure. The benefit of this approach was that by using resources of several sites one virtual construction was simulated, which, because of scale constraints, exceeded the capabilities of each of them. At the same time, the time delays of the interconnecting network were acceptable, as in pseudodynamics an extra fraction of a second added to each time-step did not matter.

MOST works in the following way. The research community has a collection of ground movement data from historical earthquakes. Engineers want to apply this to the simulated structure as if it went through the actual earthquake. The two physical beams are connected to a set of hydraulic actuators, which apply force and momentum to the structures to simulate the ground movement. Attached sensors receive the beam displacement and rotation, and pass the information on to the remote simulation components, as if

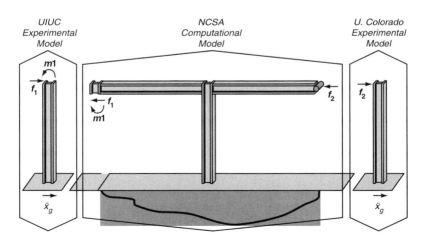

FIGURE 3.5 MOST substructures and locations

the remotely simulated parts were physically connected. In this way, the three dislocated segments take part in an experiment, which behaves as if the structure it simulates was real. This is referred to as a *hybrid* experiment (i.e., such that is simulated in part by a physical model and in part by a computational simulation).

At the same time, an array of sensors continuously registers a large number of data about the actual behavior of the structure. These data are the actual experiment results, streamed to the repository for postprocessing analysis. It can also be streamed directly to the user interface and viewed in real time.

Local and remote experiment participants also have a number of collaborative and observation tools at their disposal. The experiment progress can be monitored online by observing the behavior of each of its parts, viewing the real-time data, and watching the video. Participants also have a collaboration toolkit enabling them to chat and exchange information resources.

MOST is a reference example of types of hybrid experiments that could be done using the NEESgrid software toolkit. MOST encompassed two experimental facilities and one computational facility, separated by 1000 miles. The distributed experiment was composed of almost 1500 time steps and took several hours to complete. At the same time, it is only meant as a reference demonstrator of the NEESgrid toolkit. Future experiments using NEESgrid software could be performed at a much larger scale, with participation of tens of sites and more sophisticated physical models, heterogeneous simulations, and hardware instruments. They will belong to various institutions that would profit by virtually connecting the hardware. Grid protocols and middleware will be used as the glue interconnecting these instruments, and also to provide secure and reliable access for remote users, participants, and observers.

Hardware

The majority of NEES hardware expenses were related to the construction of physical simulation models, which are often unique and cost several thousands, and sometimes millions of dollars. Sometimes one such model is constructed for a single experiment in which it is purposely destroyed. Apart from this, the professional equipment included centrifuges, reaction wall facilities, shake tables, tsunami wave tanks, and mobile field equipment. Unlike in many other Grid project, here CPU nodes for computationally intensive tasks represented a rather small fraction of the total hardware cost. For this reason, NEESgrid is unique for today's Grid computing, as it demonstrates the variety of resources that can be connected in the Grid. From this perspective, we gain an important context to have another look at today's commercial enterprise Grid initiatives, mostly focused on integrating storage and compute clusters. Clearly, these are only very early steps on the road. The potential of Grid computing covers a much broader scope and opportunities, a glimpse of which has been shown by NEESgrid.

Software

The modular NEESgrid software is provided in a number of relatively independent components, allowing for great flexibility in composing new solutions. One major group of components provides telecontrol and teleobservation functionality for the experiment operator. It encompasses protocols and services for integrating and running the experiment and retrieving the results. The software relies on Grid middleware Globus Toolkit, and uses a number of commercial solutions such as Labview, ShoreWestern, Matlab, or DataTurbine. These are used to interface the equipment and stream the data.

Separate pieces of software include the computational simulation services, composed of several modules. One of them is based on open-source OpenSees platform, while another one includes Matlab-based simulation software. The other component is the experiment data repository. This consists of local repositories, a central repository and archiving service, and a set of service protocols interconnecting the repositories, applications, and portals.

The Web-based collaboration portal is based on CHEF, a product from the University of Michigan. It provides chat, data sharing and exchange, and facilities for browsing and viewing the repository data.

NEESgrid components use GSI security provided by Globus. The Web portal integrates with MyProxy package, which provides automatic management of user credentials. Several other protocols and tools used in the system, such as the dynamic data server DataTurbine, were also GSI-enabled. A GSI-OpenSSH facility is provided for remote log-in.

Planning the Communication with Users

In NEESgrid there was a strict division between a development team and the user community. The System Integration (SI) team, managed from the National Center for Supercomputing Applications (NCSA), was composed mostly of software engineers and computer scientists associated with Grid technologies. The user community was spread among 16 equipment sites and composed of about 1000 earthquake scientists. This clear distinction was useful for enhancing the quality of the provided solution. At the same time, the project revealed some friction between the two communities. This exemplifies what happened in many other Grid projects and proved the importance of communication with users. At the beginning of the project, the use of particular advanced computing technologies was mandated by NSF rather than required by the user community. The earthquake scientists did not understand why the cyberinfrastructure was needed, and therefore had little interest in participating. Many of them were skeptical and did not believe the project was going to succeed. For this reason, initially the IT community and the SI team had no users to talk to and ask for user requirements.

On the other hand, the SI had adopted the "spiral development" model, common to software projects in new technologies where the architecture is allowed to change after each development iteration. This was completely foreign to earthquake engineers, who were used to the fact that before building a bridge one should know where every bolt will go and how tight it must be screwed down.

On top of this, there were several other reasons for miscommunication, partly caused by schedule and procedures mandated by the NSF, which unwillingly contributed to the tension. Therefore it took a long time before the dialogue between the technology providers and the consumers was formed; however, even then the dialogue did not go smoothly. The users were not educated in Grid computing. Lacking the elementary understanding of the technology, they were not able to formulate their needs. This was sometimes badly interpreted by the IT community. As explained by Bill Spencer (NCSA), the last PI (Principal Investigator) of the NEESgrid project, the two communities spoke different languages. Grid scientists and earthquake scientists sometimes even used the same words, such as *production*, to describe different ideas, which contributed to misunderstanding. For these reasons, many thought that the progress was initially slow.

Still, the software was being gradually developed. Some active project members perceived the importance of communication and helped the community to better understand the possibilities. Finally the system had reached its critical mass, and an early demonstration of capabilities was finally possible. This happened in the summer of 2002, during an all-hands meeting for the purpose of NSF project demonstration held in Reno, Nevada. The event pushed the development process by showing what was possible to achieve. However, the real breakthrough was the preparation of the MOST experiment to be held in July 2003, which was preceded by first-time long-term work between the SI and the user community. The overwhelming success of MOST was twofold. The fact of succeeding with the simulation was of lesser importance. The real value was that MOST was the translator. The experiment was simple and effective from the engineering point of view, solved a problem with both communities understanding each other well, and, at the same time, was the manifestation and precursor of what could be accomplished in the future. The preparation to MOST took months of intensive work, where both developers and users had to be engaged and communication was forced. Eventually, the experiment caused brainstorms and a shift of opinion in the user community who now wanted to partner.

The lesson learned was that early and substantial user engagement is crucial to the project's success. In a microscale, such participation can be achieved by designing subprojects with joint responsibility and a joined objective. More generally, however, one must work on the process of community engagement and community building. On the surface, NEESgrid was about building software to connect sites. However, many project members think that it was really about bringing a community together, a process that is still not complete. The project gave the earthquake engineers and software scientists a vehicle to collaborate and think as a single community; however, engineers are not trained (and not necessarily skilled) in community building. It required tremendous effort and was possible only because of the high interpersonal skills of community champions and the engagement of personnel at all levels. Grid computing builds tools for collaboration, but its use requires collaborative thinking. Building such skills can be more challenging than building the tools.

Testing and Quality Management

Because NEES was the first cyberinfrastructure project, the metric of success was somehow difficult to define. Although the developers used various software engineering methods to maintain the module code quality (unit tests, workflow tests), the overall quality level and measure of acceptability was difficult to define because of the large number of independent components. Also, in this respect MOST turned out to be the breakthrough. For the first time, a comprehensive solution covering all aspects of the system was shown at work. From now on, MOST became a reference point. A simplified version of the experiment, called MiniMOST, was soon developed. MiniMOST needed minimal hardware resources and was inexpensive to build—the hardware model fits on a table. At the same time, its operation included all core

NEESgrid software components. A series of about a dozen specimens of MiniMOST hardware was produced and sent out to the user community in various sites, who could quickly start experimenting with NEESgrid software. This intensified the dialogue and produced important feedback streams, because now the earthquake people could actively participate in the project. At the same time, MiniMOST became an important metric for acceptability of future developments. Before the new software version appeared in January 2004, it first had to go through MiniMOST setup and testing.

Next, there was an equally important schedule of workflow and unit tests that all development groups had to adhere to. These had to be completed before the integration. The system incorporated different software modules developed by independent groups of engineers from various scientific laboratories. A common integration process was absolutely critical in bringing these efforts together.

Accomplishments

While this material is being written, NEESgrid is going through its transition phase. After a few turbulent years, the project eventually emerged successful in providing the first cyberinfrastructure toolkit, which is expected to transform the landscape of the earthquake science. In September 2004, the development completed and the NEES infrastructure and the software toolkit became operational, after the management transition to San Diego Supercomputing Center.

NEESgrid is one of most ambitious Grid projects, providing a tangible example of Grid enabling new class of research, allowing execution of engineering tasks that could not be done in the past. Apart from technological values, the project was important in crossing a psychological frontier. Grid is the abstraction that can be implemented in various ways and therefore difficult to understand without a tangible demonstration. Just like the earthquake scientists who struggled to understand the concept until they saw MOST, other branches of science and engineering are now looking at achievements of NEESgrid and planning similar activities in their field. The project has a number of follow-up initiatives, including two in Japan and Korea.

Summary

This project is an excellent example to show that tapping the compute power of the enterprise is not the main ambition of Grid computing; rather it is a humble beginning of a long and fascinating road. In the near future, Grid infrastructures will encompass and provide easy access to a wide variety of resources, such as real-time systems, scientific instruments, sensors, industrial apparatuses, and handheld devices.

The NEESgrid provided a modular software toolkit in which a number of Grid and distributed technologies interfaced with various open-source and commercial offerings. The Grid was used to glue the distributed resources together and provide safe and dependable access for remote users and observers. Using the NEESgrid toolkit, experimental sites can work together to perform simulations, which they would not be able to perform working separately. The setup and demonstration of the MOST experiment 1 year before the project delivery facilitated communication between the experts and the users.

An important lesson learned in the NEESgrid project is that the concept of Grid technology is extremely difficult to understand and accept by users until they see it deployed and become involved. If possible, engage the users early and substantially in some sort of project with joint responsibility and a joined objective. Even the best technology is of no value if users cannot conceptually relate it to their needs.

The role and support of the community are critical in collaborative projects. One should think about building the community in advance, because its backing makes the development and migration process more straightforward and less stressful.

We will use the examples of MOST and MiniMOST again in Chapter 6, as an illustration to the concept of reducing project risk management through rapid result initiatives.

CHAPTER 4

Joining the Grid

In Chapter 3 we presented the current state of the Grid market, which is currently undergoing intensive evolution. Vendors sell proprietary implementations, which constantly advance, and compete over the market segments whose opportunities for Grid-enablement have not been entirely understood. In terms of business opportunities, it seems that only the tip of the iceberg has been discovered. It is in everyone's interest that the market enters into its next phase, where everybody will start using common communication standards. Once the domains of various standard bodies get stabilized and the production quality standard implementations get developed, we should see the vendors and service providers forming relationships according to certain patterns, which are currently unavailable without adequate technology.

In this chapter we discuss how to position yourself in the Grid market. This requires understanding of the various market strategies that lead to business opportunities. You should already have some ideas here, based on the market overview from Chapter 3. However, that description did not indicate the opportunities to be pursued today. The most challenging, but also most rewarding, opportunities lie in pioneering the new market niches that are being created by today's technology advances. Therefore we should first try to envision what the market may look like in the near future. Let us reposition some elements of the market value chain diagram from Chapter 3. This time we will paint a simplified picture representing a future Grid arena where business relationships are implemented with common Grid fabric technology and standards (Figure 4.1). Note that this time we have simplified the picture by removing the entities not directly involved in producing and consuming the technology (the standard bodies, the media, etc.).

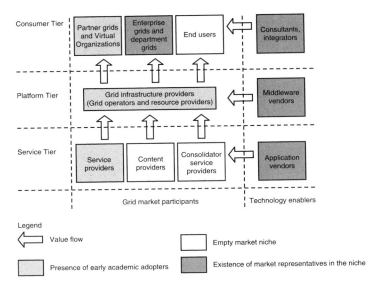

FIGURE 4.1 Possible structure of a Grid-aware market

The future Grid-aware ecosystem is centered on the standards-based communication platform for value exchange between the service providers and consumers. This platform is maintained by Grid infrastructure providers, large institutions that concentrate the resources and the infrastructure on which Grid services can be run. Example businesses that belong to the platform tier are network providers, data center providers operating the storage facilities, and supercomputing centers that sell computing time of their machines. The infrastructure providers run products purchased from the middleware vendors, which enable service virtualization and communication between the resources and the hosted services.

This Grid platform enables various businesses to offer, sell, share, and exchange their services. These companies are depicted in the service tier and most of them can be referred to as service providers. An example of a service provider is an online data mining enterprise that provides on-demand algorithms for businesses wanting to find patterns in their customer base. A travel agent, an online store, or a news channel site can all become Grid service providers. Their services live on top of the infrastructure provided by the Grid platform. For instance, the aforementioned data mining enterprise can host its intelligent services in a virtual environment provided by a resource provider (platform tier) that specializes in renting its hardware and storage in on-demand usage model. There can be other sophisticated relationships among the enterprises providing services. For instance, there may be content providers streaming data through portals maintained by the media companies. There may be service consolidators whose value will come from federating services provided by others. Generally, service providers use technology developed by application vendors.

As one might notice, the boundary between the platform tier and the service tier may not always be clear. First, in some systems there may exist several layers of consolidator services, one on top of the other, each providing some added value to the underlying functionality. Second, a service provider that hosts its services in its own hardware infrastructure remains both a service provider and an infrastructure provider. With this in mind, we will maintain the distinction between the platform and service tier in this discussion.

Finally, the consumer tier consists of the beneficiaries of Grid technology. Those are first of all institutional and individual service consumers who access services through the Grid platform. Also, the participants of partner grids belong here, as they will use a number of services, as well as the infrastructure, to successfully cooperate. Finally, the consumer tier encompasses institutions that deployed internal grids in their own domain. These entities do not need an external infrastructure provider. Nevertheless, those who use standards-compliant technology will be able to increase their operational efficiency by participating in the global resource sharing. Consumers use services of integrators and consultants, but also purchase offerings from middleware and application vendors.

Strategies for Participating

The entities shown in Figure 4.1 can be broadly divided into two categories. An entity could either consume the values from the market or add value to it. The former applies to most businesses, and possibly most readers of this book. Those individuals and institutions will find themselves in the upper left panel of the diagram, representing the consumer tier of the Grid market. They see the Grid as a possible way to improve their internal functioning, but do not necessarily need to sell it to anyone. To follow the analogy with the electrical grid, those businesses will be interested in "plugging in" to the system and use it in a way similar to the households that use electricity. This can be done either by connecting to the future ubiquitous Grid platform or by building an internal enterprise grid, which is the strategy chosen by many businesses today.

The remaining part of the diagram categorizes the enterprises that actively participate in the market by providing Grid solutions. These strategies require strong technical understanding of the technology. Especially the entities grouped in the platform tier, both Grid operators and the middleware vendors, need strong market position and profound technological foundations. For those institutions, the Grid concept is the core value of their business.

The companies in the service tier also rely on Grid technology and integrate it with their solutions. Although currently it is a rather difficult path, as there are not many examples to follow, we expect that the technology will become increasingly easy to master for the service and content providers, eventually enabling virtually anyone to publish their service on the Grid.

All those market players grouped in the platform and service tiers provide some sort of Grid-enabled product. Thus we have two generic ways to join the Grid economy. There are those who want to "plug-in," and those who want to provide Grid-enabled solution. Next we analyze what it takes to follow each of these two ways. The organization of the sections below refers to the structure of the diagram in Figure 4.1.

What Does It Mean to "Plug in"?

Build an Enterprise Grid

Currently the most popular way to Grid-enable a business is to virtualize resources inside a company by building a departmental or an enterprise grid. There are several good reasons to build an enterprise grid. Most frequently, such grids are being built to optimize usage of resources, provide easy-to-manage, virtualized application environment, and reduce total cost of ownership (TCO) of hardware assets. Also, by virtualizing the company resources in a coherent manner, grids can be applied to solving tasks that have special requirements. Often a large amount of processing power, combined with access to a database of a certain kind and specific hardware instruments, can be usefully combined together. An internal grid[1] will simplify the integration of such resources. It will also help to compose the resources on demand, which can reduce the expense of buying dedicated hardware for each task. Vendors like to contrast enterprise grids optimized for return on assets with inefficient traditional "silos" infrastructure solutions, where each company department owns a separate hardware and software stack, although the average usage rarely exceeds 10 percent of CPU time.

Thinking further, having the enterprise grid in place can prepare the company for actively participating in the on-demand market of the near future.

---

[1] In this section, we do not distinguish between departmental grids or enterprise grids because the discussion applies to both. We also use the term "internal grid" that covers both these categories.

This process will happen first of all in the technology sphere in terms of implementing proper resource abstraction, but also in the personnel sphere through educating staff, enhancing resource-sharing culture, and breaking psychological barriers.

Technologically, enterprise grids typically need:

- Distributed resource management (DRM) system with job brokering, queuing, and scheduling mechanisms
- Data management layer
- Security and access control
- Web service connectivity to access applications and various system interfaces
- Portals or other application-specific user interfaces
- Grid-enabled applications
- Hardware: server CPUs, storage, network, and workstations

In Chapter 5 we will focus on key elements of this puzzle.

Building an enterprise grid inside your organization will be simpler than participation in the Grid at large for a number of reasons. When building an enterprise grid, it is less necessary to worry about open standards and portability between the various toolkits. As a builder of an enterprise grid, you have the luxury of testing complete solutions without concern for partners or customers using kits from other vendors. Such a system may not be able to communicate with the outside grids, but depending on its purpose, this might not be needed. Having said this, many companies building enterprise grids insist on using open standard solutions for another important reason. The presence of standard-driven middleware secures a certain level of independence from the middleware vendor. A standard-driven system can be relatively easily ported to another middleware. This possibility usually motivates the vendor to maintain good customer relationship through adequate level of service. We will come back to this thread in the Wachovia use case. This advantage notwithstanding, it is also possible that after deploying an enterprise grid successfully and getting a taste for Grid computing, it will become advantageous to expand the fledgling Grid effort into an external set of resources linked to the Grid at large.

The other reason for which enterprise grids are simpler to build than open grids is the security. Several technologies used in grids today are fit for internal use but not suitable for communication external to firewalls. Another serious integration issue for open grids is that of security policies (such as concerning resource access or credential management) that tend to be highly nonuniform across enterprises. Thus although enterprise grids have perhaps

70 percent of functionality of future partner grids, this functionality has to remain internal to the enterprise.

In small companies, there will be no difference between an enterprise and a departmental grid. Assuming that the infrastructure is already in place, the initial proof-of-concept DRM setup can be pretty straightforward and be done within days. However, optimization of the working of the entire company by virtualizing the processes on the grid, as well as migrating legacy systems to the resource pool may take several months or even years and should be done in stages.

In larger companies, a pilot departmental installation will usually precede the enterprise-scale one. According to Wolfgang Gentzsch from MCNC, in most cases an enterprise grid can be built out in two phases. The first phase is to optimize the resources that already exist within the departments. This phase may take weeks to months and may not require any additional hardware. The next phase optimizes the overall enterprise environment through central management.

> **CASE STUDY:** Wachovia's Grid-Powered Trade Floor

Wachovia is among the earliest examples of Grid deployment in the financial sector. Since then the representatives of the bank have been frequent guests at the Global Grid Forum (GGF), where they enriched the community with the important consumer perspective. As we shall see, the bank did not stop after the successful launch of its trade floor department grid, but used it as a stepping-stone on the way to fulfill the vision of broader, company-wide resource virtualization.

Wachovia Corporation roots go back to the eighteenth century, when it started as a local bank in North Carolina. Today the company, headquartered in Charlotte, NC, is the fourth largest bank holding company in the United States, with 12 million customers and $437 billion in assets.

Grid computing in Wachovia started in the late nineties, when some of its in-house financial software was enhanced with distributed computing capabilities. In 2000, this was replaced with the GridServer software from DataSynapse. By February 2001, the Grid architecture supported by DataSynapse was installed on the derivative trading floor of the bank. The system used resources of 250 desktop PCs and servers, which were previously largely underutilized. The architectures included Windows 2000, Windows NT, and Sun Solaris. Collective power of these resources aided a team of five credit derivative traders in performing their simulations and trading in credit default swaps, total return swaps, and credit default obligations. Previously, the same applications had been performed on Unix SMP boxes.

The increase of performance was tremendous, ranging between one and two orders of magnitude. This means that a simulation that previously took

15 hours could now be reduced to 15 minutes, while trading volumes increased by 300 to 400 percent. Wachovia was now able to make faster risk and pricing decisions in a matter of minutes, instead of hours. This allowed for an entirely new quality of customer service. Answers to certain customers' questions requiring machine analysis could now be provided during one conversation.

The cost, which included software licenses and person-hours, was only a fraction of what would need to be spent to scale up the old SMP farm. In fact, no fixed assets purchase was needed this time.

Today Wachovia is building its next generation grid, which is based on the first positive trading floor grid experience. The new Corporate Investment Banking grid system will consist of 500 machines by the end of 2004, and eventually as many as 5000. As before, service scheduling will be provided by middleware from DataSynapse. The Corporate Investment Banking grid will provide the traders with a shared grid service platform with administration and maintenance handled by a dedicated group outside the business unit itself. The grid will become a large hosting environment for various applications. Wachovia maintains a large collection of commercial and open-source application installations and constantly develops new ones for internal use.

Most hardware will consist of Windows desktops, with possible Linux and Solaris boxes. Some new, dedicated computers will be purchased, but most of the hardware will be pooled from existing resources.

Business Case

The Corporate Investment Banking architecture and engineering group, which was leading the change, did not meet serious obstacles of a human nature when pursuing the transition plan. Grid was proposed as an improvement to the current architecture, with an aim to reduce the TCO of the infrastructure. A survey of various user communities within the company was presented to the management. A careful analysis of needs estimated the compute power lacking in the system. The purchase and maintenance cost was calculated in two variants: SMP server boxes and desktop computing grid. The latter proved to be more cost-effective. The management, convinced by the appealing business case supported by TCO calculations, supported and provided consistent backing to the project.

Transition

By 2004, Wachovia was well prepared to make the transition to the Corporate Investment Banking grid (its second generation departmental grid, supporting the Corporate Investment Banking department). The pilot grid system had been working for more than two years, allowing the staff to learn from experience. At the same time, a good relationship with the vendor and the external Grid community had been formed.

Wachovia did not choose the pilot 250-node grid for a kernel of the new Corporate Investment Banking grid infrastructure. Instead, a separate new grid was created. Currently all applications are being moved there for testing. As the next step, the production environment will be moved to the new grid, and the old one will be switched off. Only after this happens, will the resources that have so far been used in the pilot grid be added to the main resource pool. The reason for such a cautious approach is that the system's transition to the shared management coincided with the GridServer version upgrade to version 4.0. It was decided that building a new grid kernel from scratch would carry less risk.

The entire transition has been planned for about three months. As is usually the case, such a lengthy timeline was constrained more by the business process requirements than by technical problems. Competing project timelines were in the way, and certain production times did not allow for service interruption.

The Corporate Investment Banking grid has been designed so as to enable another transition to an enterprise grid (covering multiple Wachovia departments) later. However, at the current stage there is no timeline and no commitment for this step.

Applications

As explained by Brad Shea, Chief Grid architect from the new shared Corporate Investment Banking grid, there has so far been little customization effort on the application level. Applications that have been used in the Wachovia grid so far are related to risk profiling, pricing, and derivative trading. One of them is the Calypso suite, augmented by some proprietary C++ code. There will be numerous new .net, Java, and C++ applications planned in the new system.

Most of these applications, however, are either newly purchased or newly developed. Knowing that the enterprise grid architecture is on the horizon, the bank has redefined its application purchase strategy. New purchase recommendations of Wachovia Corporate Investment Banking favor those applications, which are designed for easy horizontal scaling, and have other properties facilitating deployment on the grid (we speak about these properties in the section "Provide a Grid-Enabled Product").

The DataSynapse's GridServer model for grid deployment does not force the use of custom, proprietary APIs or libraries. The original application jar files or executables can be submitted to the system as compute jobs. However, in some cases this is not enough and the application needs refactoring at the code level to manually partition it for efficient parallel execution.

Instead of custom graphical user interface, user communication with the application is done through SOAP Web services. Parallel applications developed for the grid are armed with SOAP interfaces for remote access (in the WS jargon, "consumption") by the users. Of course, users don't need to know SOAP or even realize they are using it. They use a user-friendly GUI[1] interface, which hides all the complexity from them. From the user perspective, the change is rather cosmetic (instead of the old custom GUI, users now have a new SOAP-based GUI). However, the usage of SOAP is convenient for the programmers who can easily interconnect and federate various grid applications and interfaces. Service Oriented Architecture is an integral part of the Corporate Investment Banking grid in Wachovia.

Standards

In the context of large vendors pushing for standards in the GGF, W3C, OASIS, and DMTF, it is interesting to hear how the early technology consumers view this issue. Wachovia, as a user of one of commercial Grid offerings, would like to see considerably more attention to standards coming from all the vendors. For the bank, insisting on standards is the way to ensure it will not get locked in a one-vendor solution without the negotiating power. For this reason, standards such as Open Grid Service Architecture (OGSA) are primarily important as a mechanism providing necessary abstraction layer, to which all vendors will comply.

This also implies that there should be no need to write applications with proprietary code. Clearly, a vendor policy that requires linking to its proprietary APIs is designed to perpetually bind applications with its particular middleware system. Savvy customers must be careful not to enter this path. For this reason, products supporting open, standard interfaces will be more attractive to the market, as can be clearly observed on Wachovia's example.

We should also note how the abstraction and promise of openness provided by the standards are valued by the consumer even more than the technical qualities of the standard. These are more important for the vendors, and for this reason it is the vendors who populate the GGF working groups.

Summary

Wachovia is an example of how computer clusters are the first step to true Grid architecture. Several observers did not see anything cutting-edge in the early trading floor grid built by the bank in 2000. However, this experiment

---

[1] Graphical user interface.

prepared the company for the later planning and implementation of an ambitious enterprise grid of several thousand nodes and a number of virtualized applications. It will become a company-wide resource virtualization platform, with at least two types of resources: CPUs and applications.

Wachovia's innovation, early visionary usage of such a strategy, has evolved into one of the first transactional, true utility type grids operating in an SOA fashion and providing a cost-effective scale that is charged back to the business on a usage-only basis.

A good tactical advice to follow is the intuitive baby-step approach. At the beginning of a project, it is a good practice to build a mini-scale pilot system, possibly covering all aspects of the technology. However, instead of placing it in a sterile test-bed environment, it should run in production, with real users and a clear metric of success. It takes some art to strike a balance between risk (the pilot can fail) and educational value (higher in a real environment). In Chapter 6 we address the psychological value of such short-term piloting initiatives.

With respect to the Grid middleware, Wachovia's example shows that customers are more likely to choose standards-based solutions. This gives them confidence that the relationship with the vendor will always be based on the freedom of choice and partnership.

Migration to another middleware or DRM vendor should always remain an option, although one must realize that this will usually be a sophisticated procedure. We have seen that even the fact of middleware version upgrade was a deciding factor for Wachovia to alter the migration process. An advanced Grid middleware must have a highly automated, autonomous, self-upgrading process, allowing to reconfigure the system without shutdown.

A separate, interesting observation for application developers is that soon the applications Grid-enabled by the producer will be more likely to be chosen for purchase than the competing ones without such a feature. Strong, forward-looking consumers such as Wachovia already pursue Grid-aware solutions as a more attractive option. Since there are still not many offerings like this on the market, the few solutions that exhibit Grid horizontal scalability will clearly have differential advantage over the others.

Participate in a Partner Grid

As explained in the taxonomy section in Chapter 3, partner grids are envisioned as collaborative environments spanning several institutions. In the long term, the potential for collaboration is envisioned as a more effective driver for Grid technologies than the need for computational intensity. If you have a group of business partners with whom you cooperate on some well-known tasks, building a small, closed, partner grid system may solve some of your problems. Unlike the enterprise grid, this time the system would span outside your company, but only the institutions well known to you would belong to it.

There are no set guidelines or comprehensive commercial offerings for building partner grids. The structure of a partner grid will be dictated by the particular need for which it was created. Organizations build partner grids when they need to run processes and projects involving workflows, resources, and participants from many institutions. Partner grids will ease implementing such projects, ease communication between various groups, and provide resource sharing and data sharing. All these actions are already possible today, however they are often being done manually. Virtual organizations created within partner grid frameworks will become the vehicle for streamlining these actions.

Various types of partner grids will require some of the technical features from the list below:

- The fundamental requirement for a partner grid is a security framework, which should include technology, policies, and procedures, allowing people and processes to securely share resources and communicate. Often dedicated institutions will be created to assign, manage, and control lifetime of security credentials of people and services. Virtual Organizations cannot exist without such security framework.

- Partner grids designed to share compute resources need mechanisms for central brokering of jobs or services among these resources. The entire system will usually involve independent resource pools at various organizations managed by DRM, integrated (using a toolkit such as Globus) with an external resource broker.

- Human interfaces to partner grids need to take the form of visual environments allowing users to remotely access resources, share data, and communicate with others. Currently this is done with Web and Grid portals, Java-based endpoints, and advanced collaborative environments. For instance, the NEESgrid project uses the Web-based CHEF framework that provides comprehensive environment with chat, teleobservation of experiments, and tools data sharing. The Crossgrid project promotes its Migrating Desktop interface, an install-anywhere solution with remote, Windows-style interface to the grid. Several collaborative groups worldwide use AccessGrid toolkit from Argonne National Lab that provides broadband, multichannel teleconferencing function. Partner grids today also frequently allow lowest level access to resources, such as direct login at a shell level.

- Partner grids focused on data sharing will require common data access, data transfer, data caching, and replication layer.

- Partner grids can be application specific, designed vertically to support specific applications. Their virtual organization is a system devoted for a specific purpose, such as to provide communication between different groups, to enable routing and storing of certain documents, or to provide infrastructure for solving specific engineering problems. A good contemporary example is the NEESgrid virtual organization.

- In terms of hardware, partner grids are installed on top of and have access to the infrastructure owned by the partners.

Partner grids will promote creation of Virtual Organizations (VOs), groups of people and resources, which have been organized into an administrative domain (VOs are defined in Chapter 2). They are directly analogous to the way people associate and interact in the real world. People are employees of various institutions, are members of professional organizations, belong to a church, and volunteer at the local library. As such they have certain rights.

The employee of a company has access to source code, databases, application, and tools that the company owns. The member of a professional organization has a right to that organization's training and website. The church volunteer has access to the member directory and donation history. These things are managed through a variety of mechanisms, but the point is that they are common structures. The goal of the VO structure is to duplicate these kinds of relationships through standardized technology. There are a few ways to think about achieving this goal.

There are currently several ways to administer security and access within a company, but the promise of VOs is that they can be consolidated into a single management point. At the same time, the VO security cannot conflict with the internal security policies of the stakeholders of the partner grid. However, we should note that VOs do not have to extend outside their home institution. By creating VOs within a company, different project teams can be assigned the rights necessary to do different jobs.

For instance, one common sensitive area that all companies must deal with is human resources information. Anything related to salary and benefits package must be guarded carefully and access allowed only to those with a right to know. These information resources should be available to the VO consisting of the human resources staff, as well as senior management who must oversee the company as a whole.

A development team will need access to sample hardware for the deployment platform, databases, and other resources depending on the application being developed. A VO can be created for these developers, thus allowing them access to the tools they need.

Those same developers might also be members of the VO providing support for existing production systems. As such they would be able to modify the code, run tests, and submit new versions to a workflow manager. Once the administrators of the productions systems have a chance to vet the new version, they can be put into production.

Technical-savvy readers will note that such usage of the VO is similar to the old concept of the UNIX user groups. Although this is true, now this idea is taken to a higher abstraction, above the particular operating system constraints and out of administrative boundaries of companies.

One example of already existing installations with multiple stakeholders that has advanced features of a partner grid is the NEESgrid cyberinfrastructure. There are numerous other projects, mostly of a scientific background, building virtual organizations with similar characteristics. Most national and international Grid projects identified in Chapter 3 belong to this category.

Join the Industry-Wide Grid as End-User

Eventually, it is believed that the Grid will deliver resources using the utility model, similar to the way that today's city tenants consume gas, electricity, and water. Likewise, in the near-future institutions and individuals needing compute power will be able to acquire it on demand. Those who need special applications will not install them locally, but will access remote installations through a Grid browser interface. Those wanting to start a project involving specialists of various skills will use the Grid to set up a virtual space in which participants can communicate and work.

The Grid of the future, as we envision it now, will enable such activities and much more. End-users will "plug in" to achieve better efficiency, do things cheaper and faster, but first of all to access capabilities, knowledge, data, and connectivity, which is otherwise unavailable for them at home or the local office.

We now turn to the technology that end-users of the Grid will have to cope with. It is difficult to talk in detail of something that is still an abstraction. However, we can project how users of open grids will behave by observing those who have a similar role in analogous systems today. Such environments are less powerful and smaller, but they function, deliver their goals, and bring profit.

In general, systems that work optimally allow users to focus on performing their tasks, not learning the toolkit. The complexity and internal working of the tool should be beyond users' perceptions. In the same fashion, an ideal system administrator never needs to be contacted. His role is to maintain the system available and functioning properly. The user is typically not interested how and when the maintenance actions are taking place.

In the same way, the Grid end-users will not realize how the system is working and what it takes to fulfill their requests. Earlier on we have presented the case study of Wachovia, which deployed Grid-based fixed financial applications on their trade floor. Traders access Calypso applications enhanced by the Grid power provided by the GridServer engine. Naturally, traders are not engineers and should not be bothered to decide where the compute power comes from. The only thing they know is that now, after their environment became Grid-enabled, their simulations complete within minutes instead of hours.

In the same fashion, Google users type in a keyword and receive the search result. The underlying structure of dozens of thousands of servers involved in answering the query (see case study in Chapter 1) is unknown to them. In fact, an average person would not even realize that the answer to her question was possible only because beforehand, many crawlers from Google had spent hundreds hours of caching of the entire World Wide Web! People intuitively think that Google is indeed somehow magically "searching the entire Web" for them in real time. They have a right to think so. The incredibly simple interface of Google is meant to create this illusion. Users want the answer to their questions; any additional information will only make them frustrated.

In most early examples of Grid and on-demand systems, however, the life of an end-user is not as simple as it is in the case of Wachovia or Google. Often technology consumers actually needed a lot of customization and understanding before they could benefit from reduced cost of operation. This is the case for the visual effects studio Threshold Digital who has rented compute power from IBM Deep Computing Capacity on Demand center in Poughkeepsie, NY. The rented processor cycles are being used for rendering scenes in film production. The server needed to be preconfigured for its applications, which were accessed through the virtual private network (VPN). Adding extra CPU power to the system required intervention of an administrator who preconfigured more servers and added them to the pool of machines accessible for Threshold Digital. The company benefited from the fact that it did not need to purchase expensive servers for a few weeks worth of processing. IBM was among the few technology providers advanced enough to fulfill the demand. Still, manual intervention and a certain amount of technical expertise on the customer side were necessary for effective cooperation.

These constraints are purely technical and result from the immature technology. We could easily imagine that, in the future, Threshold Digital would use Grid-enabled rendering applications that will automatically search for online cycle providers when the local resources do not answer the demand. Some applications already have similar capabilities. After Effects, a product of Adobe Systems produces motion graphics and effects for film, video, DVD, and the Web. The next release of Adobe After Effects Professional will speed up the rendering time by distributing the load among several machines. The scheduling will be done by GridIron XLR8 environment, integrated in the product. Although image rendering is not the most representative use for a Grid system (it uses embarrassingly parallel algorithms, easy to execute simultaneously on several hosts and typically not requiring advanced Grid architectures), this example shows how the system complexity should eventually be shielded from users.

We think that, just like the users of Travelocity portal, Wachovia trading applications, or Google, the end-users of Grid will not be aware of the mechanisms and scale of infrastructure providing them with Grid capabilities. Although this is not the case with the early Grid systems of today, the situation is likely to gradually improve. The burden of shielding the user from complexity, but also the associated business opportunity, is awaiting those few entrepreneurs who will provide Grid-enabled solutions.

➤ **CASE STUDY:** Synopsys: Software Release Engineering on the Grid

Synopsys is the leading provider of electronic design automation software (EDA) and services used to design complex integrated circuits (ICs), field-programmable gate arrays, and system-on-chip for the global semiconductor and electronics industries. This company, founded in 1986, currently employs about 4400 employees and reports more than $1 billion dollars of annual revenue.

The two flagship product lines of Synopsys are the Galaxy™ Design Platform and the Discovery™ Verification Platform. These product groups provide customers with an integrated suite of tools for advanced IC design and verification. These products are being developed in the company's headquarter site in Mountain View, CA. as well as in a number of R&D centers worldwide.

Software development in the Synthesis group in Synopsys is an increasingly sophisticated process. Multiple developer groups are working on multiple modules that make up the software. Code from all of the developers worldwide is eventually integrated by the release engineering team.

Regression testing is an important part of release integration. There are hundreds of thousands of tests in the code, grouped in about 5000 test suites. All need to be executed during the integration to verify functionality and quality of results. Running these on a single resource would take days. However, some of the tests allow for parallel execution. Even before commercial queuing systems came into view, the company developed its own solution to parallelize the builds and releases in an effort to reduce the time required to complete these tasks. Reducing the cycle time of the regression tests enables the Synopsys developers to release more software of higher quality. Several groups in Synopsys deployed homemade procedures and scripts to parallelize the execution of its regression tests on the compute server environment. These procedures utilized low-level UNIX tools such as cron jobs, shell scripts, or makefiles. Also, some of the Synopsys products have a built-in parallelism, which allows faster execution if they are configured to access CPUs on a defined set of machines. The software expertise to implement this environment existed in the development teams; however, it was not their primary function. Also, each of the development groups owned its own compute server resources across a heterogeneous environment. Several different architectures were in deployment, including Sun Solaris, IBM's AIX, and HP-UX from HP. As development needs have grown, 32- and 64-bit Linux systems based on processors from Intel and AMD have been added to the infrastructure.

With the infrastructure growing steadily as a result of cheaper CPU costs, the existing compute farm management using Unix tools like rsh, cron, and scripts was becoming increasing difficult. Because each development group used its own set of regression testing scripts, code integration was a nightmare. The testing and integration process did not scale, CPU utilization usage was suboptimal, and the compute server infrastructure required an undue level of administrative effort. Competitive pressures in the EDA market required Synopsys to adapt to changing business demands and scale internal processes constantly. Scalability was a key internal goal. The integration of additional products into the release management process raised serious obstacles and prompted a reengineering of the system.

Even before Sun Microsystems acquired Gridware, a group in Synopsys was using the Codine queuing system from Gridware (later to become Sun Grid Engine (SGE)). The Synopsys Grid Support Team used the scheduler on a small cluster farm. Later Synopsys also experimented with the open source version of SGE Load Sharing Facility (LSF) from Platform by installing a number of scheduling environments.

As a result of these evaluations, management decided to Grid-enable all the hardware resources and provide a common virtualized resource pool to all developers based on a common queuing system. The goal was to centralize compute resources and improve utilization within the development flow. The data center management would be centralized and simplified while regression performance improved. The company would be able to run larger regression tests faster and in a more automated fashion. The administration of a coherent system would be easier and the resource usage would be closer to optimal.

The centralized Data Center system named DesignSphere has been developed and deployed internally at Synopsys. Today it manages more than 15,000 CPUs worldwide. DesignSphere provides a single point of entry to the entire company-wide compute farms. No matter where the engineer is, the DesignSphere interface allows users to access the Synopsys Data Center where its development is being realized—Mountain View, Hillsboro, Munich, or Vienna.

Deploy Monitoring before Transition

Before introduction of the Grid-enabled system of the centralized compute farm methodology, there was no coherent way to monitor the compute resources for actual utilization. In some cases usage was sporadic; in other cases, users had to compete for the required resources. No usage statistics were collected or analyzed.

It was decided that building the grid system should be preceded by a definition of the problems that the DesignSphere could solve. However, the team needed to know about the current usage patterns to establish the improvement goal. Therefore installation of a resource monitoring system needed to precede the grid system. The resource monitoring system produced the metrics that was used as a baseline for performance improvement. Synopsys also found it helpful to deploy a user interface to graphically visualize the metrics and enable the IT management and user community to faster formulate conclusions based on this data (Figures 4.2 and 4.3). The IT department decided the best way to collect metrics on host utilization was to collect the requirements for the system and build it ground up. An enterprise class monitoring system called VigilGuard was developed to collect and visualize the utilization of all the server class CPUs at Synopsys.

The Transition

After the construction of the core grid system, largely based on Sun Grid Engine, the task was to attract new user groups and pool their resources into these collective compute farms. As noted earlier, there were several quasi-independent development groups at Synopsys who owned a large number of compute servers. By contributing its CPUs to the common pool on the grid, a group gained access to increased compute power exceeding its current resource base; however, this came with a price of lost independence.

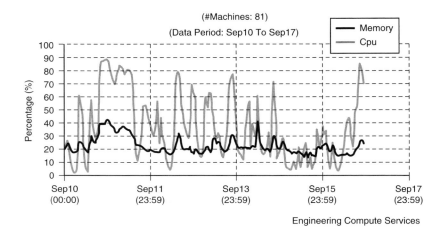

FIGURE 4.2 Farm utilization before building the grid

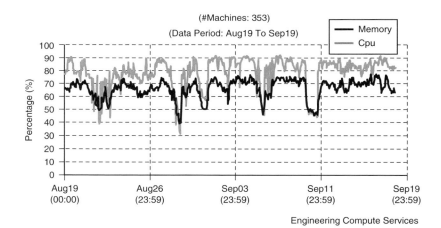

FIGURE 4.3 Farm utilization after building the grid

To initiate the transition, the Grid Support Team identified a number of groups to integrate in the virtualized compute server resource pool. As explained by Sriram Sitaraman and John Mincarelli, both the Senior IT Manager reporting to Hasmukh Ranjan, Sr. Director, IT responsible for the transition of Synopsys users to the centralized model of DesignSphere, the process of migrating a group to a centralized compute farm usually takes from 1 to 6 months, depending on the size of the target group (between 6 and 400 people) and size of their infrastructure to be relocated (between 50 and 400 CPUs). Before the transition, the group would use its in–house-developed scripts to consume its cycles. The first step is defining the requirements for the post-transition environment. Time is spent planning and educating the users. Then the queuing system is deployed on its CPUs. Afterward the group integrates the queue process into its procedures, the support team proceeds with integration of its small resource pool into the main, company-wide pool; this means centralization whenever possible. After the queuing infrastructure has been integrated, applications and data need to be migrated to the new environment.

The main obstacles in the process occur because the transition must fit within other project constraints the groups currently have in place. Naturally, the migration cannot coincide with new software releases or other important deadlines, but must be implemented at the start of a development cycle.

Some opposition to the migration to the grid came from the fact that users preferred their old environment over the new one, even if the latter was superior in some respects. The Synopsys Grid comes with a set of rules that change the processes for each of the developers. For instance, in the Grid-enabled regression test process, no direct login access to the testing machines is allowed. Also, users need to request a resource before using it. Of course, these drawbacks are minimal compared to the advantages of being able to do more tests, in various configurations, and faster. However, the developers need to change their old habits ("my computer should be under my desk!") and accept the new development paradigm. Frustration can be avoided if the process has been preceded with proper user education.

Technology

Synopsys has developed an in-house software framework called RIDGE, that includes remote access, business intelligence, data center planning, the Grid-enabled queuing systems, and environment shaping. The system uses LSF and SGE as the primary queuing systems. The latter manages a larger chunk of the grid's resources. The company chose to use the free, open-source version of the SGE scheduler.

The access to the queues is subject to a number of automatic rules that users must obey. Typically 70 percent of the nodes in the compute farm are allocated to batch processing (users submit jobs through a queue), while the rest of the nodes are devoted to interactive jobs (such as running an editor) or "heavy-interactive" tasks (jobs that consume considerable resources and need direct login access). The methodized rules and associated automation for the queuing systems is referred to as the Business Rules Monitoring system or BRM. For the interactive clusters, users are forbidden to run CPU-intensive jobs (>20% CPU) or use excessive memory (>500 MB). When using the batch clusters, the users abide by the rules of no long jobs (>5 days), no direct login to the compute servers, and no idle jobs (10% CPU over 4 hours).

It is interesting that Sun Microsystems has been very active in the project of Grid-enabling the compute resources. At first it may seem strange, because there is no obvious benefit for Sun in doing so. Synopsys used the free version of the software, and there was no need for external consulting because of the high technical value of its staff. However, the benefits of working with a very advanced user in its production environment provided the opportunity for the vendor to improve the product based on actual customer data. Because of the scale of the installation, Synopsys was able to push the limits of the software, often running into limitations years before it would have been hit by the average market user. In working with Synopsys, Sun was able to significantly improve the product. Today, Synopsys is among Sun's top Grid success stories.

Problems

The Synopsys grid faces obvious problems as a result of its worldwide distribution. The system is designed to speed up compilation and regression testing. However, as extra time must be spent on data transfer to and from the executing nodes, total performance can decrease. Currently, most of the resources have been centralized in several Data Centers worldwide to strike the optimal balance between centralization and distribution.

In the early experiments, a rigorous centralized architecture caused other technical problems. For example, a large number of jobs submitted to a single scheduler queue would crash the system. It turned out that the scheduler had built-in arbitrary limits on job numbers (in a very high range of tens of thousands of jobs), because no one had exceeded these numbers in the past. Sun worked to remove these limits to give Synopsys the necessary capabilities to meet its requirements. Also, the Synopsys grid has been partitioned into several independent job queues to avoid similar problems in the future. Queues have been segregated by job types. The single point of submission, provided by DesignSphere, is allocating jobs to particular queues.

Another nontrivial issue was to strike a balance between manpower and CPU utilization. Although it is true that DRM solutions can drastically improve the hardware utilization; maintaining the average CPU utilization at more than 80 percent comes with a price of dedicated IT effort, automation, and user education. Synopsys has been able to calculate the number of administrative staff required and economically feasible to maintain the required level of CPU utilization.

Finally, it is an ongoing challenge to continue adapting the infrastructure to meet the need for the business requirements of the company. Synopsys is growing, acquiring new companies, and increasing infrastructure. Integration of the new resources is a constant challenge. During recent months, the Grid Support Group has integrated two major business units and twelve project developer groups into the main grid resource pool. To plan and cope with constant change, the company has implemented a Continuous Improvement Program to measure infrastructure improvements and resource utilization.

Summary

Synopsys is an example of a commercial institution that has successfully implemented an enterprise grid. The grid virtualizes resources for the core activity in the company (release engineering of software product) but does not include business layer resources (on which applications such as ERP or SAP are executed). The Grid transition process executed in Synopsys was almost seamless, following a gradual change model. It migrates internal developer groups one-by-one, at the same time continually increasing the size of the central resource pool. Groups were migrated in a two-phase process. The Synopsys grid has provided the developers with extra resources and in return, benefited from simplified system management and infrastructure centralization. Currently Synopsys has about 90 percent of the compute server systems in the common resource pool. It is the management-imposed policy that all new servers purchased for the various groups be automatically assigned to this company-wide grid.

What Does It Mean to Provide a Grid-Enabled Solution?

Become a Grid Infrastructure Provider

Returning to the famous analogy of an electrical grid, we see that the core structure supporting the system is maintained by the electrical network provider. It connects the producers of the energy (power plants) and users. More recently, we can observe a similar process in the retail market, where the space between the producers and the shoppers has been dominated by large supermarket networks. They eventually grew to become the most powerful link in the value chain, able to dictate conditions to the producers of goods. In a similar way, the Internet connects the communicating parties, some of which can be clearly distinguished as service providers or consumers.

The Grid ecosystem will also need a similar backbone, a communication platform for the digital service market. We use the term *Grid infrastructure provider*, or *Grid operator* to describe an institution that owns and operates this backbone, providing the connecting tissue between the service providers and consumers. Although it is certain that the emergence of Grid infrastructure providers will be essential for the construction of the ubiquitous Grid, the exact scope of functionality provided by these institutions is difficult to predict. Will they assume an active role by delivering a wide array of Grid protocols, service-hosting hardware, and a set of public services facilitating the service exchange? Or will they simply be like today's Internet providers, whose service is transparent to most users because of the operation on the low-level abstraction of TCP/IP? In this case, there may be no difference between a Grid infrastructure provider and an Internet provider.

On one hand, the Grid operator will be able to provide a hosting environment for the service providers and a medium for communication between them. This could include an implementation of standard communication protocols, as well as public services such as the ones for service discovery, monitoring, billing, audit, and transaction management. On the other hand, the infrastructure provider will allow service consumers to connect to the system, search for the service providers, negotiate the transactions, consume the resources, and pay for them.

It is hard to tell exactly what it will take to become a Grid provider. However we can learn a lot by turning to analogous situations today. Providers of the Internet, telephony, and electricity are all large companies with substantial amounts of hardware assets. Although in many countries there also exist local, niche Internet and telephony providers, most of them simply resell services of the giant they connect to (often the former monopolist). It is difficult to become a significant player in one of these sectors by working from scratch. History shows that in many countries, even after market deregulation, for a long time it was practically impossible for newcomers to compete with the former telecommunication monopolists (Bell and SBC in the United States, BT in the United Kingdom, and TP S.A. in Poland) because of their critical mass of assets and customers. One way to enter the utility market, however, was to leverage one's strong position in another associated market. In this way, the former telephony giants often became leading mobile telephony providers. In the same way, we think that the telcos and network providers of today are natural candidates to become the Grid infrastructure providers of tomorrow. Also, other companies that have a large number of hardware assets in geographical distribution may assume the role of Grid operator.

We first said that service providers would host their services on the platform run by the Grid operator; however, this assumption is not necessarily correct. To explain what we mean, we should once again use analogies. It is true that this is the model used by the service providers present on the Web (such as Google and Travelocity). In a similar fashion, power plants use the service of an electricity network provider as a medium to deliver their services. However, if we look at the traditional telephony or television, the service provider (a telephony network, or a TV station) is often also providing the infrastructure. There is no difference between the two roles. Also, the early Grid resource providers of today (HP Utility Data Center, IBM Deep Computing Capacity on Demand, Sun Fire Capacity on Demand, Gateway, White Rose Grid, or MCNC)—see Chapter 3, "Grid Resource Providers" section—offer the grid access together with the services provided by the grid. There is no notion of third-party service hosting; the infrastructure provider is at the same time the service provider. Thus, as we have already hinted, these two functions may often be performed by the same entity.

A Grid infrastructure provider will most certainly need to deliver the following functionality:

- Critical mass of hardware infrastructure, such as the network, server nodes, and storage nodes. This would become a kernel, a hub to which resources from other providers can later be connected.

- Service registration, cataloging, and discovery facilities, enabling the parties to automatically learn about, locate, and contact other participants, services, and capabilities available on the Grid.

- Security framework, enabling users to establish each other's identity. Certificate Authorities (or equivalent bodies), who issue the security credentials and guarantee user's identities, must be associated with the Grid operator. Participants also need a mechanism for creating VOs among them.

- Entry-point interfaces for the end-users logging into the Grid. Possibly, some of them could take a form of browser-based graphical user interfaces (GUIs). However, eventually it is expected that the users should not need to be aware of the Grid. Even the process of entering into the system should take a form of an automated negotiation between the Grid provider and the Grid-enabled user-side application.

- Support for standard Grid protocols, including the higher level ones (Web services) and the lower level ones (large data transfer). In many cases, this support may be analogous to the way in which network providers today support Internet communication. The routing of IP packets is effectively transparent to the users.

- Support for standard procedures for auditing, monitoring, metering, accounting, and billing. All parties on the Grid will have to conform to these procedures to participate in the digital economy.

As we said before, however, it is difficult to say how much of this functionality will indeed be provided by the Grid operator, and what will be shifted to the service providers. For instance, it is possible that functions such as service discovery, user authentication, and billing will be operated by third-party service providers. For this reason, the notion of a Grid provider still remains largely intuitive. Some researchers even reduce the notion of a Grid provider to the network (Internet) provider, believing that the future cross-institutional federations of Grid services existing will exhibit truly peer-to-peer architectures without the need for centralized cataloging, discovery, or other form of control.

Become a Service Provider on the Grid

Grid service providers are the entities that use the Grid connectivity to offer and sell their services. As of today, there are no Grid providers operating globally, which is natural, as the presence of open grids is a prerequisite for their appearance. For this reason in this section we will continue to make use of analogies coming from other IT technologies, namely the Internet and the Web.

In regard to function, a Grid service provider will be similar to the service providers existing today on the Web. However, with the Grid technology, we should see a shift from the interfaces targeted to humans to machine-accessible interfaces. Both Google and Travelocity could easily (and probably will) become Grid service providers by redefining their public interfaces in a Grid-compliant way. In fact, this process has already started. Google has published its Web service interface, and Sabre has been offering travel agents a commercial Web services suite product.

Some providers will sell access to their physical resources. In this case, the service consumers would run applications on providers' resources. Then they would be billed for the number of CPU cycles and storage units used. Other service providers will sell access to preinstalled applications, custom logic, and private data banks. Consumers would access these applications remotely on a by-hour and by-processor license plan and also benefit from the fact that the applications would run more reliably and faster than on their home PC.

Yet other groups of service providers will likely emerge on top of the basic providers. They will provide added value to the already existing services. For instance, service consolidators (resellers) could skillfully compose services coming from many other providers. Another possible example are the content providers who could use third-party services as a framework for the data and information they sell.

Today, some similarity to Grid service providers can be observed in various service hosting plans. Application Service Providers run CRM and ERP[2] packages on behalf of their clients. Web hosting companies build virtual Web servers and allow their customers to hire them. As we have seen in Chapter 1, Sabre hosts the entire reservation systems for many airlines.

However, all these systems require human intervention to set up the remote application, operate it, and process payment. As a result, because of significant overhead in the setup and termination procedures, as well as core granularity of the hosting packages, the hosting deal makes sense only if it is signed for months or years. Grid service setup procedures are expected to change this situation dramatically, allowing for fully automatic service level agreement (SLA) negotiations of very small-grained services. Such services could possibly take a fraction of a second to complete.

Grid service providers will need to:

- Depending on their function, provide Grid-enabled backend for applications, data, or resources. Some may expose end-user GUI interfaces. Others will instead offer standards-based interfaces suitable for machine communication. On the consumer side, users will run their front-end applications, automatically connecting to the service provider backend interface over the Grid.

- Provide standards-based interfaces to access the service. It seems today that Web service standards will dominate.

- Possess the security credentials and allow for mutual authentication and setup of secure communication channels with the remote parties.

- Conform to the procedures for auditing, monitoring, metering, accounting, and billing imposed by the central Grid institutions. For instance, the users of compute cycles must be able to check that the bill reflects actual usage.

There are no Grid providers today, as the enabling technology is not fully implemented. In particular, the problems are caused by the last two bullets of the preceding list. However, a number of companies already exhibit Web

---

[2] Customer Relationship Management and Enterprise Resource Planning.

service interfaces to their backend systems. These firms will find it easier to later migrate their services to the Grid.

Provide a Grid-Enabled Product

Application vendors are adapting their products to the Grid environment. This process has been dubbed "Grid-enabling." Unlike the Grid service providers, who are few in number today, Grid-enabled products can already be observed on the market, and there are several examples to learn from.

Note that by a Grid-enabled product we mean something different than a Grid service. A Grid-enabled product could be any application, refactored so that it is easy to deploy (install), manage, and communicate with in the Grid environment. A service, instead, is an interface to a certain functionality made available by the service provider for other parties. Installations of Grid products can exhibit Grid service interfaces; however this is not mandatory.

There is no single definition for Grid-enablement. In general there are two ways to approach this concept. Many people, in particular middleware vendors, understand Grid-enabling as enhancement of the application with features of horizontal scalability. Horizontally scalable applications are such that when the demand for processing load increases, the application can use additional computational resources that are being added by as separate discrete devices (typically provided by Grid engines, or DRMs). Thus, application can easily consume Grid resources provided on demand. This way of Grid-enabling is performed for computationally intensive applications, typically integrated with a DRM system. These applications are also good candidates to an on-demand and utility computing model, where applications can be deployed on the fly and use as much resources as needed. More generally however, Grid-enabled products conform not just to the requirements of a DRM, but to the Grid environment as a whole. Grid-enabling can include refactoring of the communication channels to conform to the set of protocols and security standards used on the Grid. Let us have a closer look at these two ways of Grid-enabling.

Refactor Application for Horizontal Scalability and On-Demand Business Model

To Grid-enable an application according to the first definition, which speaks of horizontal scalability and on-demand readiness, one needs to first consider whether the application is suitable for such a model of execution. In particular:

- Assess whether the application can be managed remotely, without local access.

- Design modularity, in terms of isolation of interactive GUI modules from the backend computations. In a Grid environment, these would often have to work on separate machines.

- Analyze the feasibility of partitioning the computationally intensive part into separate parallel jobs. It is optimal if these jobs do not communicate. However, such luxury, inherent to the embarrassingly parallel problems,[3] is rare in most applications. If communication is necessary, Message Passing Interface (MPI)is still among the most frequently used internal communication technologies to consider. Alternatively, some DRM vendors require use of proprietary APIs, which can be more efficient in certain domains but not portable.

- Determine the possibility of introducing standardized and noninteractive startup and termination procedures.

- Analyze the application requirements in terms of filesystem accesses, database accesses, and other internal dependencies exhibited during execution. These dependencies need to either be removed, or refactored in a way suitable for execution in the particular hosting environment.

- Analyze application's capability to support external monitoring and runtime management tools. For example, event-driven nature and capability of issuing alerts will make the process of Grid-enabling easier.

- Design and implement communication channels between the distributed modules of the application. Communication between the computational parts must be efficient, minimal, and coordinated with the computing algorithms to avoid deadlocks. Communication with external modules such as the management modules and the user interface must be secure, standards compliant, and resilient to the obstacles such as firewalls. Web service channels are often used here.

There may be many other requirements depending on the particular use for the application hosted on the Grid. For example, in the IBM on-demand

---

[3] A class of computational problems that are by nature suitable for parallel execution, are known in the high performance computing community as "embarrassingly parallel" problems. Most applications do not share this characteristics.

readiness assessment procedure, applications are considered for vertical (apart from horizontal) scaling. Vertical scaling is the ability to use features provided by the infrastructure, such as single sign-on, directory services, or digital certificate services. Also, IBM looks at an application's multitenancy which is the ability to share one application instance among several businesses of enterprise customers.

Finally, we should note that some application vendors wanting to horizontally scale their product choose a middleware vendor to partner with and to produce an integrated solution. SAP recently shipped its new product integrated with Sun N1 Grid Engine. Sefas Innovation, a provider of enterprise software solutions for automated document production, integrated its product with DataSynapse. There are many other examples (see Chapter 3, "Applications" section). These efforts are aimed for customers who own cluster or blade servers, and can use this infrastructure to build a scalable software solution on top. Although these efforts are far from the Grid-computing ideal (because the installations are single-purpose, internal, and use proprietary communication), they can be seen as early steps in the process of refactoring the applications toward Grid compliance. Once the applications have been partitioned into jobs that run in parallel, the communication channels can be refactored to use the standard and secure technology designed for the open Grid environment.

Refactor Applications for Grid-Compliant Connectivity

Not all applications are suitable for the utility computing model. There are systems that for various reasons cannot be deployed on a server farm and take advantage of location-independent, on-demand processing. For instance, this may be the case with applications with the following characteristics:

- applications with sophisticated dependencies
- applications interfacing local, static systems
- applications that for security reasons cannot communicate externally
- application systems developed in-house, whose refactoring can be too expensive
- applications whose logic is not easily parallelized
- some mission-critical systems, for which the danger of instability caused by refactoring of the core logic in the code would outweigh advantages coming from Grid scalability. For such systems, the cost of testing of the new environment could be higher than the savings from optimal execution
- applications that work well in the current installation, deliver what they are supposed to, and would not improve after migration to the Grid

These applications can be Grid-enabled statically, through the adaptation of their external communication interfaces to the standard protocols, security schemes, Grid policies, and processes such as workflows. In this case, it is difficult to give precise guidelines, as each case will be specific to the particular application. On the high level, one needs to make sure that the newly developed interfaces are compliant to the standards or, in the absence of standards, the best practices present in the community. The process can include either integration with a common middleware libraries or development of in-house, standards-compliant interfaces. Whenever possible, the first way should be chosen, as it allows for minimal coding effort, and can be done with truly surgical changes to the code. This, in turn, guarantees minimal error rate and smaller cost of testing.

To better explain what is meant by the static Grid-enabling, the authors can quote a few examples from their own experience.

There is a long-standing idea in IT that it is advantageous to separate the interface from the implementation. This was one of the ideas behind many client/server architectures and it continues to be a valuable tool. Many applications have been written with this in mind; thus putting a Grid interface on them presents more of a technical exercise than an architectural one.

The authors are involved with building a solution for a storage company that does exactly this—adds a Grid interface to an existing software base. The interface to the system today uses the venerable old FTP standard. While this worked fine for a long time, some years ago the company realized that networking was a component in its failure to produce high-speed data movement over the Internet. Specifically, the problem was the well-known shortcoming in TCP/IP, which makes it difficult to use the full capability of the pipe as latency increases. This problem was solved some years ago by making proprietary extensions to the FTP standard, thereby creating a system that worked slowly with standard clients and quickly with proprietary clients. This was a workable solution in the short term, but as Grid standards started appearing, the company decided that it would be a better plan to start migrating to them.

Since this system had been architected with the interface layer as a separate component, it has been possible to replace this piece with one that speaks the GridFTP standard.[4] In doing these two things, the storage system now has a secure, fast, and standards-based interface. The technical advantage of GridFTP is that it can simultaneously pipe the data through several streams (*parallelism*) using separate hardware and network resources (*striping*).

---

[4] GridFTP is currently an RFC draft, submitted to the IETF through the GGF.

However, the greater advantage is that GridFTP is a standard used throughout the community; thus the new product can be easily integrated with other systems. As a result, the vendor can slowly phase out its existing solution and replace it with one for which a number of client tools already exist and for which its customers have the ability to program to in an open fashion.

Another example of static Grid-enabling involves DataTurbine, a product from Creare, Inc. which is a data stream dispatcher and dynamic data server. DataTurbine has been successfully used in a number of installations, however most of them were running inside firewalled systems of Creare's customers. However, in 2003, DataTurbine was chosen as a solution for data streaming in NEESgrid and needed to conform to the common Grid mechanisms for authentication, authorization, transfer integrity, and encryption required by the policy of the project. For this reason, DataTurbine was enhanced with a layer of Grid Security Infrastructure (GSI) authentication based on PKI, X.509 certificates, and proxy certificates. The Open Source GSI libraries from the Globus project were used. Once the architectural details of the integration had been hashed out, a very small number of lines of code and less than a week of work was enough to complete the task. The integrated solution allows users with Grid certificates to securely send and receive streams of data. Because in the traditional Grid environment, GSI is a de facto standard, all participants possess GSI credentials. Therefore they do not need to do anything to secure the DataTurbine connection between them—authentication is performed automatically. The integrated solution is completely transparent to users. Once they obtain valid Grid certificates, they can use DataTurbine exactly as they were doing it before. Also, the security feature is switched off by default for other customers who do not want to use GSI.

The most common way for static Grid-enablement of applications in the future will probably include adapting them to Web service interfaces. As Web services have been adopted as the platform of choice for the Grid, the community is currently in the process of deciding what Web service extensions are needed by an application to become Grid-compliant. These will certainly include the security schemes, the WSRF collection of standards, and elements of OGSA. Applications with external interfaces compliant to these guidelines will be available for exposure as Grid resources.

Become a Middleware Vendor

Middleware vendors have a key role in enabling Grid technologies. Enterprise grid builders, Grid infrastructure providers, service providers, and application developers are using Grid middleware to integrate their offerings with standard protocols. Fewer than a dozen companies have products that could be classified as generic Grid middleware. Many more companies provide similar products to niche markets, such as cluster or high performance computing. Clearly, becoming a middleware vendor is one way to become a player in the Grid market. We mention this here for completeness. Providing any guidelines would require more profound technical discussion, which is out of the scope of this book. Also, the market for middleware vendors seems to fill up rapidly.

➤ **CASE STUDY:** Rolls-Royce and Data Systems & Solutions Develop Grid for Equipment Health Monitoring

> One hundred years ago the Eton graduate and car enthusiast Charles Rolls was introduced to the skilled automotive engineer Henry Royce. The two men shared the belief that the car could replace the horse or the train as a major means of transportation, and they decided to prove this by building the most technologically advanced cars in the world. Their meeting in Manchester in 1904 ultimately led to the partnership that formed one of the great global names in quality engineering—initially in the automotive industry but later in aviation. Today, the company remains one of the world's best-known technology brands, widely admired for its products, innovations, and business practices.
>
> Today the UK-based company has annual sales of approximately €8.7bn drawn from operations in civil and defense aerospace, marine power, and energy. The market for which it is best known today is aerospace solutions (the motor cars are now made by a different company). Rolls-Royce currently serves approximately 500 airlines, 4000 corporate and utility aviation operators, and approximately 160 armed forces.
>
> Since 1987, the company has greatly expanded its product range and actively moved into providing support services. This redefinition of its strategy was a move away from its traditional sales model of simply selling new equipment and associated spare parts. This new revenue model has proven remarkably successful; now about half the company's revenue comes from support services for the 50,000 or so turbines currently in service around the world.
>
> ## The Support Services Model
>
> Demand for support services has risen as customers attempt to drive down their own operating costs by looking to lease engines directly from the manufacturer. Responding to its customers' demands, Rolls-Royce developed Power By The Hour™ service, where a customer simply leases an engine from Rolls-Royce and pays a fee for each hour the engine is in

operation. Rolls-Royce then becomes responsible for the maintenance and servicing of the engine throughout its lifetime, and assumes the cost risks involved instead of passing them onto the customer.

Power By The Hour™ means that Rolls-Royce now has to balance the cost of maintaining and repairing its turbines, their initial build cost, their life-expectancy, and their maintenance against the amount of money it can reasonably charge the customer for the service. As far as the customer is concerned, all he wants is an engine to power his asset; anything else is Rolls-Royce's problem. With large engines costing up to several million euros each, along with the massive cost penalties imposed by canceling a flight or any overrunning maintenance delays to aircraft, it is imperative that Rolls-Royce keep as many engines running as possible and that downtime on each one is kept to an absolute minimum, without ever compromising reliability or safety. It is also essential that all required maintenance is done on time to an optimized build standard to avoid any unplanned outages. Such outages cost money to fix, disrupt carefully balanced repair line capacity plans, are an embarrassment for the company, and so must be avoided at all costs.

Rolls-Royce found that the answer to this problem is to collect as much data as necessary on each and every engine in operation so that its condition, performance, configuration, and state of maintenance can be ascertained in near real time. This information must cover physical wear and tear, operational statistics, fuel burn, operational profiles, temperatures and vibration recordings, and so on. Once these data are captured from the engines, they are then used in various off-line analyses.

Data Systems & Solutions

Because of the data and IT requirements intensity of this problem, and the desire to rapidly develop solutions to it, Rolls-Royce teamed up with U.S. information systems developer Science Applications International Corporation (SAIC), a Fortune 500 giant with a history of innovative and robust installations for many U.S. government departments. The two companies rolled out their joint venture company, Data Systems & Solutions, in 1999 and charged it with developing enterprise asset management systems that made the best use of predictive maintenance technologies for an enterprise's complex or expensive assets.

The young company began expanding its area of expertise to supply decision support information for asset management organizations covering such diverse assets as ships, aircraft, trains, and power stations, seeing these markets as areas of growth. Data Systems & Solutions' monitoring systems are now so advanced that they can automatically make predictions based solely on snapshots of data taken from the asset. To increase the quality and timeliness of fault detection, however, there are plans to increase the frequency of data sampling to real-time, continuous streams of data, initially involving full spectrum vibration and speed data derived from each shaft of the gas turbine. The ideal solution would be sampling each sensor at a rate of 10 to 15 samples per second. The majority of the value for a condition or health monitoring system is directly proportional to the time available after detecting incipient failure, which is used to avoid or mitigate that failure. Sampling the data, in near real time and at high frequency, enables the earliest detection of incipient failure, thereby maximizing the time for mitigation. The volume of data this level of monitoring produces places great demands on systems required to transport, store, and analyze the resultant data, but Data Systems & Solutions believes it has found the solution.

Equipment Health Monitoring (EHM) Problem Description

To understand the solution, it is important to first understand the problem. Data Systems & Solutions has produced a comprehensive asset optimization decision support tool called CoreControl™ that covers both the EHM and the Ground Support Station (GSS) aspects of asset management. Built-in sensors monitor, in real time, the performance, health, and usage of the engine. These data are also supplemented by other sources such as pilot logs from where anecdotal information may be gathered to illustrate the data. This extra knowledge, combined with the collected data, is then converted into explicit heuristic rules that help diagnostic and prognostic analysis. The parameter data are initially used in real time on the aircraft itself to provide cockpit alerts, or to optimize the engine's performance, but can later be downloaded into a GSS computer, where it can be analyzed to support maintenance planning and further asset management activities.

The onboard reporting is generally handled by the aircraft's embedded communication systems; however, transmission of the data to the GSS systems is a little more problematic. At present, a snapshot of data is taken several times during the flight and transmitted, either by cell-phone link or by Aircraft Communications Addressing and Reporting System (ACARS), back to the waiting GSS systems. ACARS was developed during the 1980s to provide a digital link between commercial aircraft. Advanced avionics equipment would then automatically produce reports and transmit them via ACARS to its GSS, reducing the need for regular reporting to be made by the crew. Today, aircraft send standard ACARS messages back and forth to confirm undertaken procedures or to request information. These messages are received by ACARS operators and relayed to appropriate address. Data Systems & Solutions' data snapshots follow this route to its servers.

The main problem with the ACARS system is that not all of the data can be sent, as there is an upper limit of only 3520 characters per packet. This limited capacity is inadequate when the envisioned continuous stream of collected raw data could be around 1GB per flight or higher! The relative cost of bulk data transmission would also be prohibitive at today's rates. To solve this issue, a policy of preprocessing, or partially processing data onboard, along with data reduction algorithms to transmit minimal data packets, has been adopted. If bulk raw data need to be retrieved for more intensive analysis or to form a complete historical record, this will have to be done by retrieving the data when the aircraft is on the ground and available. This technique will require onboard storage and retrieval methods that are compatible with the low cost-base of the existing EHM systems in operation today.

Once the data are transferred from the aircraft (by whatever method), it is delivered to the data center system where it is analyzed and then trended. Initially, the data are "washed" though an automatic system that looks for potential trends that indicate abnormal behavior. Each instance of abnormal behavior is called a *feature*. A group of similar *features* occurring over a period of time may be indicative of a developing fault condition or a failure mode. The central EHM system is able to automatically classify features to known failure modes to complete the diagnosis part of the process. The system then determines the severity of the incipient fault along with the most probable time where unacceptable consequences are incurred for the prognosis. This information, along with remedial action advice, is packaged up in alerts, which are then transmitted to the appropriate recipients who may take action to avoid or mitigate the consequences of the failure.

This automatic data analysis "washing" is a complex, multistep process. The first step is to look for trends within the data, and it is important for all the data to be normalized. Because engine performance varies from flight to flight as a result of changes in conditions such as altitude, temperature, thrust setting, and the like, along with sensor sensitivities and systemic errors introduced by processing, the data need to be adjusted to compensate for these differences. To accomplish this adjustment, Data Systems & Solutions uses a system called COMPASS Navigator allied with a Computational Intelligence (CI) toolkit, which was developed by the company and Rolls-Royce. Between them, COMPASS and CI normalizes the data and reduce any statistical "noise" to obtain a level required for comparison.

The Distributed Aircraft Maintenance Environment (DAME) project has introduced a new tool and process into the existing setup, with the development of continuous sampled vibration data using an advanced pattern-matching application called AURA. If the automated system detects abnormal behavior that has not been classified in a diagnosis before, it will be necessary to conduct the diagnosis offline from the automated system. AURA enables an extremely rapid search through the historical vibration and performance data of the whole monitored fleet of assets, searching for previous instances of similar abnormal behavior. This historical database may be many terabytes in size, and the search must return matches within a few minutes to be viable. When matches are found, the asset identifier and date time stamp data fields of the historical matches are used to query and extract the associated historical maintenance and event data records into a case based reasoning (CBR) application. The CBR tool sorts and ranks the maintenance and event data so that the most likely diagnosis becomes easily apparent to the user. Once the diagnosis is confirmed by domain experts working together in the DAME collaborative environment, the online diagnostic classifier may be "trained" to automatically diagnose any subsequent occurrence of that particular failure mode.

Data Systems & Solutions has hundreds of customers for its equipment health monitoring services, which has necessitated a great deal of investment to the data management aspects of ensuring each customer's data are automatically processed in accordance with agreed service levels and that the data are accessible to authorized users, but never to its business rivals or any other unauthorized user. The environment that automates this is called the 24/7 system. It also automatically schedules and dispatches jobs to the application servers and is self-sensing for internal faults in the hardware and software. If faults are sensed, the system will dynamically reconfigure itself to guarantee compliance with customer SLA requirements and send alerts to the appropriate Data Systems & Solutions support and operational staff. The 24/7 system also breaks down each job into small transactions, with the ability to roll back or bring forward processing transactions to ensure compliance with the SLAs. The 24/7 system delivers the scalability that allows Data Systems & Solutions to continue expanding its EHM services to a much wider set of customers and assets. The attractiveness of the Grid is that some of the functionality within the 24/7 system is an inherent feature of the Grid paradigm.

This EHM system improves as more data are supplied to it; it effectively learns as it goes along. Thus the more data that are captured, the more accurate the system becomes, so increasing the throughput of information is an area that Rolls-Royce is keen to improve. The main bottleneck to obtaining data is not so much the collection of the data, but more the transmission and later storage of the data at the GSS. In addition to the problems of data transmission and storage, the very nature of aircraft is that they travel, so any solution would have to make use of a distributed architecture. This allows data to be downloaded or accessed from any aircraft or asset at any location and even partially or completely processed locally so that decisions can be made before the aircraft flies again. Also, because of the number of stakeholders involved in the operation—Data Systems & Solutions, Rolls-Royce, the airlines, the airports, the maintenance companies, and so on—it was decided to use Grid computing technology.

DAME

Both Data Systems & Solutions and its parent company, Rolls-Royce, are principal industrial partners in the DAME project in conjunction with the White Rose Consortium (Universities of Leeds, York, and Sheffield), University of Oxford and Cybula. The DAME project, which began in January 2002 at a cost of €5m, will deliver a working demonstrator of a Grid-based gas turbine fault diagnostic system.

This system relies on the Globus Toolkit 3 Grid services, which provide a deployable, virtual diagnostic workbench that can be accessed through a GSI-secured web portal—a portal that looks to be in a single place on the Internet, but is actually distributed across the entire grid. The sensor system on the aircraft and the air-to-ground communication links are controlled and represented by the Engine Data Service, a localized service that would be used in real time at various locations around the world to collect the aircraft data from the plane and deliver it to the database on the GSS. The larger datasets will probably be downloaded by wired connection once the aircraft has landed to avoid any transmission bottleneck, but other options are being investigated. The Engine Data Service will also control the data replication, as there may be a requirement to have data cached in many different locations. The Engine Data Service is called into operation only when and where required and is switched off at all other times.

All the engine data gathered are stored in a multiterabyte database, which is represented in the DAME system through the OGSA-DAI interface, the SOAP and Grid service-standardized way to access data sources over the Grid. This database is searched by the Data Mining Service, which uses the AURA pattern matching system. It is possible for many Data Mining Services to be run in parallel on data intensive problems, a feature of the Grid service that allows a dynamic approach to distribution.

A number of other services can be started on demand to allow various processing and analysis operations to be performed on the downloaded data, for example, modeling services that allow the downloaded data to be applied to a "virtual" engine. Also, the ground staff can access a number of case-based reasoning applications or expert level data analysis services, which can simulate and analyze the behavior of an engine in operation, or perform an off-line analysis.

Generalization

For Data Systems & Solutions, the implications of this system are as far reaching as the Grid on which it is based. The predictive maintenance process (analysis of the asset data to provide the operators with information to avoid any potential problems) is applied across the entire fleet managed by Data Systems & Solutions—assets such as ships, trains, aircraft, and power plants. Add into this wide diversity of assets the company's geographic distribution, and it is easy to see why Data Systems & Solutions is looking for a distributive solution.

This type of solution can lead to difficulties from customers; for example, some are concerned about the privacy of their data and are unwilling to allow anyone outside their operations to view it, even Data Systems & Solutions. Also there are restrictions on bandwidth; whether too small to efficiently handle large datasets, or military in purpose and under a communications blackout during operation. In these cases, the assets must be able to operate autonomously, free from the central hub, and send data in when they can.

Security is another issue. If a third party got hold of a dataset it could conceivably "reverse engineer" confidential information such as asset performance or failure statistics without actually having any engineering knowledge or study the asset itself. Data Systems & Solutions is looking for a flexible distributed technology that will allow it to perform prediction analysis at the customers site, with the customer solely responsible downloading, storing, and starting analysis runs and raw data, independent of any centralized control. When you apply this idea across an entire fleet of assets—say a fleet of aircraft—you can see that a localized processing operation can upload its results to the central hub only when conditions allow. This lack of a requirement to keep the centralized hub always connected and updated improves security and operation flexibility of the system, and increases its attractiveness to customers.

Analysis

This architecture is driven by the need for on-demand processing of business-critical information. When dealing with civil aviation, cost optimization calls for a very short time between the arrival and departure of an aircraft as the company only makes money when the aircraft are airborne. This ever-narrowing timescale must be enough for the download of all engine performance data recorded in flight, its analysis, and for decisions to be made on the recommended maintenance actions. This process will be repeated at various locations around the world, at different times of the day; but the data collected must be synchronized with the static, centrally located historical data held at the hub of the system. The Grid computing technology allows for dynamic processing locally, with support for more complicated and in-depth analysis to be performed on-demand. In addition, Grid provides methods for dealing with large datasets, data access, data caching, replication, and transport.

Operational Grid-based Engine Health Monitoring systems would have to be globally distributed and include airport facilities, network links, and central processing and storage facilities. As yet neither Rolls-Royce nor Data Systems & Solutions has the IT infrastructure in place to support such a massive system. Indeed, under two agreements signed in 1996 and 2000 Rolls-Royce has outsourced approximately 90 percent of its IT infrastructure and support to the giant EDS corporation. To turn this plan into a reality, both companies know that they have to seek partnerships with network and resource providers. In addition, they will have to look to other third parties for support, such as airlines, the ACARS providers, and airport authorities. With so many companies involved, security and safety of business-critical data are essential; these are issues that the Grid is already equipped to address through the concept of virtual organizations and the associated GSI security model. Using these services, trusted entities can be automatically created on-demand in the required location, can perform their job, can send the resulting data to a secure location, and can then erase themselves without threatening the integrity or confidentiality of the data.

Finally, in the operational environment, the available resources, as well as urgent questions that require answers, will be subject to minute-by-minute dynamic changes. A local service provider may not have allocated a set of resources solely for Rolls-Royce, but instead provision them depending on availability and need in the same way that conference attendees have to share a single wireless access point. In this environment, the dynamic capabilities of the Grid services are crucial and provide the platform for such situation-adaptive processing schemes.

Could such a project be solved without the Grid? Of course, and in many different ways. Security can be provided by public and private encryption key schemes or tunneling through SSL-encrypted channels. Another option would be a VPN running over the Internet. Dynamic behavior can be achieved by hosting the services in application servers such as JBoss, Sun Java System, IBM WebSphere, Orion, Apache Axis, or Tomcat. Alternatives could include the highly researched agent programming paradigm.

Communication between distributed components has been successfully implemented in several business architectures using CORBA, DCOM, Java, RMI, or proprietary protocols over TCP or UDP. The problem of cross-platform compatibility can also be solved using compact operating systems, such as Inferno from Vita Nuova, which is currently being evaluated by Data Systems & Solutions. As for the use of the Internet with this kind of system, Data Systems & Solutions' CoreControl already uses a secure Web portal for the delivery of its business critical data. Finally, there are countless commercial solutions offering data caching, replication and transportation of large datasets, as well as powerful data processing architectures from supercomputers to PC clusters.

You could combine all of the above technologies and build this system, but there are at least three reasons to seriously consider the Grid-based alternative:

- Multidomain concept: The problem of sharing resources over organizational boundaries has always been the driving factor of the Grid. By design it is better addressed for solving the issue.

- Completeness: By definition, Grid computing encompasses integrated solutions to the problems listed previously such as distribution, dynamics, security, and so on. Though their level of development varies greatly, the solutions are being gradually improved, and solving these problems comprehensively is one of the aims of the grid community.

- Standard approach: As stated in Foster's three-point checklist, the Grid relies on open standards. Historically, it has been proven that such tactics guarantee a high survival rate, for example, TCP, e-mail, and the World Wide Web. Adopting open technology is the right step for creating a maintainable system with a healthy future, which is able to integrate with other companies' IT infrastructure, as well as other partnering organizations.

Grid is not the only reasonable solution for the problem of a distributed EHM system. However, it is a strong candidate, especially for a company that is slowly building a long-term vision for its system. As this book is being written, the White Rose Consortium is presenting its EHM demonstrator to the Rolls-Royce management for approval. The follow-up project from Rolls-Royce and Data Systems & Solutions is expected to pave the way for a production system, possibly within the next three years. During this development period, current problems with the middleware quality of service will need to be fixed; perhaps the first implementation will use only a single service provider for the central processing facility and data warehouse. During this period, the relationships between the partners need to be strengthened and the strategy mapped out between all interested parties. Once the industrialists are confident of what the Grid has to offer, both Rolls-Royce and Data Systems & Solutions see their place at the center of the global computing resources market, using automated service level agreements to broker Grid services with their clients and making their client's data work to save money, time, and effort in the asset management field.

Summary

In this chapter, we have enumerated a number of roles in the Grid computing environment. For some of these roles, such as the partner grid participant or the end-customer, it is hard to find functioning examples today. Some other roles, such as the infrastructure provider or the service provider, are in the very early stage of the evolution, and the institutions undertaking such mission are able to provide solutions with only partial functionality. Finally, there are a number of roles companies can already assume today, such as the enterprise grid owner, or the vendor of a Grid-aware application.

Although many of the boxes in Figure 4.1 are white, thus designating an empty market niche, we have a reason to expect that this will not be the case a few years from now. The same picture drawn five years ago would have been completely white. However, it is entirely possible that the relationships in the mature Grid market will not be as simplistic as we have presented here.

This chapter tried to isolate several practical concepts people associate with grids and explain business opportunities associated with each concept. Clearly, a vendor of a Grid-enabled image-rendering application, an online provider of per-hour cycles of such an application, and an enterprise grid builder where this application would be installed will each see a different opportunity, choose a different path to achieve the goal, and establish a different metrics of success. We hope we have explained these differences clearly enough. You should now clearly see where your business belongs in the Grid computing business model, and where there may be a business opportunity.

For those who learn better through examples, the five use cases provided in Chapters 3 and 4 illustrate some of the strategies described previously. The earthquake engineering infrastructure and the community created by the NEESgrid project is an early example of a partner grid, or a virtual organization. MCNC Grid & Networking Services plays the role of an early Grid infrastructure provider as well as a service provider. Wachovia has built a departmental grid; the system constructed by Synopsys has features of an enterprise grid. The research project of DS&S escapes easy classification. The early Grid EHM prototype certainly aims to be an advanced Grid-aware application suite. The future production infrastructure involving several stakeholders will possibly resemble a partner grid.

CHAPTER 5

Technical Issues

This chapter focuses on technical considerations needed for building enterprise grids, departmental grids, partner grids, or for participating in the Grid at large. As seen in Chapter 4, such participation may involve providing resources and digital services as commodities.

Given the profile of the audience for this book, the amount of products currently available, and the rapid evolution of products, this discussion deals more with principles than the nuts and bolts of particular products. On occasion, particular features of various toolkits are briefly touched on to give a flavor of the current state of things. Further investigation is essential for those who endeavor to select and deploy resources based on any particular toolkit.

High-Level System Design

At the highest level, a Grid system is either confined to its home institution (department or enterprise grids) or spreading across several institutions (partner or open grids). The process of creating a Grid architecture is conceptually similar to any other system construction effort, especially when building highly distributed systems, but some issues play a more central role in designing a grid installation than others. This is particularly true for systems that are going to operate on the Grid at large. In making these decisions, a number of technical factors are important:

- Organizational security requirements
- Data sensitivity
- CPU peak requirements and duty cycles
- Data storage

- Internet bandwidth availability
- Existing resources
- Custom resources
- Potential for porting
- Potential for partnering

In the process of designing a grid, depending on the experience and subjective preference of the architect, it is possible to begin at the lowest levels (e.g., determining the storage and replication requirements of a given application) or the highest level (e.g., constrain the design by data center location and networking, then work down from there and see what might be done). One point that will come into play for some architects is that the relative newness of the technology can make it easier for most to start at the top and work their way down. This is just a heuristic though. In particular, people who like to build small prototypes as part of the institutional education process may well find it most productive to take a small well-known problem domain and render it in Grid technology.

One should not feel intimidated by the task of designing a grid. It is a common practice to think big, but start small. This "baby-steps" approach lowers the burden of delivering the complete design at the start. Chapter 6, as well as several use cases, promotes exactly this approach.

Organizational Security Requirements and Firewalls

Standard business data, business practices, and business resources must be protected from damage, cracking, and theft. Even when the data itself are not so valuable as to require the kinds of measures as those used in finance or health care, the cost in terms of employee time, customer attrition, and competition is still valuable. With this in mind, nearly all companies have security rules designed to allow their staff access to internal data without allowing just anyone to do "bad things."

One of the first approaches to secure systems was the deployment of firewalls on networks. This was a quick and easy approach, but done at the expense of flexibility. The Internet is a peer network, meaning that no node on the Internet is architecturally more significant than any other. Any node can run a service, and any node can contact any other. The upside is that this is a very flexible platform on which things like the Web and the Grid can be built. The downside is that it isn't the easiest environment to secure systems from attack. A firewall takes a white list approach. Specifically, it only allows traffic that has been approved by the network administrators. The assumption is that an action that has not been specifically approved is considered an attack. In practice, this means is that even widely deployed protocols like RFC-959 FTP, which has been around since nearly the beginning of time, often operate in a degenerate mode to be able to function at all within a fire-walled architecture. With GridFTP (the Grid-enabled extension of FTP) the situation actually gets a bit worse, because while it can fall back to something like RFC-959 FTP and at least move data, it is possible that every through-put improvement of GridFTP is unavailable thanks to the firewall.

There are solutions to this class of problem. The most common one is to white list given port ranges for certain nodes. In the case of GridFTP, the pro-tocol specification places no requirements for which ports are used, particu-larly for the data channel. Thus whoever is setting up the service can specify on which ports the service should listen for the incoming data connections. This information can then be passed to the network administrator and those ports blessed in the firewall configuration. The problems here are obvious. On the Grid, like the Internet, there are no special nodes and each can be used for any purpose. Thus it may well be true that a particular node is being used as a semipermanent GridFTP server today, but tomorrow there may be a tem-porary GridFTP server started on another node to provide load balancing for some temporarily highly demanded data. In this scenario, the only practical thing to do is to allow all nodes that might one day be hosting a GridFTP service to do so from a firewall configuration perspective. This is a practical but suboptimal solution because now an additional port is open to all machines, even those not currently running GridFTP services. Another solu-tion, one which the authors have implemented for a client, is to increase the smartness of the firewall in such a manner that it becomes aware of the data flowing across it and can take independent action based on what it sees. In this instance, what it means is inspecting the control channel of the GridFTP connection and looking for the port information about the data channel(s). By knowing this information, the firewall can dynamically open the ports necessary for the data transfer; there is no bureaucratic overhead from the per-spective of the users and everything "just works."[1]

Today, this is a bit more difficult than it should be because there are no off-the-shelf components with such functionality. There are two reasons why this should get a bit easier going forward. First, a few years ago the infra-structure of the Grid moved to Web Services and XML. These make it easier

---

[1] The authors have a client who is fond of saying that "just" is a four letter word.

for the firewall to do inspection of the data being passed. Second, there is a proposal slowly making its way through the standards process called WS-Agreement, which would allow for this kind of negotiation to take place in a common way for all services. The potential exists here for the firewall to itself present open standards-based interfaces and allow client applications to first contact it to negotiate an agreement, then contact their end data provider for the GridFTP transfer. Because the firewall was explicitly involved in the setup for the transfer, all ports necessary to facilitate the transfer will be open and able to receive data. Security is discussed in more detail later in the chapter.

Data Sensitivity

Many grid decisions today are being made almost exclusively on the basis of the sensitivity of the data involved. Currently there is a well-established security model for authentication and delegation. This model can be used in a number of different arenas. However, there are only the beginnings of a comprehensive model for securing data while it is in use. If the data are especially sensitive, then the Grid is still a difficult place to ensure safety. That said, all the tools that are needed exist; there just isn't yet a single point of entry that can be used to bootstrap the process. Security, in particular the ability to give certain jobs to certain hosts or providers, can mitigate much of the risk; but, depending on the application, issues can remain.

In terms of securing sensitive data, enterprise grids can be an effective solution. In addition to giving much of the power of the Grid, this flavor of solution is much easier to secure. On the other hand, when building partner grids, one needs to cope with three resource-level areas that open a potential threat for exposing sensitive data. First, a job may run on any authorized node on the Grid. Much of the risk here can be mitigated by using virtual organizations (VOs) to indicate which nodes are trusted. These might be nodes owned by partners or independent software vendors. In either case, there is a contractual relationship in place demanding a certain level of physical security at those nodes. Second is the storage on which data are archived and replicated. For the most part, the primary storage is not difficult to secure, as it is likely to be owned by the institution that is most concerned about it. An issue can arise when changing focus to replication. As with the nodes that are permitted to run jobs, a VO can be useful to specify where a piece of data is allowed to be stored. Finally, there is the issue of securing the data as they go across the network. Using secure channels based on secure socket layer (SSL) or Web services security standards (in short WS-Security, or WSS), it is possible to encrypt data as they are transferred between nodes. GridFTP is an example of such a channel.

Although it is true that all three of these issues have potential solutions, it is also true that each is of varying maturity in various Grid toolkits, and certainly developers have to exercise great diligence in designing solutions that make use of the appropriate toolkits at the appropriate times. As the beginning of this section stated, one way to deal with this Gordian knot is to simply cut it wide open. Instead of trying to deploy a solution on the Grid, build an enterprise grid and put the application back in a domain that is better understood by both the developers already on staff and the security people responsible for approving the implementation. For those leaning toward a partner grid architecture, the Grid security model introduced in Chapter 1 is discussed in detail further in this chapter.

CPU Peak Requirements and Duty Cycles

One of the fun things about Grid computing is that it lets a manager think at an enterprise level more easily than the last generation technology manager was able to do. It used to be that CPU was purchased at a node, cluster, or supercomputer level, and it was usually deployed for a particular application. As an example, a department with overnight processing would often purchase whatever power was needed to get that job done in a half or a quarter the time actually required; this ensured a safety margin in case of problems. The same organization might have jobs running during the day either on behalf of users or services they use. This system also would usually be purchased by the department to support its specific requirements.

With the advent of Grid computing, it becomes possible to use the same systems for both the overnight batch jobs and the ad hoc jobs run during the day. Instead of stopping at a department level, the analysis continues to the enterprise level, determining the organizational peak load. Eventually, with the use of a Grid scheduler, jobs will be deployed in a manner consistent with their load and privileges during the course of the day and night.

In addition to simply buying the peak horsepower needed, it may be that an organization has a peak that is fairly short in duration, but requires tons of CPUs during that peak. In this case, it might make sense to subscribe to one of the emerging product offerings from vendors like IBM and Sun, who will sell on-demand CPU access to those with short-term needs. Clearly, the rates being charged for these machines are quite high if the need stretches beyond a small portion of the year, but for intermittent high-demand period, they can make sense. As the Grid continues to evolve, these services are expected to have standards-based Grid interfaces.

Finally, it is also possible to do load balancing based on more dynamic criteria. As load grows for a given application, it is possible to create more instances of that application in order to bring more CPU to bear on a load.

Today, accomplishing this process is toolkit or even installation dependent, but this kind of balancing is a key need for many applications and thus is expected to emerge quickly in standards.

Data Storage

A wide range of storage solutions are available in the market today. From RAID systems on stand-alone machines to SANs (Storage Area Networks) to robotic tape systems and climate-controlled caves, any storage need can be met. With Grid standards there are a few different ways to think about these options.

Since the Grid is a flat architecture with all nodes being equal, storage follows the same pattern, and any data can be placed anywhere. How the decision is made to put a piece of data at a particular location is based on the capacity available on the storage system, data rates, costs of storage, lifetime of the data, and, of course, policy.

One of the emerging standards for storage is the SRM (Storage Resource Manager). This standard specifies a multitiered protocol for engaging a storage system to the requests of a client. The client isn't aware of the mechanism in place to store its file, it only knows the promises that the SRM is making with regard to the file. For example, a client can specify that a particular file be stored temporarily or permanently. The canonical implementation of an SRM is one that has a tape system and a layer of disk cache. If a client specifies that a file be stored permanently, the SRM might allow the client to transfer the file first to cache and later to a tape system (see "Storage Management" later in this chapter for a more detailed discussion of such systems). The client, however, knows none of this. If the permanent storage facility is tape, disk, or punch card, the client doesn't care. All that matters is that the SRM has made a contract with the client concerning the longevity of the file.

When planning for storage on the Grid or in an enterprise grid the four main criteria are capacity, latency, throughput, and longevity. Although it is true that these four are found in combination, the issues surrounding each are sufficiently distinct so that talking about them independently is useful.

Capacity is the total amount of storage that will ultimately be needed. This much is obvious. What is less obvious is that some storage solutions do not scale effectively to large capacities. For example, it is difficult today to provide petabytes of disk and create a cost-efficient, long-term storage system. Latency dictates the media that are used. If the latency requirements dictate quick response, it is impossible to use tape-based systems. If latency is best effort, then tape still wins the economic battles. Throughput is less of a concern in grid systems than in many other systems. Because of the inherent scaling in the Grid, throughput can often be achieved through usually slow technology (e.g., tape) by using many instances at once to achieve the needed aggregate data delivery. Finally, longevity will often push to a tape system instead of disk. Most of these issues are data-center specific rather than issues local to the Grid, so this book does not deal with them in great depth. The take-away message here is that the Grid, and particularly standards like SRM, allows a variety of storage solutions to be used in a uniform fashion. Thus, as emerging standards such as WS-Agreement make it into production environments, a client will be able to request a class of service and a standard library instead of having to purpose build each solution for each application.

Internet Bandwidth Availability

Because the Grid operates over the Internet, the available bandwidth can be important. This is one of several reasons why many first projects are enterprise grids. Enterprise grids, because they operate within the confines of an internal network, generally either have enough bandwidth available already or can be trivially upgraded. In the more controlled environment of an enterprise grid, there is nearly unlimited bandwidth. Even where additional capacity must be added, it is far less expensive than a comparable fat pipe to the Internet with its monthly maintenance fees.

That said, for either an enterprise grid with Internet requirements or for an application running on the Grid the size of the pipe matters. When buying access to CPU resources, there must be sufficient bandwidth to push the job out to the CPU. A job running on Grid technology must bring along its own environment, and this can make the size of the package (i.e., the application, files, and libraries it depends on) quite large. Especially when running many smaller jobs, this can be a considerable amount of data.

More obviously, if the application produces or consumes a lot of data, this will be a serious consideration. An application that is packaged into a 10 MB execution unit, consumes a 2 GB file, and produces a 100 MB output in 5 minutes requires a throughput of about 6 MB/sec to the node to sustain the input stream. This adds up quickly if the jobs are run at an on-demand facility by a 100 node farm.

Consider that in the world of scientific applications it is not uncommon for Internet links to be in the tens of Gigabits per second in speed. A typical host, however, is only able to move data at about a 1Gbps so there is generally more bandwidth available that that node can use. This gives the theoretical ability to move that 2GB file in 16 seconds. This is the world most scientific users are familiar with.

As we move into the Grid things change a bit as links become better used. Let's expand that example to being a 100 node farm instead of a single host. If we launch all 100 jobs at once it will take about three minutes to deliver all the data across the 10Gbps link provisioned in that lab. This is the worst case scenario; savings begin to appear with data reuse and if the job takes longer than five minutes to run, but given the nature of network provisioning, it is probably the one worth planning for. In production environments, it is, of course, common for there to be opportunities for data reuse, for it to take longer than three minutes to process the data, and for some machines to process secondary datasets.

Because this is one of the typical characteristics of the Grid, it is possible to have large volumes of data and data consumers distributed geographically. With this assumption in mind, these are some of the issues that need to be considered:

A. Design a data architecture to serve the needs.

   1. What are the characteristics of data consumers (users) in the application architecture?

   2. Where are they geographically?

   3. What data volume is expected?

   4. What bandwidth and quality of service (QoS) is required?

B. Data caching is often necessary to optimize access time. Typically caching challenges include these questions:

   1. Is the copy up to date?

   2. How often to refresh the cache?

   3. Also, with distributed caching system, which copy is closer to the user?

   4. How can the system proactively move data to the "right places" and thus have it available when the requests are made?

C. For reliability, data redundancy can be used to ensure that data are always available. If a data repository host fails, user requests will be routed to a backup system in a transparent manner.

D. For transferring the data between the repositories, you will need a medium that provides fast, reliable, and secure transfers. You can consider using GridFTP or something similar.

E. Security and privacy needs will change:

   1. Who owns the data?

   2. Which user groups or virtual organizations have permission to view the data?

3. Which users can write/delete the data?

F. Depending on complexity of the system, meta-data to describe the database structure and the data itself are often necessary. This meta-data will be of smaller volume than the "real" data, but will have similar needs, such as accessibility and reliability.

Besides this list, there are also advanced data management issues specific to the higher level applications. For example, there are highly advanced work flow management systems specific to the high-energy physics community.

Related to the subject of Internet bandwidth are the issues surrounding connectivity failures. For mission-critical applications, the failure of a link can be a high-profile event. Grid technology provides some recourse because load can be shifted to alternate data centers or alternate links. These issues are largely unrelated to Grid technology specifically, however, and are thus outside the scope of this book.

Existing Resources

The potential for reusing existing resources, typically computers, was one of the driving forces in the acceptance of Grid technology. The first step in planning for Grid technology is to get an inventory of existing resources and their duty cycles. There are a few classes of computers that are worth considering separately.

Desktop machines are those littered around any organization of even modest size. Taken together, they represent both a considerable financial investment and a lot of idle power. The ability to leverage these existing resources is appealing; however, this power will likely only be available during off hours for the company. During daytime hours, demand will be the highest and the resources will be least available. Also, desktop machines are characterized by high maintenance cost per processor, and they can handle only certain types of Grid processing. Still, having these resources available for 12 or 16 hours a day, when fewer people are sitting at their desks, is still a powerful tool for overnight batch jobs.

Farms and clusters, for the sake of this discussion, can be considered equivalent. It is true that there are significant structural differences between the two, but from a standpoint of planning for a new grid effort, they are both resources with certain hardware characteristics. Knowing about these attributes, schedulers can match jobs to the appropriate resources. For jobs that require the specialized resources of each, schedulers can match them to the appropriate resources. One difference between this class of resource and desktop machines is that they are available 24 hours a day. Typically, they are also more reliable, manageable, and secure. There are two modes of setting up an existing cluster as a Grid resource. One is non-dedicated: previous users will still be able to use the cluster as they always have, but its CPUs will also be available to other Grid users when they are idle. An alternative is a dedicated mode, where the cluster is being exclusively assigned to the Grid jobs. Old users loose their exclusive access rights, but gain unlimited access to other resources in the enterprise grid pool. We have seen example of such migration in the Synopsys case study, Chapter 4.

Planning in this instance includes not only the analysis suggested for desktop machines of determining what their duty cycles are, but also determining what class of jobs might take advantage of the specialized capabilities of each of these classes of deployment. Once an inventory has been made of the resources currently available, the demand that can be met by making the resources available on the Grid, and the priorities of those jobs, it can be determined whether the currently available infrastructure is sufficient for the demand and where additional money would be best spent. Particularly in the case of farms, these additional resources can be efficiently provisioned when compared to the traditional style of computing, with each work group buying whatever resources they need to accomplish their mission.

Finally, the last resources that many organizations have that should be considered are the symmetric multiprocessing (SMP) machines and other specialized compute resources. These are especially interesting because they are resources that previously were difficult to exploit outside of a limited set of people with accounts on them. Because of this fact, these machines often either sit idle or are used for things that make suboptimal use of their time, such as real-time, mission-critical applications. In these situations, there is frequently not just one, but two of these resources. The second machine acts as a hot spare for the first, but is rarely used effectively. Often this second machine does little but serving console sessions for developers doing tests or, running dozens of instances of Netscape Web browser. Far better use of the resources in general, and the backups in particular, can be made by utilizing them in a grid that allows jobs that require these kinds of specialized capabilities be conveniently accessed.

Custom Resources

Many organizations have resources that were custom built for a given task or class of tasks. These can range from measurement devices to custom hardware to software. In traditional IT, these resources would be accessible via custom protocols, conventional networks, or even, in many cases, proprietary networks.

Access to these devices is, in fact, an engineering effort itself. Examples of this class of device include measurement devices in process control and many data acquisition systems used in the NEESgrid system (case study, Chapter 3).

With the advent of Grid computing, much of this load can be absorbed by the toolkits that have been and are being developed to implement new services using open underpinnings. This a loaded statement; there are three critical pieces. First is the issue of "have been and are being developed." When it comes to custom resources, there are two main classes of device, those that are highly capable (i.e., PC or better CPU and memory) and those that are less capable (i.e., embedded systems and other platforms with small memory or CPU footprints).

In the case of highly capable platforms, those with plenty of memory and CPU, it is possible with the toolkits available today from a variety of vendors to write new services that implement interfaces to these resources using Grid protocols. In this instance the service writer gains built-in security, distribution, notification, and all the other bells and whistles discussed in earlier chapters. Writing a new service in this scenario differs little from writing one for any other highly capable platform such as exposing analytical processes on conventional compute platforms. Where things get more interesting is when the platforms get smaller.

Embedded systems and other small footprint platforms present challenges. We are aware that some middleware providers are working toward having small footprint Grid technology available, but none have thus far shipped a product that will run on even comparatively capable platforms. This is the "are being developed" portion of the summary. These tools are in the works today and as the standards continue to settle, more options should become available. Until then, those with less capable platforms can either write their own minihosting environments or write resource wrappers on more capable platforms that communicate via the existing proprietary interfaces. Writing a minihosting environment is not completely trivial, but thanks to the Web Services and XML underpinnings, a tremendous amount of existing library support is available that can be cobbled together into code that meets the needs immediately at hand.

Another option is to run the Grid service on a highly capable machine and have it relay information to the custom resource through a proprietary mechanism. Given the likely emergence of proper embedded Grid middleware in the near future, this second option becomes especially appealing, as it is likely to be much less expensive. The proprietary libraries necessary to talk to the platform already exist; the support necessary to write the new services already exists. This approach hits the "sweet spot" of both platforms. In the future, when native support exists for developing Grid services on the embedded platform, you can rewrite the service using the tools available at that time.

The next idea is implementing new services. Most of this book deals with the services associated with standardized resources. While it is beyond the scope of this book to discuss the process of developing proprietary interfaces, it is worth mentioning again that Grid standards are multitiered (see Chapter 2). There are the Web Services underpinnings, the Grid infrastructure that are built upon, and, finally, services built on those underpinnings. In the case of custom resources not all layers must necessarily be implemented, but it is still possible to efficiently build services that share common communication and security models with the rest of the resources both internal and external to the organization.

The last point "using open underpinnings" is discussed in previous chapters. The Grid does not work as a collection of isolated islands of communication; tools from multiple vendors can speak to each other, just as a browser from any vendor can surf the Web and retrieve content from any Web server. In this fashion, a custom resource can be used by any client on the Grid.

Potential for Porting

One of the common ways to join the Grid is to take existing applications and port them to a Grid middleware platform. Previously this book has talked about the idea of putting a Grid wrapper on an existing application; surely that is one way to derive quick value. However, to take advantage of a wider set of Grid construction tools, it is necessary to do more work. Grid service layer concepts such as lifetime, notification, and faults can be better expressed with tighter integration into an existing code base than with wrappers. Doing so allows more functionality from the original application to be exposed.

There are two basic kinds of components in a grid: those that use the services of others and those that stand alone, providing a service without necessarily contacting other grid services. In both cases, to develop such a component, it is necessary to iterate through the user and software requirements of the legacy system. Some classes of requirements, like security, will require a new method of handling. In contrast, some other requirements (performance, resources) may become less restrictive because of the broader capabilities provided by the Grid.

Map the legacy system to components. Encapsulate the old system elements as Grid services. Some existing applications may well sit comfortably behind an interface defined in a standards organization. A couple examples are storage systems and data movers. In the first case, the SRM standard might be used; in the second, the aforementioned GridFTP is used. By adopting those interfaces instead of creating proprietary new ones, you can use existing off-the-shelf clients instead of having to write new ones. There are, for example, several implementations of GridFTP clients available from various places. This obviates the need for the organization to maintain the client themselves.

In other situations, the legacy system is unlike anything for which there is an existing standardized interface. In this case, the application will be wrapped with an interface that is proprietary, but use Grid technology as the plumbing. Depending on the nature of the application, it might makes sense to create a standard proposal and thus enrich the global Grid space. If the application is proprietary or otherwise gives the company a competitive advantage, then this makes less sense, but using Grid technology as a strategic tool is still reasonable, as it continues in the direction of having the entire enterprise be based on a single set of standards. This is how several of the existing standards began. People realized they would like to put one of their services on the Grid and built an interface that they then took to standards bodies to propose as a standards effort.

As the porting begins, it can be valuable to look at third-party resources. Depending on the system, being on a grid can be beneficial because it provides access to more resources, and some of these resources may come from other organizations.

Side Trip: Analogies

There have been dozens of examples of successful enterprise grids around the world. A system designer in such a situation looks for analogies in other branches of engineering. Such a process requires both the ability of abstract thinking and multidisciplinary technical proficiency. In this case, the design team should optimally consist of engineers coming from other branches of computing or telecommunication. In this section we provide hints of interesting technologies that you may consider as examples.

The Web

The Web standards provide the base technology for Grid services. The basic concept of current Grid standards is to extend already existing platforms rather than invent new ones from whole cloth. This idea is worth mentioning explicitly because the earliest work in the field did not reflect this attitude. The earliest work predates widespread Web services and was done at a time when the plumbing was built nearly from scratch thanks to the dearth of existing foundational work.

The analogy here is that just as the Grid is based on open standards so too was the work done on HTTP and HTML, and once it became apparent that there was some traction for the ideas, the world of networking changed. It is becoming increasingly easy to argue that the Grid is getting close to this same kind of a tipping point. There have been dozens of examples of successful enterprise grids around the world, and thus far there has been no loss of momentum. The Grid is still a speculative bet in a number of ways, but it seems clear that the next few years will continue to see growth and provide enough examples to create new thought leaders in the field.

Peer to Peer

In fact, Grid systems will often have peer-to-peer (P2P) characteristics. This is an important point and one in which managers can gain an early competitive advantage. A survey of the projects and technology in the world (this book providing one) shows that a great deal of work is being done in the area of peer systems, be it either for computing on demand, file sharing, or peer-topology information systems. Peer-to-peer architectures share a number of Grid concepts, such as a number of management points, ability to cross the organizational frontiers, or collective resistance for network failures. Some of these technologies have been directly incorporated in commerical Grid products, such as the desktop computing systems. A leader who has products that can exploit this vacuum in the market is going to have a much more clear chance to move ahead quickly and make a mark on this emerging aspect of the art.

CORBA, DCOM

There are other connectivity layers that were recently popular and served a similar purpose to Grid services. Many systems built on CORBA exist today. This is also true to some extent of DCOM, .Net, Java RMI, and other similar technologies. They all lacked one thing or another to make them the premier standard of the Grid. Some were overly complex, some weren't open, some weren't human readable, and some didn't go through firewalls effectively. At least one had all those "misfeatures." As the Internet revolution has shown us, open standards will generally win the day. Second to that is the requirement that any closed standard be available on all needed platforms.

The phrase word *effectively* deserves some extra attention here. One of the problems with previous generations of application distribution mechanisms was that they used protocols that made it difficult to get them through a firewall. It is true that there were work-arounds for some of them, but even in these instances the solutions were proprietary. Anyone who wanted to do application construction in the large was confined to virtual private networks

(VPNs) or huge holes in the security infrastructure. Grid technology works past these issues by using open standards, so that infrastructure providers can do stateful inspection as data passes through them.[2] Although this approach will lead to a requirement that firewalls run on more powerful hardware, that is a small price to pay for the advantages of the Grid.

Technology Areas

Development of any Grid-based system will interface a number of IT technologies. Some of them are tightly integrated with the concept of the Grid. In the following sections we enumerate those most frequently quoted and explain how they are being extended in the Grid architectures. Data, storage, resource management, and security are the most obvious parts of this section.

One of the challenges in adopting Grid technology is deciding where in the fairly large landscape projects fit. This challenge is compounded because some of the tools that exist in this young field are narrowly focused on a small subset of the Grid space. These tools are useful, especially those that are tracking standards, but they are not by themselves fully realized visions of the Grid. In this section we look at examples of the kinds of resources being developed in isolation of their larger implementations. As appropriate we present some context for these examples and touch briefly on areas of overlap, whether conceptual or implementational.

Data Management and Databases

The role of databases in IT has evolved over the last 30 years. From the first business applications (at least), there has been a need to store lots of data in a structured format. In the case of these earliest examples, the database frequently consisted of proprietary routines developed in-house. There were two reasons for this. First, the companies saw IT as a strategic advantage in a competitive world. They believed that by investing heavily in these one-of-a-kind systems, they would be able to operate the rest of their business more efficiently than the other vendors in their market. In many cases this was true. Second, there were often no packages available that would meet their needs. Between the two, a whole lot of custom development was occurring.

---

[2] This does not mean that data needs to be sent in clear for anyone to read. Open standards define the structure of the communication, but do not interfere with the data. Knowing the standard, a firewall software could read the network-specific communication metadata while the rest of the transferred information would remain opaque to it.

This requirement for custom development was indeed an expensive way to run an operation. Those with the skills necessary to build such systems in a reliable fashion were rare, and the code needed to implement such an environment was complex. Although the data volumes of the day were very small compared to the petabyte systems that are becoming more common today, they both were on the edge of what was usable and controllable by the then state-of-the-art computers and programming methodologies.

Early in the IT life cycle, databases were researched and a pretty stable set of core theory was accepted by the community as useful and capable of being implemented. With this work progressing, several early database products were brought to market. Corporate programmers were able to focus on application development rather than database development. One significant advantage to this was that the new, off-the-shelf databases were generally much more efficient and less expensive than the home brew that had previously been used. One disadvantage was that the databases from the various vendors still had proprietary interfaces. This disadvantage was for the most part acceptable because application development was still largely a corporate task, and choosing a platform and doing all development on it was a long-term commitment.

The next generation of databases began using standard interfaces. Specifically, the SQL standard was developed and became mature enough that a variety of clients could be developed that spoke to a given database. Similarly, the well-known programming environment developed standard database access programmer interfaces. For instance, a Java programmer can use JDBC libraries to access in the same way as Oracle, MySQL, or Postgress databases. This multistep process closely follows that of the Grid where over the course of decades, a successive set of standards was developed that allowed greater and greater abstraction. Beginning with TCP/IP and leading through HTTP and Web services, there are layers of increasing abstraction that allow programmers to assemble larger and larger systems.

Just as databases of previous generations have become increasingly open and standardized, so too the database vendors of today are beginning to adopt Grid technology.

Secure Remote Access

One area in the database community that is not well standardized is security. Each vendor is currently solving the problem of secure remote database access in its own fashion. This means that each implementation has to be dealt with in turn, and users cannot easily gather information from multiple databases of different kinds. With a commonly accepted Grid security scheme such as the Grid Security Infrastructure (GSI), this could be solved in a uniform manner.

Taking Advantage of Clusters

Historically, databases have run on single machines. Getting improvements in speed typically meant buying more expensive hardware with more CPUs and vastly more memory. Just getting enough memory often proved difficult and expensive because the commodity platforms either did not physically support enough memory, or their operating systems did not know what to do with it. As a consequence, mainframes and SMP boxes from Sun, IBM, and HP were the only game in town. More recently, database vendors have been delivering products that can run on rack-mounted commodity systems. This has some immediate cost advantages. Early in 2004, Oracle delivered its first-generation Grid database using this kind of metaphor.

Oracle proposes to attack the problem of large database load balancing using a cluster technology, instead of having a machine for Human Resources and another for Sales. It is possible to have a cluster-based database that serves both purposes and dynamically allocates the needed horsepower to the database instance currently demanding more resources.

With this initial generation of cluster-based database engine products built there are some additional ways in which databases and database tools can incorporate more advanced Grid concepts.

Secure Delegation

As we explain in the security section, besides the basic access security, Grid technology also permits a user to securely delegate authority to another entity. This might allow a user to connect to a database that also uses real-time data from another tool to satisfy queries. Because the database can act as a delegate of the user, it can look up information in a manner consistent with that user's ability to access the other tools. Figure 5.1 shows such an interaction. The key is that the administration of the sensor array does not have to take into account the existence of an entity called *Grid Database*. When the request in this scenario is made, the Grid Database is passing a delegated credential, identifying itself as a proxy credential for the user that initiated the request (the concept of a proxy credential is explained further in the Security section of this chapter). Thus the sensor need only check whether that user has permission to query for status.

Federated Databases

The first step a database executes when a request comes in is to determine how to process it. This is the execution plan that it will ultimately use to satisfy the

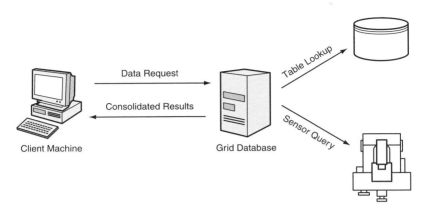

FIGURE 5.1   Grid Database Interaction

query. By using Grid technology, it is possible to take the plan and determine what nodes in a federated database are best suited to returning the results most efficiently. This determination can take into account a number of different factors such as the locality of the data to given nodes, access to tertiary information, and the estimated length of time a query will take. For example, in Figure 5.2 the Grid Database has two replicas to choose from for getting manufacturing data but must get other pieces of the query results from singletons. This picture looks very much like what people do every day using tools from several different

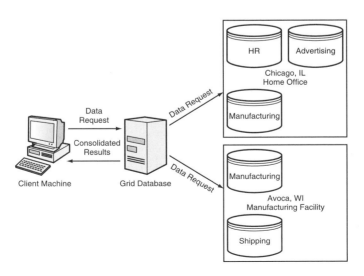

FIGURE 5.2

database vendors. The difference here is that the protocols being developed for doing things like this on the Grid make it possible to have each of those databases hosted by implementations from different vendors.

Another way to leverage Grid architecture in databases is to have a multitier implementation in which the first resource contacted presents a federated view of the entire corporate environment. This is particularly advantageous in situations where various databases are located throughout an enterprise and are implemented using products from different vendors.

In this example, a user would create a Grid proxy for himself and contact the federation master with his query. The federation master would evaluate the query and create a plan. This might include data from several different sources that can be queried concurrently or must be serialized depending on the nature of the result sets so that the federation master might contact each of the databases (themselves Grid resources) and ask them for their plans. A plan is an indication of the steps that which will be taken to satisfy the query. By evaluating the plans from various data sources, a federation master can determine which will be able to most quickly satisfy the query.

Next the federation master would dispatch various pieces of the query to the appropriate databases and accumulate interim results. The results could vary wildly depending on the query, so it is likely the federation master would be able to create temporary tables to cache the working set just as modern relational databases do today.

Finally, the federation master would complete its plan and return the results to the user. Because these steps took place within a secure framework, the results that the user eventually receives are only those that she has authorization to access.

Storage Management

There is an enormous amount of work to be done in the field of unstructured data. It is an art at about the same stage as databases were in the 1970s. A number of solutions are available, but none are standardized. Companies are still at a state where they can gain a competitive advantage by implementing storage systems that allow for the efficient management of documents, instrument readings, e-mail, and workflow results. There are even a number of legitimate reasons to consider building these systems in-house instead of buying off-the-shelf solutions.

This problem domain can be cut into two pieces at a high level, meta-data storage and data storage. Meta-data storage is the cataloging of the properties of the data being stored. Data storage is the core storage infrastructure itself. Both are interesting topics.

Meta-data can consist of any number of elements. For a banking application, data might include the name of a person receiving a loan, vital statistics, and credit history attached to the scans of the loan documents signed. For a pharmaceutical company, it might be the workflow that ended up producing the FDA (Food and Drug Administration) filing. The pharmaceutical example is a particularly interesting one, because it can be used to show how workflow management in Grid systems can be tied to storage systems.

In a vastly simplified view of the process, in the development of new drugs and diagnostic agents, scientists must document each step in the process. This information, along with the results of animal and clinical trials, are submitted to the FDA to gain approval to manufacture and ship the product. Much of the data associated with this process is unstructured. It can be instrumentation results (e.g., radiographs, chemical analysis results, photos), documentation (e.g., test plans, laboratory notes, FDA filings), and information about how the rest of that fits together. This last bit is particularly true in the computer modeling part of the process.

When a new drug is developed, models are frequently built to study how the agent will work within the context of the body. These models are growing ever more sophisticated and are usually incredibly CPU-intensive. Moreover, sometimes it is necessary to reprocess a job for a variety of reasons. The results may be lost or on a server that is down. The requirements of the job that produced the data may have changed and needs to be rerun. Additional input may be available.

In each of these examples it is important to know the path that produced the original data. The meta-data system is the component that tracks this information. The meta-data, logically organized into a DAG (directed acyclical graph) can be used by the Grid scheduler to optimize the process. For example, take the case of a prerequisite dataset not being available because a server is down. The scheduler can use the workflow data to determine that by going back a generation, it can recreate the dataset and thus proceed with the analysis currently being requested. Storage systems for this kind of usage have typically been tape based. For a long time, the demise of tape systems has been predicted, but each time denser hard disk is released or primary storage has caught up with the needs of users, something new comes along to demand more storage. It seems likely that this trend will continue.

A problem with this scenario is that tape systems are not only expensive to purchase initially, but they tend to scale in giant leaps rather than a bit at a time as needed. To deal with these shortcomings, people have built disk caching systems that keep frequently accessed files on some fast storage. This cache is usually disk, but occasionally memory, depending on the data volume and access patterns. Even systems with disk cache tend to be centralized overall.

Most desktop PCs today come with hard drives much larger than the people using them will need. Assuming that 25 percent of the disk is being used on a typical 80 GB drive, an organization with as few as a hundred PCs has 6 TB of storage available to be exploited.

One of the emerging standards from the Global Grid Forum (GGF) is the SRM. This standard specifies how clients can interact with storage resources on a Grid. The principle is one of giving the users the ability to request as much data as they need, but also giving the SRM the information it needs to make decisions about how to manage its physical resources.

One area in which SRMs are useful is in the management of tape systems. Some tape systems cost in the millions of dollars, and all have limitations on how quickly they can process requests. Usually this limitation is a result of how long it takes the robot to move along its track, find the volume with the data being requested, grab the volume, move to an open drive, insert the volume, and finally position the tape to the spot on which the data reside. These process are mechanical and occur slowly. It is common for administrators to try to optimize the system by reducing the number of times the robot must mount[3] a given volume. One way to do this is to demand that users tell the robot all the files they will be interested in when they make their initial request. This system, when such information is available, is very effective as it allows the robot to spend time mounting the volume only once, but read all the files that will be needed before unmounting it. In situations where such prior knowledge is not available, another common idiom is to simply read the entire volume into a cache. If later a client makes a request of another file from the same volume, it can essentially be served immediately. Modern systems also use caching because they can act as a rate adaptation layer between the expensive tape drives—sometimes tens of thousands of dollars a piece—and the client who may be at the other end of a slow link, or because application semantics is only interested in reading a small portion of the file. Later it might return for another piece. Finally, an SRM allows administrators to make policy decisions. These can be decisions affecting the management of the tape system, cache, or network. Each has a slightly different set of important characteristics.

In managing the tape system, the goal is often to reduce mounts, but there are also concerns regarding quota and drive usage. For example, the

---

[3] In technical jargon, a storage device must be "mounted" to the system before one can read or write data to it. In particular, this is the case with multivolume storage systems. In robot-operated tape storage archives, the act of mounting is associated with physical move of the robotic arm that reaches for the given tape and places it in the drive. Then the tape must be sequentially read. This is a very time-consuming operation.

authors are familiar with a system in which the various drives in the tape system were purchased by different departments. Although the department that paid $120,000 for four drives, is likely happy or obligated to share with the rest of the enterprise when they are not using them, it is also true that the department spent that money to satisfy certain requirements that it has in terms of data movement. This kind of scenario is common in systems that cannot afford to lose information during the acquisition of data from live feeds. If the information is lost, it is lost for good. So having all the bandwidth necessary, plus a spare, is a demand that must be accommodated.

Similarly quota must be allocated to people based on administrative policy. This is true for both the tape system and cache. For tape, the concern is often monetary, like that of the drive purchase. For cache, the concern is balancing the needs of large dataset users against those who tend to churn through lots of data.

To balance these concerns, and taking into account the large latency between the time of the users' request and when the last file will be delivered, the SRM standard was developed so that a user can request all the data she knows she will need at once. Knowing the load for the system, an SRM can then schedule tape mounts, cache policies, and run the overall system more efficiently.

Taking this idea to the next level, some of the SRM implementations in existence today also allow for third-party transfers. In this instance, a user will make a request for a file that exists in another SRM, and his local SRM will orchestrate a third-party transfer between the remote SRM and one of the storage systems under its control.

In keeping with the idea that the SRM standard only dictates what is necessary to operate an SRM effectively, the standard says very little about how to actually transfer the data. This was done to allow different implementations to take advantage of transfer protocols best suited to their environment.

On the surface, this mechanism seems like it works contrary to the Grid goal of using standardized protocols, but that is not really true. Although it is possible for a malicious administrator to install only the protocols he wants to advance, what is so far universally common in SRMs is to have several protocols available. For example, it is common for sites to have some protocol that they developed in-house, have used for a long time, and have built confidence with. It is also universally common for the SRM implementations the authors are aware of to use the GridFTP protocol. Sometimes legacy FTP, SCP, HTTP, and others are also available. When the user submits his request, he also includes a list of the protocols that client knows how to speak. The SRM uses this information to determine which of the protocols it wants to use to give the data to the client. Finally, after the data have been staged into cache, the SRM tells the client how to retrieve it and what protocol to use.

This brings the story back to where this section began. If an organization has terabytes of extra disk floating around how can this potential be used? One challenge is that not every node can speak every transfer protocol. By allowing the use of multiple protocols, the SRM can not only choose what is best but can move data to the appropriate nodes. If a user can only speak GridFTP, but ten of the disk caches speak only HTTP, then moving a file to one of those ten machines does not make much sense. Conversely, if a client can speak HTTP and the data she wants are already on a node that speaks that protocol, then immediate access can be granted instead of having to move data to other cache locations.

Load balancing can be achieved in SRMs quite easily in this manner. When an SRM sees that a many requests are coming in for a set of data, it makes additional copies on other nodes. In this fashion many users can be served the same data without the cache node becoming a bottleneck in the system.

Although many of these features exist in some proprietary storage systems, the SRM standard makes it possible to have a single client that speaks to a number of servers running, not only within an organization but also with partner firms or other people in the VO. Thus, again, open standards become the key to elucidating the difference between the Grid and more primitive modes of doing distributed systems work.

Resource Management

System sharing and load balancing are probably the most hyped aspect of Grid computing, and thus are an area of extensive existing experience. In fact, in reading about the Grid, it is common to see people make the mistake of thinking of the Grid as a mechanism for doing distributed load balancing and "by the seat of my pants" supercomputer assembly. It is thus imperative that this section begins by reiterating that the Grid is not a cluster. A cluster can be a resource on the Grid, but it is certainly not itself a grid, nor is it even an enterprise grid in any but the most simple sense of the word.

Many interesting things can be done by making either idle desktops or purpose built clusters available as Grid resources (Wachovia is an excellent example of the former; Synopsys is an example of the latter. Both were presented in Chapter 4). There are two ways to approach this aspect of Grid computing. One is to scavenge cycles from existing resources that are not fully utilized. The other is to build custom facilities and make them available as CPU resources.

The first case, scavenging cycles from existing resources, is how a lot of people get started in Grid computing. At a high level, it is appealing that, as people leave for the day, their desktop computers can seamlessly become part of an enterprise grid, an installation of Grid technology insulated from the Internet by a firewall or other such network protection, for whatever compute intensive jobs they may have. The advantages of this model are mostly obvious. Because the budget requirements are modest, success is easy to demonstrate. One less obvious by-product is that this is a one-time gain. Enterprise grids are first of all constructed to ensure proper return on assets. People with these sorts of motivations initially point to this type of CPU scavenging, or desktop grids, as their goal architecture. This is especially true at an early stage of grid construction. Often, this is followed by a more advanced architecture where groups of existing resources are moved out of departmental control. Instead, they are added to a centralized pool of resources to provide dedicated support for virtualized service architecture.

People can save money doing desktop computing. Desktop computing is a good way to dip the organizations feet in the water. The challenge comes in repeating the monetary success. Once the first Grid efforts are shown to be successful, people will invariably demand more. As the demand for more resources continues, organizations will need to provide additional machines and clusters just to meet the increasing demands from their users. This is still a very good thing because this style of deployment is still much less expensive and easier to make good use of older kinds of software. Perhaps just as important, ultimately Grid computing is not only about CPU, but access to resources in general, and CPU is the thin end of the wedge driving adoption.

The other way to gain access to large amounts of horsepower is to buy it. In this instance Grid technology becomes a useful way to deploy new resources. As with older styles of computing, there are a number of different ways to provide such power. At a high level, these are: supercomputers, clusters (recently also available in a new, more advanced incarnation as blade servers), and farms of nodes.

Supercomputers

There are still many jobs that cannot be successfully deployed on PC-style hardware; for these cases, supercomputers are still a requirement. Typically, these are jobs defined in platform-specific software built for particular architecture either for their performance, or for historical reasons. In particular, applications with large working sets in memory that cannot be easily broken down into pieces that can be processed independently are still the domain of supercomputers.[4] In these instances, the supercomputer is advertised as a resource on the Grid, and jobs that need these particular kinds of capabilities say so at their submission. The advantage of using Grid technology is that the supercomputer can be managed using the same infrastructure as the rest of the resources at the site.

Clusters and Farms

The distinction between clusters and farms can be a little more subtle, but the essence of a cluster is that it is structured such that it can be used as a single unit. In particular, it will generally have high speed, low latency networking between the nodes. A farm, however, is built for more general purpose computing. In the case of clusters, they will often be managed as a single resource. Farms and clusters are usually managed as a collection of resources that can be parsed out in the quantities necessary for a particular job.

On-Demand CPU Resources

As cluster and farm styles of computing have taken off over the last few years, a new kind of business has grown more viable. To understand it, we should briefly revisit the power grid analogy, where the bulk of the energy provided comes from large and expensive generation facilities. These are powered by a number of different fuels, but one thing that holds true is that they are a hassle to manage in the face of differing loads from one hour to the next and from one weather front to the next. They take a long time to start up in particular. In response, small generators are built local to the energy consumers and can be started up for a few days or weeks during a heat wave to supply energy to the highest demand times. These so-called peaker plants are external to the main generation facilities, but are accessible to the consumer via the standard interface.

Similarly to this power grid topology, there are vendors now offering peaker compute facilities (IBM, Sun, HP—see "Grid Resource Providers" in Chapter 3). These peaker plants allow businesses to buy access to additional facilities only as their needs demand. Instead of having to buy a couple hundred nodes for a twice yearly forecasting job before the board meetings, a company could instead rent time on the peaker and not have to pay for and house those nodes themselves. It is true that renting is more expensive than

---

[4] The problems of domain decomposition and emburassingly parallel tasks have been explained in Chapter 1.

buying if the need is more pervasive, but for some jobs this has the promise to become an interesting way of accommodating periodic demand. Given the nature of this kind of arrangement, it is likely that the resources being rented will become available using the standardized Grid interfaces.

One example of the class of application that can take advantage of this kind of increase in CPU availability is forecasting. A robust model can take an enormous number of cycles and could run for days on any but the most powerful computers. Supercomputers can solve the problems more quickly, but at great expense. One interesting aspect of this kind of application is that people sometimes need to simplify their study to make the problem tractable for the hardware they own. If they had more power, they might run simulations with greater detail, more variations of assumptions, or with more kinds of inputs.

The term *utility computing* is also used to describe this style of resource provisioning. Utility computing is the idea that instead of buying everything that an organization might need, they instead rent power on an as needed basis to satisfy peak demands. In principle, this means that a company will be able to rent power at the end of a quarter or year to run its peak loads. It will pay a premium for that time, but compared to owning the equipment, it will cost a lot less. The problem is that many organizations have time-based peaks that match (e.g., quarterly and yearly). This means that the utility computing vendors will have to create suitably large peaker plants to handle this load. It is unclear to many in the community how this will ultimately pan out.

Workflow Management

The state of the art in workflow management is still primitive, but this example gives a glimpse of the power that can be realized as the Grid matures. There are several implications of this example that make it best suited for Grid solutions.

One of the originators in this aspect of the Grid is the Condor project (see Chapter 2, "Early Proto-Grids"). This project is more than a decade old and was one of the early scientific projects responsible for early thought about Grid computing. One piece of its system is the DAGMan (directed acyclical graph manager). This tool allows for specification of a sequence of jobs where dependencies exist between the output of one job to the input of the next. Once the order of execution has been specified, the Condor system manages the execution of jobs on resources around the site. There are several groups working to bring this kind of functionality into standards group for broader acceptance. Among the well-known efforts with industry acceptance is the BPEL standard.

Guaranteed Execution

In Grid computing users are giving up local control to take advantage of resources in a broader environment. As a consequence, the new environment needs to guarantee at least the same level of reliability as the old local environment. At a minimum, the submitted jobs must always run. If things get lost along the way, then the whole idea falls flat on its face.

One early example of a resource that provides this feature is the reliable file transfer (RFT) component in the Globus toolkit. This service manages file transfers in such a manner that moving data becomes a fire-and-forget type of activity. When a client contacts the RFT, it presents the files it wants to transfer. In most cases this is a few very large files or a many smaller ones. The case for using an RFT becomes less compelling for smaller amounts of data.

Security

Lack of adequate security is among the most frequently quoted reasons for delaying implementation of Grid solutions. Just as Grid computing has been received with hype, security for Grid computing is greeted with disbelief. Both reactions entered into a stereotype. In both cases, the association is more often intuitive than supported by arguments.

Security is the absolute central topic in Grid computing. Because of the open and ubiquitous nature of Grid installations, every function provided by the Grid must be "secure." This topic includes secure and scalable virtualization, secure workload scheduling, and secure collaborations.

Although the subject is so crucial, it is rather difficult to cover it methodically. There are many ways to approach perimeter solutions, but it is difficult to describe these in terms of a fit-all security model. The best-known attempt to do so has been summarized by Ian Foster and his colleagues in the article "A Security Architecture for Computational Grids" published at the ACM Conference on Computers and Security in 1998. This model has been later rephrased in the VO terminology (see Chapter 2, "Security for Virtual Organizations"). As covered there, the three important functions of the VO security are:

- To interoperate with local security solutions
- To manage on-demand trust domains
- To dynamically create new entities and assign secure identities to them

The GSI based on the Public Key Infrastructure (PKI) has been developed as the most popular implementation of this model. This scheme remains the main conceptual model for implementing the grids today. However, the community has rapidly evolved since 1998, and the model does not include the new concepts, obstacles, and solutions that have since been developed. In particular, important work has been done on the centralized authorization policies, federations of users and resources, and the Open Grid Service Architecture (OGSA) service computing model. Today there is plenty of Grid security-related research going on, with little synchronization.

We feel that security is so closely interwoven with every aspect of Grid computing that it should be covered in more detail than any other component of the technology. Therefore we will devote this section to it. We first explain some key concepts of Grid security jargon. Next we revisit GSI and other technologies. We then present and comment on the problems faced by the technology. Finally, current standards and best practices are reviewed for those intending to design a security infrastructure for their grid deployment.

Internal versus External Security

The security of IT systems can be divided into internal and external security. Internal security deals with threats that come from inside the system (e.g., a malicious employee accessing internal resources); external security covers the dangers that come from outside (e.g., an intruder trying to penetrate the system by using vulnerabilities of the interfaces that he can access remotely).

Departmental and enterprise grids involve systems that are protected by firewalls. The security of such systems is no different than that of any other company-wide installations. The design and maintenance of the internal security include actions such as assignment of privileges to user groups, dividing the system into access zones, defining the routing of sensitive data, and ensuring that the hardware itself is not vulnerable to uncontrolled physical access. The latter includes protecting desktops with passwords, securing wireless networks from spoofing, and such mundane actions as locking the offices and monitoring the access to the corporate buildings.

The presence of a corporate-wide grid will not significantly change these procedures. With common access to the central pool of resources, data with various levels of sensitivity may be processed in the same place. However, data will never exit the internal company systems. Moreover, the processing will take place on the central facility, very possibly owned and monitored by the corporate grid administration unit, imposing certain usage restrictions such as no direct user login. Securing these systems is similar to securing other central facilities in the company.

As the enterprise grid is usually enclosed with firewalls, it does not significantly interfere with the external security management. The organization may, but does not have to, choose to allow external access to resources. In this case a secure shell login, a VPN, or a browser-based limited interface may be chosen as the access technology. None of these solutions, perhaps with the exception of a Grid portal (see Chapter 3), is Grid-specific. With telecommuting increasing in popularity, all these technologies have already been implemented and successfully used by many companies whose employees need to connect to corporate systems from home, from a conference, or from a customer site.

To summarize, the enterprise grids are not free of security threats. However, the encountered problems are generic, similar to other enterprise-wide systems, and not Grid-specific. This is true to the point that there are organizations which desire to remove security from the Globus Toolkit in their enterprise grids, considering it redundant to their existing security infrastructure when used in such protected environments.

The situation is different with the partner grids or the Grid. The Grid, like the Internet, will connect smaller, enterprise-wide structures (grids) into a larger domain. For this reason, the problem of the external security needs serious consideration. In fact, this problem contributes to the fact that few commercial partner grids are available. Moreover, because Grid computing usually allows execution of guest code at the local resources, partner grids introduce new issues to the internal security. To understand better the elements of the security culture that needs to be present in partner grids, let us analyze a simple example. We return to the imaginary Techman & Robotix use case from Chapter 1.

Techman Case Revisited

As we remember, Techman was an engineering company, charged with running complex simulations for its client Robotix. Techman suffered for lack of resources, such as the adequate number of powerful machines to perform the simulations. Let us imagine Techman being part of an industry-wide partner grid, where it can hire the resources it needs using the on-demand computing model. We will track down the steps the company needs to take to launch and complete a simulation (Figure 5.3).

The VO that Techman joined is an organization for companies with a common area of interest. They are all involved in similar types of engineering tasks and therefore are interested in sharing access to specialized software tuned for this purpose.

There are several Application Service Providers (ASPs) in the partner grid offering to run computations for someone else. These organizations regularly

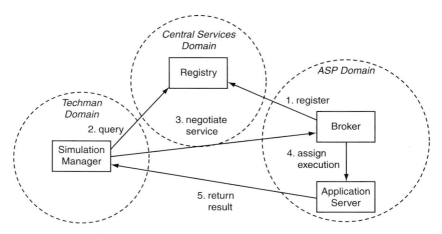

FIGURE 5.3 The process of launching the simulation on a partner grid

advertise their capabilities to a well-known central registry (1) maintained by the partner grid management institution.

Techman runs a Simulation Manager. It is a Grid-enabled front-end for its simulation. The application is not designed to perform the simulations locally. It only formulates the parameterized simulation requests and submits them on the Grid. The Simulation Manager first needs to discover who has available resources matching the simulation requirements. It queries the central registry (2) and receives in return a list of currently available ASPs. The Simulation Manager contacts one of the ASPs and negotiates the conditions of service (3). The ASP uses the resource broker to setup a virtual application server, which would perform the simulation for Techman (4). When the simulation is complete, the application server sends Techman the results (5).

This simple scenario involves three stakeholders, with three separate administrative domains. What are the procedures and requirements needed to maintain the satisfactory security level?

At the beginning of the service negotiations in step 3, Techman needs to establish the identity of the party it contacted. Although the contact address of the ASP has been provided by the directory, this alone does not guarantee anything. For instance, this does not guard against a man-in-the-middle attack.[5] Therefore a secure procedure is needed to ensure that the remote

---

[5] This jargon term indicates a type of attack when an intruder is able to intercept the communication between the two parties by placing himself in the middle of the communication channel.

party is indeed the one it claims to be. Such a process of asserting the identity is called the *authentication*.

Once the remote party has been authenticated, Techman needs to initiate an internal procedure to check whether it is okay to let that particular ASP run the simulation. The algorithm depends on Techman's local authorization policy. For instance, the policy may only allow sending data to members of its VO, companies certified by some third party, or those recommended by other partners. The process of accepting the communication with the other party is called the *authorization*.

The other party will also perform the similar procedure, namely it will authenticate and authorize Techman. In particular, the authentication will be necessary. Later the ASP will need to send back the simulation results, and so it must assert that the identity of the receiver is the same as that of the requester. In Grid computing, we frequently speak about *mutual authentication*.

The entire subsequent negotiation needs to go over a secure channel. The most important characteristics of such a channel include the features of *protection* (encryption) and *integrity* (warranting that the data stream has not been tampered with by a third party who may have intercepted it on the way).

Once the negotiation is over, the Simulation Manager allows the ASP to perform the simulation on its behalf. This is called the *delegation*. Delegation is also closely related with security. The party with the delegated responsibility (the ASP) receives a subset of privileges of the delegating party (Techman). With such privileges, it is possible to prearrange the simulation procedure so that no one but Techman can decode the results.

The ASP's service broker creates a dedicated virtual resource for Techman. This resource needs to be trusted, but it should have an identity separate from the broker. Since the broker may receive hundreds of similar requests from various customers, each request is being immediately handled to such a dedicated resource. In this fashion, customers can be certain that their data are not exposed to a third party by executing on a common resource. In Grid computing, there are procedures for *on-demand creation of secure entities*, which includes assigning identities to these entities.

The broker again delegates its role, previously assigned by Techman, to the newly created virtual Application Server. The server performs the simulation in question, which may possibly last many hours. Before it starts, the Application Server needs to secure the local environment to ensure that the guest code does not affect the local system, and vice versa. This includes security (e.g., ensuring that no local data are exposed to the guest code, and no data of the guest program can be seen by local applications) as well as safety (guarding against the situations when badly written guest code may drive out of control of the local system). The art of isolating the guest applications from local environment has been frequently referred to as *sandboxing.*

Before the results can travel back to Techman, the procedure of authentication, authorization, and securing the connection is performed again. This time, it is primarily the ASP who wants to ensure that it exposes the results only to the same party who requested the service. Techman wants to check that the results come from the same simulation it had requested. It will do so by checking whether the Application Server can present the credentials originally assigned by Techman. This can be proved using the same PKI that was used in every previous step, and the entire mechanism is called the *certificate chain of responsibility.*

Feasibility Study

How much of the preceding scenario is possible today, and what is still missing? The short answer can be provided immediately. The entire scenario can be implemented and executed using today's technology. In the Grid computing community, the use of the standard PKI and the X.509 certificates is a norm. All Grid users identify themselves with such certificates, which they typically receive from a central Certificate Authority, institutions trusted by all participants of the Grid. These certificates allow for mutual authentication and authorization. PKI and X.509 certificate standard are also the base for the popular GSI (Chapter 2) developed initially by the Globus Alliance. The transport level security (encryption, integrity) in GSI is based on other open standards: SSL (TLS), and more recently, the Web services Security (WS-Security).

To many people, GSI is synonymous with Grid security. However, it is important to remember that GSI itself is not an official standard, but a de facto most popular implementation gluing several standards together.

To implement delegation, on-demand creation of secure entities, and certificate chain of responsibility, GSI introduced the notion of a proxy certificate, in short referred to as proxy. A user's proxy represents a subset of user's privileges. For instance, the ASP in the preceding example would be given Techman's proxy certificate, allowing it to perform the job on Techman's behalf. Typically, the proxy certificate would expire and become invalid after a short time.

Sandboxing is a separate issue from the PKI, and the methods are specific for the local hosting environment. A number of sandboxing solutions exist and are discussed later in more detail.

To summarize, in general the Techman scenario is entirely feasible using today's technology (at least on the security plane). However, because the devil is in the details, we should look at the particular concerns about the GSI that are being raised on the Grid community forum.

Authorization Scalability and Federations

One frequently quoted concern is that of scalability. We address this issue here in detail, as it is related to the concept of federations, one of the important Grid computing terms.

As an example, the Globus GSI implementation bases the authorization on the *gridmap* file, which is a form of access control list (ACL). The gridmap file contains local mapping for names of users allowed to enter the system. In fact, this is a limited form of an authorization *policy*. Many researchers point out that sites may have more advanced requirements of building access or use policies than a checklist that defines whether a user is allowed to enter. For instance, policies could state what kind of operations the user is allowed to perform, impose time and performance limits on resource usage, allow or disallow users to delegate their credentials to other machines, or perform a series of security checks on certain user actions.

It is argued that the gridmap is an authorization mechanism not manageable in larger installations. In this approach, each single external trusted user must be present in the gridmap file, which contains local mapping of all such user names. It is enough to imagine that Techman having one thousand engineers, and the partner grid containing a hundred companies like Techman, to see that the solution does not scale. In the extreme, on each staff change, Techman would need to immediately notify all its grid partners to update its access lists.

The Community Authorization Service (CAS), which is also part of the Globus Toolkit, is one solution to overcome this problem. Services and resources from one organization participating in a partner grid can outsource all their authorizing decisions to CAS, which is a centralized authorization policy management within this organization. Another approach would be to consult a Security Assertion Markup Language (SAML) authorization server with each authorization decision. The OASIS SAML is an XML standard, defining a framework for exchanging authentication and authorization information.

The advantage of having an authorization server is that many access control lists can be replaced by one service. Another approach to simplify the problem would link Grid entities into federations. The concept of federations has been gaining popularity in the Grid community.

The goal is to achieve simplicity and manageability by grouping both users and resources into federations (groups). By assigning secure identities to such groups, management of mapping of access rights between the Grid actors and resources becomes simpler (Figures 5.4 and 5.5). In our example, the ASP would federate its computational resources available for the partner grid and make it available for a number of user groups. One such group would be managed by Techman and include all its employees allowed to run simulations. To make things simpler, however, such a group could as well

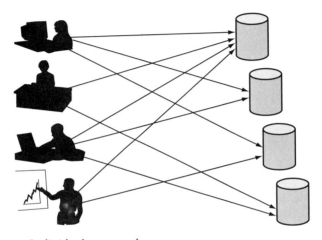

FIGURE 5.4 Individual users and resources

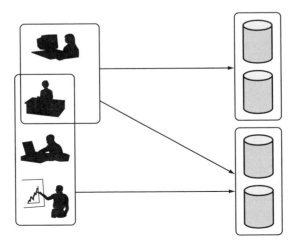

FIGURE 5.5 Federated users and resources

contain all participants of the partner grid. In such a case, a new company joining the grid could automatically and securely start using the resources of the ASP without a single human intervention. By implementing federations, scalability of authorization procedures can be achieved.

Other Security Concerns

Vulnerability of the proxy certificate has been raised as another security concern against GSI. The proxy certificate is not as secure as the user or service certificate. Basically, the proxies are typically solely defended by UNIX filesystem permissions. Although the proxy certificates typically have a short life span of a few hours, even this time can be enough for the intruder to harm the system or access sensitive data.

Critics of the GSI also include the underlying technologies. For instance, there are well-known deficiencies of the PKI certificate scheme. The weak elements of the system include the Certificate Authority (CA), a third-party trusted by all users. PKI does not specify how the CA should assess the identity of a person applying for certificates. Some CAs require that a passport or driving license be faxed, but this exposes the system to counterfeiting. Also, in a case of identity theft, there are technical difficulties to revoke the certificate (basically, all remaining Grid users and services should be notified). There are also other recognized problems with X.509 scheme, such as difficulties with roaming, or some disagreements in standardization. Also, according to the best security practices, passwords should be changed every few weeks. In the PKI context, the role of passwords is being taken over by the private key of similar sensitivity.

Pragmatic View

Having seen such a long list of complaints, you might indeed conclude that the Grid security is a long way from reaching stability; however, such reasoning would be incorrect. In fact, a pragmatic analysis of these concerns proves that the use of PKI certificates in the Grid environment is no less secure than most non-Grid IT technologies used today. In fact, all ecommerce on the Internet uses even less restrictive forms of PKI-based encryption to process nearly $100 billion in annual purchases.

First, note that most of the problems reported here involve perimeter problems, not the core of the certificate chain system. This includes the problem of the CA assessing people's identities. In fact, the same problem exists in any other IT system, where at some point credentials (such as passwords) need to be mapped to physical persons. The local administrator creating a new account either needs to see the person's ID, or ask co-workers to identify the person. Both methods are potentially risky. However, in practice, it is rather rare to hear of someone breaking into an IT system by forging someone else's ID.

The requirement for frequent renewal of the certificates should be contrasted with the similar requirement in regard to the passwords used in most IT systems today. As we all know, this requirement is being commonly ignored even by most professional users. Today, when each of us needs to remember a dozen PIN codes or passwords to credit cards, online services, bank accounts, e-mail accounts, and IT systems, the requirement for regular renewing of each of these secret words is simply impractical. Guidelines exist, but they are being ignored.

In this context, the problem of Grid certificate keys renewal is not such a big issue, because in other systems where similar functionality exists, it is not being executed. In contrast, there are reasons to believe that the technology for automatic key renewal could be developed in the future, while the analogous problem of password renewal will never be solved at a global level.

The other technical problem, which concerns revoking a compromised certificate is indeed among the important arguments against certificate-based systems. Intensive work is being done in this area. For instance, recent distributions of GSI support a certificate revocation list, which is one method to solve the problem.

It is doubtful whether perfect security systems will ever be invented. Although there certainly are holes in the Grid security as it is being used today, we do not think they will nor should significantly block the adoption of Grid computing. The GSI is not worse than many other security solutions available in production today. One convincing example that can be quoted is the credit card payment system, which has dominated the world, although it does not even pretend to be secure. The world where knowing someone else's credit card number is enough to draw money from his account could be compared to a world where knowing someone's Web domain name would be sufficient to break into his system.

Other Grid Security Solutions

We have mentioned GSI a number of times, but have not named any competing solutions. There are no obvious contenders of GSI in the field of Grid security. It is hard to explain reasons for such uniformity, which is not the case in other related technologies such as the scheduling solutions, brokers, Web service containers, or data transfer solutions.

Kerberos has often been quoted as an alternative approach. Kerberos does not use certificates. Users use Kerberos tickets to perform operations in a secure fashion. Because Kerberos is strong in academic, scientific, and national defense communities, bridging solutions have been made between it and PKI, such as KX.509. However, the adoption rate for Kerberos is not comparable to GSI in the Grid environment.

Akenti, another open-source project from the Lawrence Berkeley National Laboratory, takes an approach to site access policies opposite to CAS. Instead of centralizing the policy management, Akenti brings the access control down to the resource level. The architects of Akenti argue that in grids, a resource (such as an industrial apparatus) may have multiple stakeholders (such as the sponsor, the operating technician, the work safety unit, or the management of production processes). Each stakeholder may want to set up access policies according to their area of interest. Therefore Akenti makes it possible to implement advanced policies on each resource separately.

There are also a number of commercial and academic niche solutions in Grid security, some of which are successful. In particular, there is a wide choice of solutions for sandboxing applications so that they do not interfere with the local system, and vice versa. In UNIX or Linux, the operating system itself provides a barebones sandbox solution, by separating userland programs from the kernel, and isolating users from each other in the process space as well as the filesystem. Small-grained, but less perfect application level sandboxes are available through various hosting environments provided by commercial or open-source application servers (see Chapter 3). Most of these run on the Java Virtual Machine, with embedded sandboxing technology.

Those who fear that the application- and filesystem-level isolation is still inadequate can build core-grained isolated containers by virtualizing the entire operating system instance. Most advanced in this direction is the Sun Solaris 10 operating system, where containers can be rapidly created and administered with a GUI console. With more effort, similar virtual operating systems can be set up on top of Linux or FreeBSD. In this approach, the isolation of the guest code is close to perfect.

One example of similar solution in Windows is GridMP, a product from United Devices. GridMP is marketed as a secure solution for open grids. The product implements a secure sandbox inside which remote applications are run. According to the vendor, because the framework has been closely integrated with the Microsoft technology, the guest applications cannot harm the local operating system.

Where Do the Standards Go?

Before the merge of Grid and Web technologies, PKI, X.509, GSS-API, and SSL (TLS) were the main security standards that the Grid community was using. With the shift in the Grid community toward the Web services, the security groups worked hard to work out the standards and best practices to fill the gap.

Security for Web services is built on a collection of semi-independent standards. Often, these standards are first conceived inside large companies who have enough momentum to induce the community usage by pushing the initial development process. Most notably, Microsoft, IBM, and Verisign have been active in creating new versions of the WSS (Web service security) standards. The documents are then usually transferred to the standardization bodies where they are being reviewed and officially released. Therefore, when searching for standards and best practices, it is wise to first consult the recognized standard bodies such as the IETF, OASIS, WS-I, and W3C, where the stable documents can be found, and then learn about the research done by the large companies and academic groups for the newer ideas with possible future market impact.

WSS is the OASIS standard, officially announced in 2004, that creates background for secure SOAP and Web services communication. OASIS only confirmed what has been practiced in the community for at least 2 years. The previous, unofficial version of WSS has been available from the Microsoft Web Service Development Center. WS-Trust (from IBM et al.) specifies how security tokens get created and used, and defines security credential dissemination among different domains. WS-Secure Conversation standard, also available from IBM, built on top of the two previously mentioned, describes how the security context is shared between two parties.

A joint mission between two standard bodies, W3C and IETF, has defined WS-Signature procedures for representing digital signatures of resources or portions of messages. The protection of the XML traffic is defined by WS-Encryption standard published by W3C.

Another important organization is the WS-I, which deals with interoperability between various Web service implementations. The Basic Security Profile Working Group produces recommendations for the interoperable use of WS-Security.

GGF recommendations are built on top of these standards. Documents published by the GGF Security area are categorized as informational, those describing community best practices, and those giving recommendations.

There are currently three active working groups in the GGF security area:

- Authorization Frameworks and Mechanisms
- Certificate Authority Operations
- Open Grid Service Architecture Authorization

Two other groups have completed their activities: Site Authentication, Authorization and Accounting Requirements, and Authority Recognition Research Group. They have published a number of recommendation and informational documents in a draft or final form. All are available from the categorized repository at GridForge.org.

More generic guidelines can be found in the Architecture area of the GGF. The OGSA document (Chapter 2) contains a list of functionalities for the security services.

Current efforts of the GGF are proceeding along various topics. Several groups have been successful in developing niche recommendations for solving particular problems; however, a bird's eye vision with a global security model for Grid computing is not yet complete. The last such effort was made in 1998 and is not covering most security work that is being done today. Some community members argue that this situation is natural, because the Grid technology is so complex that a suit-all solution is impossible to construct. In any case, it seems likely that a cohesive whole is unavoidable in the long term.

Security Summary

Grids have been intuitively feared for exposing resources externally, thus posing security threats to organizations. In this chapter, we argue that although this may partly be the case, any general statements on inadequate or immature Grid security are false because of the complex nature of the security in Grid computing. Internal grids do not pose special security risks. External grids need to be constructed carefully. Their typical functionality requires providing secure authentication, authorization, message protection, sandboxing, as well as ways for establishing secure identities on demand and delegating work to such entities. PKI and X.509 certificate schemes, commonly used in Grid computing, provide solutions to most of these problems except for sandboxing, which can be solved locally. However, this scheme has been criticized for various perimeter solutions, such as the lack of good CA procedures of assigning and revoking certificates. Although this critique is important, we have to admit that other IT solutions that are commonly used today, such as password-based remote shell login or the worldwide credit card payment systems, pose comparable or higher security concerns.

In terms of the user base and installations, the GSI is the uncontested leader in academic Grid security implementations. There are a number of other solutions that have not won comparable popularity. Possibly, commercial competition should also be expected soon.

The added value of the GSI lies is the proxy certificate scheme, which provides for single sign-on, delegation, and creation of simple trust domains. Another idea that is being currently developed in the community is that of federating resources to minimize complexity of the security rights management.

In designing secure solution for a grid, it is important to check whether the proposed system adheres to the standards and best community practices, and what level of interoperability it implements. One should consult WS-I, W3C, IETF, OASIS, GGF Architecture, and GGF Security areas.

CHAPTER 6

Management Issues

Building and Selling Grid Business Case

Grid migration or development projects should be preceded by construction of a compelling business case. Such work helps not only to convince others to support and fund the project, but also to better understand your own goal, motivation, available resources, obstacles, and possible tactics.

There is a difference between selling the Grid as a concept and selling Grid technology as a solution for a particular problem. Depending on the people who need to be convinced, the approach can be different. One of the major lines of demarcation is the difference between solution providers and solution consumers. Here are two examples demonstrating this difference.

British Telecommunications (BT) wants to become a Grid technology provider. BT already has a great deal of IT and telecommunication resources, scattered around various locations. The company plans to use these as a base for Grid hardware infrastructure, on top of which Grid middleware would be built. Customers and partners on the Grid will be able to use these resources but also contribute their own. The massive hardware potential available for BT today will become a kernel of a much larger infrastructure, operated, but not necessarily owned, by BT. BT sees the Grid as the kind of technology they could champion at leveraging their telephony provider's infrastructure and know-how. The Grid, at an architectural level, is all about highly available access to metered resources. The similarities between the Grid and the switched network BT is already operating are obvious.

BT decision makers need to understand the potential of the technology. In the future, they will be selling Grid "as is"; therefore it needs to be certain of the value it brings to be able to estimate the revenue. BT technical visionaries need to sell "Grid as a concept" to their management.

Procter and Gamble (P&G) is a key player in the field of cosmetics. P&G has three data centers worldwide. Operations of these three centers could be brought under single management using Grid technology to improve productivity and optimize resource use. Also, virtualization of several resources would improve abstractions and make the management of those resources more flexible; however, this would be an internal development only for in-house P&G use. Eventually, what counts is the savings brought by the new technology. The same hardware base would afford for more operations, being managed by less staff. Thus P&G management would welcome a business case on "database operational cost reduction." The subtitle could possibly read "with Grid technology." However, it is not the Grid that is being sold, because it is likely that another case "database operational cost reduction by outsourcing IT administration" would meet with similar management enthusiasm, if only the case realistically proved equally efficient way of cutting cost. By contrast, a proposal entitled "migrating P&G infrastructure to the Grid technology" but the solution would likely see zero interest, because being on the Grid as such is not recognized as a strategic goal for P&G. What needs to be sold here is not the Grid itself, but the solution for a particular problem: how to pay less for the resource maintenance, without hampering the R&D potential of the corporation.

The difference between "Grid as a concept" and "Grid as a solution" is important to understand. Depending on the audience you are trying to reach, you would use one of the two concepts, or balance between the two. The first standpoint should be taken by those trying to become Grid infrastructure providers, administrators, developers or service operators, or ship Grid-enabled products. This category was collectively referred to in Chapter 4 as providers of Grid-enabled solutions. The second approach is suitable for consumers who primarily hope to profit from the technology by improving the working and/or economy of their own infrastructure. In Chapter 4, they identified themselves as the ones who want to "plug in." We foresee that the majority of the readers of this book would belong to the second category.

It must be noted, however, that regardless of the company strategic goals, technologists tend to lean toward "Grid as a concept" approach, putting unnecessary, and perhaps counterproductive, emphasis on the fascinating (to them) technical details of the solution. Management is typically not interested in these, as the majority of companies, unlike BT, are not natural candidates for future Grid infrastructure providers. Therefore, a word of caution: if your company is not an IT company, chances are you should be selling "Grid as a solution," no matter how fascinating the technological implications seem.

The following section focuses on building a business case for those who do want to plug in and Grid-improve their infrastructure. Another case should be built by those who want to sell Grid as a concept. However, because the members of the first category are natural customers for the second one, the material should be beneficial to everyone.

When writing this chapter, we consulted a number of sources from both the Grid computing and business arenas. Our first source comes from numerous conversations with the management of firms that implemented or were planning to implement Grid solutions. To build the coherent model of managing the transition into a Grid architecture, we confronted this knowledge with generic literature on the subject of the IT project management and change and transition management. Good introductory source of such knowledge are the books and materials from the *Harvard Business Review.* We also consulted the work *Managing Change and Transition* by Harvard Business School Press. A more advanced reference that we used is *A Guide to Project Management Body of Knowledge* (PMBOK Guide).We also relied on the advice of specialists in this field listed in the Ackowledgments. The online companion at www.savvygrid.com contains references to those materials that are available online.

Identify Problems to Solve

In marketing in general, an "outside-in" approach is favored over a product-centered or process-centered focus. In other words, "make what you can sell," rather than "sell what you can make." In this approach, marketing means first discovering customer needs and then profitably supplying them with a solution. We often are asked the following question: What would be the reason to implement Grid computing in the company? Apart from the fact of Grid technology being "cool" and "cutting edge" (both of which are true), how would the company benefit from new Grid architecture?

If you sell "Grid as a solution," the question should be inverted. Start by describing problems currently encountered with the IT infrastructure. Ask this question: What problems is the organization's infrastructure encountering? Analysis of these problems may or may not point to Grid as one possible solution. Further refinement of all available options will point out whether it is the best one.

To assist with such an analysis, we have prepared a list of most frequently quoted problems that led to research or implementation of a Grid architecture.

- *There is a need to attack a new emerging class of problems:* The company would see benefit in being able to tackle problems that require capabilities exceeding, by many orders of magnitude, what is available today. The on-wing engine monitoring system from DS&S currently operates on 220-byte messages, but should eventually interface petabyte databases (10 orders of magnitude). Such a dramatic increase involves not just scaling up of the system, but a range of new methods to cope with it. On the other hand, it brings opportunities to do things that could not be done in the past. In the future version of DS&S engine health monitoring solution, a new range of mathematical formulae could be used for analysis of the improved system. This is not possible in the current solution, which only records discrete measurement values, and these are only suitable for a limited number of analytical methods.

- *The system runs too slow because of inadequate resources:* Move to a scalable infrastructure and Grid-enabled applications, ensuring access to overflow resources in hours of peak demand.

- *Resource utilization is not optimal:* This is the most frequently quoted reason to move to Grid. Systems that have enough resources for peak processing are usually built with silos architecture. When peak demand is over, most of the resources run idle, which is unacceptable with today's three-year amortization time for hardware. Deploy one of the various Grid middleware tools that will allow the company to take advantage of existing resources before having to buy new ones. Another class of resource optimization is found when considering the amount of overprovisioning found in most data centers. When application A requires 16 machines for peak loading and application B requires 24, most of the time both applications have far more nodes than are necessary. Grid technology can help managers use those excess nodes for useful purposes during the times when they aren't needed to match the standard load on both applications. Finally, it is worth mentioning that some in the Grid community are latching on to the idea of using the Grid to manage software license costs. In a world where applications are often tied to usage-based metrics (e.g., CPU or concurrent users), having an ability to spread a peak load across a longer time can make economic sense.

- *Hardware cost per operation is too high:* Design Grid infrastructure so that the per-operation cost can decrease because a lot of functionality is consolidated on less hardware. The corollary is that when existing equipment is used more effectively, the business case for buying new equipment becomes more compelling. It is harder to justify a $100K server to run a single application once a month than it is to justify that same server when knowing it can be easily put into service running applications from around the enterprise during the other 29 days.

- *Tightly coupled architecture is not flexible:* Migrate to a modular Service-Oriented Architecture (SOA), which improves maintainability, adaptability, and change readiness.

- *Too high cost of integration and adaptation:* Minimize future integration cost thanks to an SOA.

- *Legacy security (or no security) not adequate for open systems:* Legacy security design is often only suitable for behind-the-firewall systems, but not for highly distributed environments. Move to a virtual organization model, where Grid technology provides solutions that suit the needs of dynamic enterprises with several geographically distributed locations.

- *Monolithic applications require dedicated hardware, sophisticated upgrade process, and long development cycle:* Reduce application size and speed up their development cycle by splitting functionality into various resources using Grid middleware to host the different pieces.

- *Applications are not portable to operating systems or environment used by some resource providers:* Introduce a Grid middleware layer between the application and the resource, thus allowing to abstract the logic from the execution environment. Such middleware, virtualizing the resources into standardized services (see Chapter 2), should decouple the application from the hardware, allowing usage of alternative resources. For instance, an application directly accessing a particular proprietary queuing system is far more difficult for porting than a similar application accessing the resources through a generic resource broker.

- *Applications are not interoperable and require adapters:* Enable interoperability and data exchange between various applications through introduction of standardized data and protocol formats.

- *Static architecture is not prepared for IT outsourcing:* Move toward dynamic architecture, easy for partial outsourcing leading to cost saving when necessary.

- *Enterprise is highly dependent on current hardware infrastructure providers:* Become less dependent on hardware infrastructure providers by introducing Grid middleware layer. Open standards allow interoperability between solutions from various vendors.

Marketing Mix

A common part of the business case is the marketing mix, aka 4Ps (Product, Price, Promotion, and Place). This mix is product-specific and any kind of suit-all recipe would be inappropriate. What follows is a short discussion on how the marketing mix can be approached in Grid context and what aspects are strongly related to the technology itself.

Product and Product Differential Advantage

Grid application developers are selling the application or middleware; Grid infrastructure providers are selling the service; a Grid customer company is selling the new infrastructure design to management.

In each case, market positioning of the product is important. It usually helps to start with an analysis of the positioning of the predecessor product, and then draw a list of added value in the new product. Such a list helps to define the differential advantage over competing products or over the preceding versions of the same product.

The list of core features can be drawn with the help of the list from the previous section. Core features of Grid technology will usually revolve around the themes of resource utilization, modularity, service orientation, architectural advantages of middleware, adaptation to geographical distribution, and standard compliance. There are also augmented features of the Grid solution. These are the features that do not add to the core system functionality, but make it more attractive thanks to beneficial side effects. Some possible augmented features are:

- *Learning the technology before the competition does:* Many estimates say that the constant rise of Grid and Web services technology adoption will eventually make it ubiquitous technology that everybody will be forced to use. Introducing elements of this technology beforehand will introduce necessary know-how to the technical culture of the company. This will allow smoother and faster adaptation to future ubiquitous solutions, thus "beating out" the competition.

- *Building an image of an innovator and thought leader:* An enterprise that not only introduces the cutting edge technology but also is able to present it to the media wins respect and opinion as a thought leader. At the same time, the competition will be perceived as blind followers desperately trying to keep pace with, but not having intellectual capital comparable to, the innovator. Such opinion provides a strong argument for contacts with media and partners. With some marketing effort, this image can radiate a beneficial effect toward current and potential customers.

- *Potential for government financial aid:* Many governments (United States, Europe, Asia/Pacific) strongly financially support the development of Grid computing in the private sector through various programs. In Europe, Grid computing is among the key goals of the Sixth Framework Programme.[1] Financial support for Grid investments can be as high as 80 percent of the total expenditure on agreeable terms.

- *Possibility for joining forces with academic know-how:* Academic institutions involved in Grid research for the past few years or as long as a decade are looking for commercial partners to prove usability of their solutions. Enormous opportunities are to be found there; Grid test beds are available, as well as piles of cutting edge academic software awaiting technology transfer. Partnership in such a program involves financial aid, recognition by media, contact with thought leaders in the field, and access to skilled staff from academic institutions.

- *Influence on standards:* As can be observed, even small companies who were first to adapt the technology were able to influentially position themselves in institutions such as the Global Grid Forum (GGF). The GGF has several beneficial effects such as the ease of networking, advance knowledge of the direction of the changes, and influence on the way standards are evolving.

- *Prepare for globalization:* To be a viable business in the future, more and more companies are paying closer attention to how they will work with foreign partners. Grid technology is built on international standards that will allow for an easier transition.

- *Use of a Grid technology:* In most cases, the sole fact of using the Grid technology can only be placed among the augmented features. As explained previously, in most business cases being on the Grid is not a goal, but a means to achieve a goal; however, using the Grid can be an advantage. As we can observe, the word "Grid" has good technological connotations and therefore represents marketing power. Several products that have been out there for a while are now being remarketed as Grid aware, or even rebranded. HP is offering Grid solution suite, although several components of the solutions are more than a decade old. Oracle has shipped Oracle 10g, where "g" stands for Grid, although add-on Grid features do not affect the core functionality of the database engine. There are tens of examples of products using

---

[1] The Sixth Framework Programme has been put together to strengthen the scientific and technological bases of industry and encourage its international competitiveness while promoting research activities in support of other EU policies.

various versions of distributed or cluster technology, which recently are being remarketed as Grid products. This is a double-edged sword, as this trend contributes to the overall confusion. We may observe vulgarization of the word *Grid*, and it is entirely possible that, if it becomes meaningless in the eyes of the public, it will be replaced by another term. At the moment, however, it still seems to bear huge potential for positive meaning. Using Grid technology can be a vehicle to win both the end-consumers of the product and the management to whom the business case is directed.

Depending on the focus of the business case, some features will shift from the core to an augmented list and vice versa. For instance, consider an image-rendering application, which so far has been used in a single server environment. The new version adapts to the Grid architecture, being able to outsource the rendering jobs to schedulers such as the LSF, N1GE, or PBS through GRAM, or meta-scheduler such as CSF. The primary core feature of this product is that it is faster than its predecessor. Another feature can be the ability of using any computing resource independent of the underlying architecture, which lowers the entry barrier for a new user (no need for new hardware purchase). Other features such as intuitive interface should be classified as augmented features of the product, because they do not directly improve the primary goal—being able to render images.

Planning for a new Grid product requires similar analysis of differential advantage based on core and augmented features. On one hand, such analysis must compare the product against the competition's products. On the other hand, similar technical analysis needs to be performed, comparing the Grid-based solution with other potential technologies. There is no need to go Grid if the goal can be achieved with simpler techniques. However, we should also note that as standards mature and become more commonplace, people may choose to use Grid solutions for their simplicity just as they chose a pure WS implementation in place of a CORBA one.

Price

In general, there are two ways to price a product. Cost-plus pricing is a system of calculating the cost as the sum of the production cost and the required profit. This method is easy and precise, but also "precisely wrong" for ignoring the market forces. Market-related pricing determines the price by analyzing the market forces, such as the price the customer would be willing to pay and the expected competition reaction. Although fundamentally imprecise, this method is often preferable for its outside-in focus (make what you can sell, not the other way around). Normally, pricing is done by combining both methods.

Market-related pricing is so specific to the particular product, that it is impossible to discuss in this book focused on Grid computing in general. We will restrain from any attempts to give any but the most generic guidelines in this direction, but there are some things worth touching on here.

If selling "Grid as a solution," it is likely that market-related pricing methods will have nothing to do with Grid computing at all, because it is not the Grid technology that the customer is buying. To return to the earlier example of a rendering engine, market-related pricing would need to estimate the value of the faster processing in the customer's eyes, and how the market would react to the new product (would the competition lower their licensing fees?). This assessment of the financial opportunity can be performed by an analyst who knows nothing about the Grid.

If selling "Grid as a concept," the market and competition analysis can be aided by the starting points from this book (see Chapter 3). Products entering the traditional Grid markets, such as the financial sector, pharmaceuticals, or industrial manufacturing, will need to find a more specific market niche or will face strong and well-established competition. Grid service companies will compete with strong players such as IBM, HP, and Sun. The combination of strategy, right alliances, and further refining of the target market will be necessary to survive. However, although the field is getting more crowded every month, vast areas still await exploration. Widespread acceptance of forming virtual organizations (VOs) with partners is still a step away. Commercial implementations of WS-Resource Framework (WSRF) and Open Grid Service Architecture are incomplete. Product companies focus on the handful of key markets, while the remaining part of the market is left to find their own in-house solutions. Entertainment, shopping, telecommunication, military, and earth sciences are only the beginning of a long list of opportunities.

Cost-plus pricing must be done in parallel to market-related pricing to make the project feasible. By contrast, when designing an in-house Grid architecture for internal consumption, this is the only pricing method available.

In general, a few important aspects must be taken in account when estimating the cost of a Grid project.

Usually, the core of a Grid architecture consists of the middleware. In the section "Technical Issues" we discuss choosing the right middleware. Several options are available, including both commercial and open-source licenses. Differentiating between the two is beyond the scope of this book. We think that open-source Grid solutions carry undervalued potential. The Globus Toolkit is the most popular academic middleware. There are a number of solutions built on top of Globus by distinct user communities, such as the LCG2 from EDG/EGEE (used mainly by physicists), or the NEESgrid software for earthquake science. Well-known open-source Grid components include Sun Grid Engine, OpenPBS, Globus Toolkit, Unicore, GridSphere, OCGE, and many more. Organizations that choose open-source software usually look less at the license price, more at flexibility and control that such distribution model gives. In terms of cost, proprietary solutions are less expensive in the short term as a result of fast and easy integration, but can be more expensive in the long term as a result of the lack of flexibility in development. This generic statement needs not to be true in each case. Also, if one of the motives for implementing Grid architecture is to gain certain independence from the hardware vendors, it would not be wise to get too close to the middleware vendor instead. Unfortunately, the solutions available today are far from compatible, and migration from one to the other is a significant endeavor; however, it is worth noting that proprietary solutions from Platform, SUN, or DataSynapse are far more popular in the business environment than their freely available academic counter parts, especially because the latter lack ease of use and clearly defined support plan.

The technical qualities of the products, such as adaptability and ease of integration, can be more important than the license cost or even the licensing model. Analysts and CEOs agree that grids are built, not bought. Currently, there aren't many cases when an out-of-the-box solution solves the problem. In terms of pricing, this means that the licenses, as well as the hardware cost, are only a small fraction of the project cost.

The majority of the cost will go to the integration and customization effort. The main component of these is staffing. To estimate it, the cost of the experts in the field needs to be known. This is a difficult task, as there are not many specialists out there. Those engineers who claim "Grid" knowledge have often specialized in some specific Grid middleware, remaining ignorant in the rest of the field. In general, more know-how can be found in academia where variants of Grid computing have been active for years. Comprehensive technical knowledge of industrial Grid computing is rare. In terms of finances, this means that the real Grid specialists will be extremely expensive, and, in many cases, simply unavailable other than by contracting through specializing service companies.

As explained in the section "Technical Issues," the proof-of-concept solution usually precedes the full-fledged system. This means that the company adoption of the technology will be growing in several evolution steps. The emergence and growth of the company grid culture should follow the same pace. Initially, external specialists should be consulted for the strategic decisions. They should be involved in preparing the business case itself. If the case is successful, the follow-up contract with external Grid engineers should involve two parallel actions: work on the proof-of-concept and intensive training of the company's full time technical staff.

The staff does not have to be experienced in industrial Grid, but experience in related technologies is desirable. Web services, Java, and parallel processing are examples.

Although academic projects have mostly been based on the Globus Toolkit, people who have worked on them acquired general understanding of the concept; thus they will learn conceptually related commercial technologies more quickly. In general, an experienced engineer may need an average of six months to acquire enough Grid knowledge to provide substantial productivity without guidance.

Promotion

As a result of the relative newness of the subject of Grid computing and the confusion that reigns in the media (in no small part fostered by some in the vendor community relabeling whatever software they are already marketing as "Grid"), proper emphasis needs to be put on promotion of the chosen solution. Management needs to understand how the Grid would improve the company's ability to work efficiently, and how it would influence the current hardware topology. If we talk about the internal solution, this first of all means educating management as well as staff members. An understanding of the real technical value is necessary for correct judgment of available options.

Classes are the standard method of learning. Two types of Grid computing classes are available from consulting and training companies: managerial and technical.

The AIDA (Awareness/Interest/Decision/Action) model generally cannot be applied to the process of purchasing a Grid solution. More suitable is the Adoption Model, in which the Interest phase is followed by phases of Evaluation, Trial, and Adoption. General confusion present in the market contributes to lack of understanding and distrust. Also, since grids interact differently with legacy infrastructure than do the existing applications, it is usually desirable to go through a trial period before introducing irreversible changes in the infrastructure. In this period, a proof-of-concept solution is built, operated, and observed. As we learn best by experience, this prototype is important for providing the ability to tune the system before making it into a production environment. At the same time, it serves as the tangible element of the promotion campaign.

The cost of building the proof-of-concept prototype can be reduced by using evaluation licenses available from vendors. Although in general, the standard 30-day period will not be enough for building and meaningful analysis of proof-of-concept installation, vendors are often flexible with the license period.

In some cases, it is not easy to build a prototype of the Grid environment locally, especially if the system is meant to have geographical distribution. Several well-known organizations offer their resources for the purpose of testing Grid products. Most notably, IBM has introduced its Solutions Grid strategy. In solutions Grid centers, vendors partnering with IBM receive access to hardware and software stacks of various Grid middleware, as well as assistance of personal staff. Also, some scientific grids, such as the White Rose Grid and MCNC Enterprise grid, offer similar services to companies.

Many vendors aggressively promote their Grid offerings. This often includes giving out for free an open-source version of the product, with limited functionality but production quality (Sun Grid Engine). Others distribute free licenses for developers (Oracle). In some other cases (IBM), most revenue in this area comes from service, integration, and consulting, rather than from license fees.

A nonprofit Grid infrastructure provider, MCNC in North Carolina, recently launched a special plan to attract enterprises for their infrastructure. Customers receive necessary hardware and middleware installation plus one-year free subscription to Grid services, followed by another year of discounts.

The importance of a proper promotion plan for Grid offerings comes mainly from the fact that several Grid offerings will, by nature, have high-entry barriers for first-time customers. These barriers need to be minimized by attractive promotion.

Place (Channels)

Although selling the internal Grid solution business case does not require much attention to the place, selling a Grid-enabled product needs consideration. In most cases, Grid-enabling would only be an augmented feature of a product. Therefore, traditional channels usually take precedence over Grid-related channels. If a database product becomes Grid enabled, it is first of all supposed to become more attractive for the existing user base. Channeling of promotion will not change. Similarly, if a rendering engine acquires a Grid feature, the customer base will not shift dramatically. However, the situation is different for new products or those whose core function is being Grid-enabled. For those, sales channels associated with Grid computing community need to be considered.

Press The first and possibly easiest step to consider is building the presence in press. Grid computing press is largely, if not exclusively, Internet-based. Tabor Communications has a long history of publishing in high-performance computing industry, with its HPCwire newsletter (initially owned by TGC) electronically distributed to the IT community for many years. Since 2002, Tabor also ships GRIDtoday, a weekly e-mail-based newsletter, devoted to Grid computing in general. GRIDtoday offers an amazing amount of content at regular intervals, which on one hand ensures their brand recognition, and on the other discourages thorough reading of anything but the feature material.

GridComputingPlanet.com is an online portal publishing Grid news. However, they mostly focus on computational aspects of Grid, solving large problems by combining the power of several computer units.

The Grid Report is a non-profit Slashdot-style forum, started by Scott Gose from the Globus team. Articles there are submitted by the community, which ensures less bias but also more of an academic flavor.

Gridstart (www.gridstart.org) is a news center for all the Fifth Framework[2] research projects focusing on Grid. These are mostly academic projects funded by the European Union.

EnterTheGrid (enterthegrid.com), apart from the industry-focused *Primeur* magazine, provides an online directory of Grid-related solutions, companies and projects.

Grid-scape.org is another portal for Grid news and discussion, associated with the online companion of this book.

The general problem this online press sector suffers from is the vulgarization of the meaning of the Grid. As summarized by Forrester Research, it has become a trendy term that no longer has one meaning. Indeed, some "specialized" news sources define it broadly enough to be able to deliver daily news portion. However, doing this they also shape their reader base, so the eventual readers are those interested in generic level information. One has to take this fact into account when evaluating the news sources as marketing channels for Grid solutions.

Complete selection of the available news channels can be found at the online companion to this book at www.savvygrid.com.

There are also Grid-devoted special editions of several paper magazines, both technical (*Communications of the ACM,* IEEE Computer Society's newsletter) and management-oriented (*EuropeanCEO*). These are usually more difficult to track, especially for the market newcomers.

---

[2] Predecessor for the Sixth Framework Programme.

Events A separate channel for sales and market presence can be associated with specialized conferences; however, the choice is difficult. The GGF, to which more attention was devoted in Chapter 2, is the world's best-recognized Grid conference. The GGF meets three times in a year and attracts both industry professionals and academics. However, until lately the strict focus on standards did not make it attractive for a general audience. Recently, the new GGF management under the leadership of Mark Linesch from HP introduced changes in this policy. The conference is now actively supporting the broader Grid community by organizing newcomer tutorials, management level event track and other activities for users not directly involved in producing standards. Recently, a number of industry-related events appeared independently in the three most developed parts of the world. The first edition of a GridToday conference (now a regular event) took place in Philadelphia during three days in May 2004. It was considered a promising start, with some 500 attendees, 20-plus exhibitors, and speakers from most vendor companies. In Europe, the Grid computing effort so far has been largely driven by the centrally funded Information Society Technologies projects. As a result, most conferences and events there lean toward academic audiences associated with massive multinational projects such as the EGEE (Enabling Grids for E-science in Europe), or the former GridLab, CrossGrid and European Data Grid (EDG) projects. One of the driving forces here is the strong high-energy physics community in CERN and several scientific institutions. Although these projects are aimed to eventually spark the industrial interest, the efforts to attract large industry have so far only been partially successful. By contrast, a number of today's commercial Grid solutions have been born in Europe, such as the Sun Grid Engine (previously from Genias and GridWare), Fujitsu's Unicore (also associated with Pallas GmbH, Germany), or less known solutions from Spanish GridSystems. The first European Grid Conference (EGC05) was held in Amsterdam in February 2005, with a dedicated business and industry track. This was a successor to the earlier series of AcrossGrid events. In the Asia-Pacific region, Japan is witnessing the most dynamic progress of the Grid technologies. The Grid World 2004 conference held in April 2004 in Tokyo drew massive interest, with 2000 visitors and several vendors. The somewhat hermetic market in Japan is dominated by large companies such as Fujitsu or Hitachi on one side and large government-sponsored consortia such as Business Grid Computing Project and NAREGI (National Research Grid Initiative). NEC, Fujitsu, and Hitachi are also part of the Business Grid Computing Project formed by Japan's Ministry of Economy, Trade and Industry.

The online companion to this book (www.savvygrid.com) is a good place to look for updated information about events as the industry evolves.

Still, more of an audience is attracted by events that cover broader context than Grid. Trade shows focusing solely on Grid computing are by nature young and thus difficult to estimate in terms of target audience. Many key players in the Grid industry aim for the annual Supercomputing Conference held in various places in the United States, or its European counterpart, the International Supercomputer Conference in Heidelberg, Germany. The Grid computing movement has a traditionally strong presence at these events, while the differentiated audience ensures better visibility.

Partnering Although the market is very young, there has already been an intense competition between the vendors, especially in the traditional Grid-aware sectors. Newcomers to the market would either have to significantly differentiate their products or consider partnering with organizations whose position, contacts, and channels to customers are already established.

Strong vendors, such as Platform or DataSynapse, typically partner with service companies such as IBM, who have established channels to the customer. There aren't many product-agnostic technical consulting companies out there; Sun and HP apart from services also sell their Grid products. Smaller players in the field include BestSystems (Japan), Grid Technology Partners (United States), and Gridwise Technologies (Europe, United States).[3]

There are also a number of management consulting companies who do not deal with technical consulting, but focus on market analytic reports. These include Gartner Group, Forrester Research, The 451 Group, The Economic Strategy Institute, and The Tabb Group. Each of these published at least one public report analyzing various sectors and aspects of market for Grid computing. In most cases, these reports are available only for a fee, although sometimes they are distributed freely among participants of the core Grid conferences.

Partnership is not needed for those organizations who plan to investigate Grid solutions for their internal infrastructure. Instead, they would focus on finding the right group of experts to advise them of optimal solutions. Knowing the structure and relationships on the market would help these technology users choose an unbiased group not associated with particular vendors.

---

[3] Discloser: The authors of this book are partners in Gridwise Technologies.

SWOT Matrix

SWOT analysis is another frequent part of the business case. The SWOT matrix itself is product specific, and any general guidance is impossible. comprehensive However, there are features common to many Grid solutions that have been discussed throughout this book. Next we list the most commonly quoted strengths, weaknesses, opportunities, and threats that can serve as entries to such matrix.

Strengths

- Do things not doable today. Solve a class of problems, which today cannot be attacked because of limited processing performance.
- Improve resource utilization.
- Improve reliability.
- Improve interoperability.
- Reduce hardware cost per operation.
- Improve maintainability, adaptability, and change readiness by modular SOA.
- Minimize future integration cost thanks to SOA.
- Build flexible security adaptable to highly distributed environments.
- Reduce application size and speed up development cycle by splitting functionality into resource layer, Grid middleware, and application layer.
- Enable portability of applications, as well as interoperability with other resource providers, resulting from the standardized Grid middleware layer.
- Move toward dynamic architecture, easy for partial outsourcing when necessary.
- Become less dependent on hardware infrastructure providers, as Grid middleware layer promises to interoperate with many of them.

Weaknesses

- Integration of legacy code may be difficult with respect to vertical cross-cutting issues such as security.
- Qualified personnel are scarce, and those knowledgeable come from academia and are often ignorant of business environment.
- There are not many examples to learn from, the literature is missing, and companies who have implemented grids keep it to themselves.

Opportunities

- Learn the technology before the competition does.
- Build an image of innovator and thought leader.
- Many governments (United States, Europe, Asia-Pacific) strongly financially support the development of Grid computing in the private sector through various programs.
- Join forces with academic know-how.

Risks

- Immature standards: although key standards are supported by the big industry, fully standardized examples are lacking.
- Exposing internal working of the company, resources, and confidential data.
- Transition time and cost difficult to estimate.
- Psychological problem: management does not want to hear that external code would be run inside their systems.
- Internal billing problem: how to account for use of department A's resources for department B's purposes.
- Infrastructure vendors will not like the move toward Grid, as this makes systems independent from particular hardware platform.
- Change may be opposed internally.
- Extra risk (white space risk) is associated with new technologies.
- Reduction of local control.

Change and Transition Period Management

Moving to a Grid infrastructure is one of a series of inevitable changes that organizations go through today. Globalization of economy and culture, evolution of lifestyle, and rapid advancements of technology all impose changes in the functionality of enterprise. Firms that are not innovation leaders are later often forced into reforms in much less convenient conditions to keep up with more effective competition.

The ubiquitous need for corporate reforms became so visible in recent decades that a dedicated discipline, *Change Management*, elbowed its way into management schools and consultancy shops. Change management takes a holistic view on planning and implementing the transition phase, stressing the impact of change on the corporate structure, culture, personnel relationships, and morale. Thus apart from the technological implications of change, change management deals with the people factor.

A typical office looked quite different before the introduction of personal computers. Accessibility and affordability of the network allowed a number of people to work from home. Mobile phones, digital photography, and e-mail allowed sharing information within seconds rather than weeks. All these changes were traumatic for many enterprises. Also, they usually went in line with personnel restructuring and often layoffs. Lack of motivation or understanding of the process, disbelief in success, stress related to deteriorated conditions of work, or even fear of possible personnel reduction create company-wide resistance to change and opposition, which eventually threatens the probability of success.

Introducing a Grid architecture can be a dramatic change for the organization, just like any new technology that recasts the work environment.

Change Driven by Technology

Enterprise grids look at productivity; there will be fewer people administrating more powerful equipment. Because of the removal of silos and departmental grid architectures, horizontal relationships within organization will be strengthened. Later, VOs that go outside from the home company will introduce new dimension to cooperation. Teams from various organizations will be brought much closer in cooperation, which will influence the relationship within organizations and threaten hierarchical structures. The practice of service outsourcing and on-demand resource leasing will bring new complex business relationship patterns between service providers and consumers. New management methods will need to be developed to control and monitor dynamic dependencies between several layers of providers, necessary for critical operation of the enterprise. Thus, although eventually the structure of the Grid may become invisible to the end user (like in the famous electric grid analogy), the indirect side effects will affect and transform the style of work.

Change Driven by Organization

Researchers point out that Grid computing often results from fusions and mergers, where new technology is being sought to replace the incompatible systems used by the two organizations. By contrast, creation of a Grid processing facility for the whole enterprise must be backed by formation of specialized units of support and maintenance groups. Thus, the move to Grid technology often goes hand in hand with transforming structures of organization.

Change Resulting from Introduction of New Product

Whether the company introduces a Grid product, or Grid-enables an old one, this will always be followed by the change in the market position. These actions will push the company toward new market niche, and often, new competition. Adaptation and learning will be necessary.

It has been historically proven that predictions of the future are often inaccurate. Therefore we will restrain from speculating further what long-term changes Grid technology will bring to organizations. Instead, we will say a few words about the organizational change readiness that smoothes whatever remodeling the company needs to go through. The structure of the following sections is largely influenced by the work *Managing Change and Transition* by Harvard Business School Press. The few quoted numbers come from the same source.

Change Readiness

Organizations achieve change readiness through their strong and respected leaders, motivated crew, and structures built on cooperation rather than hierarchy. We briefly explore these three aspects.

Identify Charismatic Leaders

Grid computing is a vision, and the vehicle to convey the vision to the people is a motivated leader. Naturally, companies are usually motivated to the change by pragmatic, short-term goals ("cut capital expenditure by 30 percent"). However, if the short-term goal is supported by long-term vision ("become top player in the global Grid resource market"), the plan becomes more appealing, convincing, and eventually effective. The evangelization and implementation of the vision must originate from a clear leadership. Identification of such a leader should be among the organization's first goals.

The leader must be convincing and respected. The leader must carry enthusiasm and constant belief in the vision she personifies. The leader's role is to guide the crew through the period of transition when motivation is most needed.

It is usually a good practice to select the leader from among the technologists. One obvious reason for this is that the vision of Grid-enabled enterprise needs a strong technical background. The concept is complicated enough that the relationship between the day-to-day details and the vision sometimes needs constant reassuring. When the technology becomes the daily bread for the team, it is easy to lose sight of the long-run perspective. The role of the change leader is to make this relationship clear in reassuring the team of the special role of the transition project. The other reason is that the leader's position is defined by the respect from the team. Technical personnel will not respect a nontechnical leader, just like the barbarians would not elect another king but the bloodiest warrior. Only he is capable of leading the attack to the enemy ranks where any sign of weakness may shake the morale of the entire army.

The leader may not take the role of the manager, where other skills are needed. The leader's role is to point the direction, create the vision, prepare the strategy, and motivate the team. The manager's role is to make sure that things go smoothly and take care of the details. In small organizations both roles may be performed by a single person, while in larger groups the distinction can be made. Long-term goals will be achieved only with both strong leadership and management.

The Grid computing community has many prominent examples of change leaders. A decade ago a number of skilled leaders such as Ian Foster (Globus), Wolfgang Gentzsch (Genias, later Sun Microsystems and MCNC), Andrew Grimshaw (University of Virginia, later Avaki) and Songnian Zhou (Platform) drew the vision of ubiquitous resource sharing. Then they attracted the community and consequently carried the torch through the transition period. Today we have begun to see results of the first Grid systems, and Grid computing is on everybody's minds.

Motivate people

Grids will change organizations technologically. However, as we noted previously, the change will also be seen in people's style of work and interactions. Team members must understand the need for change, or they may oppose it. A move to Grid computing can be motivated either by opportunity ("We could win new markets") or threat ("the competition is ahead of us technologically"). In the first case, motivation must be explained in terms of new opportunities that also affect the team personally (bonuses). In the latter case, it is likely that the employees themselves are concerned that something needs to change. This energy only needs to be channeled in the right direction.

Minimize hierarchy

Hierarchical organizations are less successful in promoting and implementing change. Hierarchy tends to conserve bureaucracy and the status quo. On the contrary, decentralization and local autonomy produce incentive and stimulation. Organizations today tend to move toward a flat management model, where team members are assigned responsible roles instead of being subject to the manager. For instance, a popular methodology for code inspections recommends four-person teams composed of moderator, reader, recorder, and author. Each role carries different responsibility and encourages incentive. The only subject of the review is the code itself (not the author). There are no vertical relationships in the team.

Grid computing is a relatively new technology, and, as such, competent personnel are not easy to find. Those who are competent often come from academic backgrounds and are inexperienced in other commercial technologies or practices. The move to Grid-based architecture brings changes difficult to predict. Experience from all layers of personnel should be considered in the planning and transition phase. Hierarchy, which builds up comfort for upper management layers by minimizing contact with personnel, does not encourage such communication. Reduce hierarchy to eliminate fear and give people the right to speak.

Planning the Change

Engage Team to Identifying Solutions

Problems and/or opportunities leading to the Grid solution need a clear definition. It should be known and understood by the personnel affected by the anticipated change. However, their support for the change will be incomparably higher if people take an active role in identifying problems and solutions.

Teams charged with the task of planning the move must include the change leader, representatives of management, and representatives of technical staff who will implement the change and take over the maintenance. Because of a lack of experienced Grid experts in the job market, hiring external Grid consultants may be necessary. However, consultancy shops often tend to sell one-size-fits-all recipes that have worked in other organizations. Unfortunately, complex solutions such as new Grid architecture involve many aspects of organization's work; therefore what worked for one can be devastating for another. For this reason, it is important to be careful with out-of-the-box solutions. The analysis and planning team should work with a coalition of multiple layers of personnel who often understand the problems better than management. Employees from various sections working with the planning group must be faced with the problem and understand the possible consequences of leaving the problem unsolved, especially those affecting them personally (such as the prospect of the company being sold).

Naturally, with all the effort toward engaging the lower layers of employees in identifying with the problem and having their voices heard, management's participation cannot be neglected. While the engagement of all affected employees is a good practice, the engagement of management is an absolute must. Change cannot succeed without the active support of a majority of managers.

Construct the Vision Shared by Everyone

It certainly is a challenge for the change leader to communicate the vision in a way so that people accept it as their own and identify with it. However, if there is visible tension between the vision of management and the rest of the team, this may signal the problem in the proposed solution itself, or in the ways it was communicated. The goals of employees may differ from the goal of the company, but the employees may better understand the problem.

In communicating the vision, make sure to be clear in explaining the tangible profit it will bring to the company and the employees. The vision must be appealing, convincing, and realistic. The vision should concentrate on particular aspects of the organization's work that is visible today. For instance, the attempts to explain the general notion of resources abstracted as services for easier sharing may fail for being too detached. Instead, the vision should focus on the tangible results of this process. Virtualized data resources will allow consultants to access important data from other departments at runtime during telephone conversations with the customer. This will attract infrequent customers to strengthen relationship with the company and achieve an advantage over the competition.

Statistics show that 20 percent of employees usually support the change from the beginning, and 30 percent oppose it. Successful vision improves these statistics by convincing the remaining 50 percent to take an active role in implementing the vision.

Build a Sensible Deployment Plan

The plan of transition, constructed by the planning team, will describe what to do in what order. The plan must be simple and consist of realistic stages. A simple plan must be presentable as a diagram.

The myth and confusion covering the concepts of Grid computing contribute to the tendency to speak of it with sophisticated terms and incomprehensible lingo. A number of articles from scientific conferences and the popular press are examples of the common belief that professional matters such as Grid computing cannot be explained in simple terms. This is not true, and we hope that this book demonstrates that fact. Do not follow this trend.

The vision of transition must be explained in simple words and clearly state how it improves the situation of today. The deployment plan must consist of clear steps that logically lead to implementing the vision. Stages of the plan must be achievable with a realistic effort. The plan must state roles and responsibilities, and identified persons must assume these roles, which implies understanding of the goals. The ability to write a simple and comprehensible plan must be among the skills of the future change leader.

Start Transition from Peripheries and Let It Radiate

This guideline may not be practical in some organizations. However, if the organization structure allows for it, probes of the planned Grid architecture should be first built at a peripheral unit that, if possible, is small and autonomous and where the risk factor is smaller than at the organization's core. Such a strategy also leaves time for people to build necessary skills before the major transformation occurs. Staff who worked on the pilot project will later be strategically promoted to the roles of change innovators leading the transition phase.

Apart from the risk issue, the start-from-periphery tactics carries an important psychological value. The probability of success in a small, independent unit is more likely than making a first Grid project large and important to the core business. Such success observed by the rest of the company will contribute to the morale of employees and ease common acceptance of the Grid strategy.

Adjust Strategy to the Observed Transition Process

Experience shows that larger changes rarely follow the expected plan. In Grid technology, each deployment is different and organization-specific. Be elastic in your expectations and ensure that the transition plan takes into account possible modifications in sequence of events, technology, or personnel. Observe and monitor the situation. An organizational culture that enhances autonomy and responsibility and minimizes hierarchy will help adjust the plan to the reality.

Address Human Factor

Change management practices largely focus on the human factor of the process. Do not rely on technology solutions. Technology will change the environment, but how people will react to the change is a completely separate topic. New process may theoretically improve productivity, but if it destroys the relationships people have built by years of working together, the effect may be far from positive. Stress on two-way communication is important during the transition. Change involves a variety of behaviors such as opposition, skepticism, and conservatism, which sometimes need treatment. Also, each change involves beneficiaries and losers; thus anticipation of a certain course of action may induce strategic behavior within the team affected by the change. These are the areas specific to generic change management practices, which are out of the scope here, but experienced managers will be aware of them.

Single Change versus Constant Change

Best practices in the field of change management show that gradual transition performed in many small steps is always better than changing everything at once. Unfortunately, we are moving in an inherently imprecise area, where the best advice that can be given is: do not attempt to blindly repeat someone else's success story—too many factors differ between that environment and yours. There is no suit-all recipe for moving into Grid computing. Instead, try to implement your own vision in a microscale, learn on your own mistakes, and gradually extend the area of innovation.

Theoretically, gradual change is always preferred for several reasons: (1) it is easier to manage, (2) the chances of success are higher, (3) problems and side effects have a shorter time span and are thus easier to predict and cope with, (4) the change does not block the entire organization in its state of alert and market readiness, and (5) gradual change allows the chance of spotting unexpected effects of the chosen strategy early on. Then corrections can be applied to the plan during its execution. Unfortunately, it is almost certain that there will be side effects. Mistakes must be anticipated. The larger the undertaking, the larger the danger that the organization lacks all needed abilities for the change.

In migrating to a Grid environment, the gradual change theory has been verbalized by the phrase "start small, think big." It can be applied in at least three respects described next.

Migrate in Three Stages

We have already mentioned that the project should start with a proof-of-concept demonstrator. The next phase could be deployment of a pilot system in production, but in an outlaying organizational unit. After that the target system can be built to supply the main processing capacity. Such a two- or three-step strategy has been adopted as the best practice in the field and adopted by several corporations successful in pioneering Grid computing, such as Charles Schwab. Also NEESgrid, an ambitious Grid project for earthquake science, first connected three pilot sites into the distributed experiment.

The successful experiment was repeated in almost the same configuration in a dozen sites. After achieving experience and confidence, the earthquake science experiments would be run with greater flexibility in multiple configuration variants and a number of cooperating parties.

Scale Up the Pilot System

An alternative solution would start with a small but scalable pilot system, which would later gradually be expanded to become the main resource center of the organization. This is the plan successfully implemented by Google, which has to grow its processing capabilities at the speed of the growing Web. Such a plan may not seem suitable for organizations who already have a processing center; thus the massive migration needs to happen at once. Even so, this plan has several attractive aspects. The gradual growth of the new system will be a great test of how scalable the new Grid architecture is. After all, scalability and ease of transition are two of the driving factors to move to Grid.

Internal Change First, External Later

Enterprise grids being implemented now allow for optimal resource consumption within the organization. Opening an organization to the Grid at large will enable sharing these resources with partnering organizations. However, to effectively share with others, it is important to first put things in order within one's own realm. Therefore building enterprise grids can be thought as preparatory step toward taking part in the global resource market of the future. Building internal structures with middleware available today can prepare organization technologically and culturally for successful competing in the future on the Grid at large. This is how the future is understood by visionaries and change leaders in corporations evaluating grids nowadays. GlobXplorer has built an enterprise grid image processing facility, but is looking at exchanging XML-formatted data with other vendors from Open GIS Consortium. DS&S and Rolls-Royce have just completed the first pilot project of a Grid-enabled turbine health monitoring system, but the bigger vision is to trade the computing resources in the future. British Telecommunications has been running a Grid computing research team for years, hoping to become a major operator and hub on the open Grid.

Role of Consultants

Since the 1950s, management consulting shops have increased their importance in the market, gradually overtaking more important segments of large enterprises. In the move toward outsourcing, some companies decided to entrust the entire management to an external power. In this context, it is tempting to hire consultants for the entire transition period.

As mentioned earlier, for many organizations the need for expertise will lead to hiring of external experts. Where should the responsibility of a consultant end, and what strategic areas should be managed by full-time staff?

For the convenience of our discussion, the change management activity of a management consultant can be divided into four phases:

- During the diagnosis phase, the consulting team will learn about the organization. They find out about the state of the company and the problems it copes with.

- This is followed by assessment of abilities, where the company resources and structures are measured with respect to change readiness.

- The next task is the development of a strategy, which usually consists of a combination of staff training and technical development.

- The transition phase itself follows last, and entails major spending.

In each of these periods, involvement of external consulting resources must be kept at a certain level, which we explore in subsequent sections.

Do You Need a Consultant?

Generally, consultants are hired in two types of situations: (1) if the company copes with a particular problem for which the expertise of internal staff is not sufficient, for example, an old transaction processing system that may need enhancement because of increased request load, and (2) if management is about to make a strategic decision, such as planning a new product, and professional advice is needed. In a Grid context, the common denominator of both situations is the lack of objective technical expertise in Grid technology and the market. This problem awaits both short-term (the immediate advice) and long-term (building internal skills to master the technology) solution. Make sure that the advisor helps to resolve both needs. (There is also a third way to use technical consultants. They can be used to augment staff in situations when there aren't enough internal people and additional help is needed. This can usually be resolved on the fly and is not the kind of a strategic engagement we talk about in this section.)

Firms with sound technical focus can also adapt to the technology with their internal resources. Several organizations chose this way by regularly sending their representatives to the GGF to participate in standards development and by assigning staff to analyze the available market solutions. This tactic is possible only with the presence of change leader with a solid understanding of technology who could coordinate such an effort.

In many cases, partnering with Grid development shop is the preferable to hiring management consultants. When an existing product needs Grid-enabling, several companies choose constant partnership with a Grid specialty firm, who provide development, integration, and maintenance of the Grid-specific part of the product. In this model, strategic partnership is assumed; thus technology transfer is needed only in a limited form. Time and resources can be saved on education because the skills needed are already represented by the strategic partner. Also, it should be expected that infiltration of these skills should be a beneficial side effect of long-term cooperation. A drawback of the partnering approach is the need to give away control of potentially strategic technical areas and products.

Precisely Define the Consultant's Mission

The program of consulting must have clear goals. This is difficult, especially for an organization that does not have the Grid know-how. Management must understand, at least at a high level, the role Grid technology can play in the future of the enterprise before asking the consultant for a diagnosis. If only one side (the consultant) has such understanding, it is possible that his opinion on his own role will differ from that of a management. In other words, the problem to be solved needs to be determined by the company in conjunction with consultants, not by the consultant in isolation.

Understand the Interest of the Consultant

Consulting agencies are being pushed by the same market forces as any other enterprise. They have a complex relationship with other entities and organizations; they have allies and competitors. The Grid computing community is rather small, and those who have been there for years have usually built relationship with each other. The choice of the right consulting shop should be influenced by analysis of how the interest of the consultant may diverge from your interests. For example, if the choice of the middleware vendor has already been made, the consulting shop cooperating with the respective vendor is a reasonable choice. However, if the consultant is expected to come out with product recommendation, any vendor association can signal potential conflict of interest.

Be Actively Involved in the Mission

Management needs to be convinced of the importance and role the consultant plays, and support it throughout the mission. Once management and the consulting team get out of touch, failure is guaranteed.

Engage External Resources for Diagnosis

As said earlier, there are compelling reasons to engage low level staff in the problem diagnosis, such as their comprehensive knowledge and need of their support in the change. However, external consultants may represent a more objective birds-eye view on the issues because of their emotional detachment, weaker personal relations in the team, and different interest from the staff.

Gradually Transfer Responsibilities

In the subsequent phases of the project, the role of the consultant will usually diminish and the staff should assume most responsibilities. Eventually, they will have to cope with the new system. The project plan must contain staff training. Think of the entire project as less of a new system construction and more of a knowledge transfer process. If you are using a two- or three-stage deployment model, have the consultants manage the proof-of-concept phase, and then ask your own staff to build the periphery production system, with consultants playing the advisory monitoring role. This approach will prepare the staff to take full responsibility of the main task, which will involve building the central production system. When it comes to training, timing is important. New skills are rapidly lost if not applied immediately; therefore plan the training sessions that terminate shortly before or actually overlap with deployment activities.

Be Prepared to Take Over

The moment of delivery has extreme importance and should be agreed to at the beginning of the cooperation. One can build Grid services using external resources, but at the same time internal staff need to spend time preparing to overtake the maintenance. The entire effort will be wasted if the company is not prepared in terms of staff and know-how to overtake the results.

Risk Mitigation

Grid computing projects inherently belong to the high risk area as a result of the technological immaturity of the standards and implementations. On one hand, high risk is being justified with potential for high reward. On the other hand, there are known methods for minimizing the risk even in brand new areas and disciplines. In this section, we look at best practices of risk management in Grid projects.

Execution Risk Management: The Traditional Approach

Risk management in general has been a subject of research for years. One good source of collective knowledge in this matter is the Project Management Body of Knowledge (PMBOK). PMBOK has standardized best practices in project management in a series of schemes and procedures. They are generic enough to be applied to any discipline. Risk management is part of the development process where it coexists with simultaneous practices such as staffing, procurement, project scope management, and quality management. Risk management cannot be taken out of this context, because the procedures require interactions with other spheres of project management. The process consists of risk identification, risk quantification, risk response development, and risk control.

Risk Identification

Risk identification starts from analyzing what is already known about the project. There are both internal (project may be delayed because of bad management) and external risks (funds can disappear because of economy changes). External risks include fluctuation in the employment market, economy forces, legal issues, competition factor, and others. External risks are easier to identify because they are not inherent to the use of a particular technology; however, this is not always the case. An example of an external risk that must be considered when building the Grid is the possibility that a new invention, practice or standard will make the technology in the project obsolete.

Internal risks are more difficult to identify, partly because this requires an objective view of one's own plan. Apart from intuition, historical information about what happened in other "new technology" projects can provide some guidance. Experience with other technology endeavors usually helps to identify project time planning and cost estimates as aggressive or realistic, with a certain degree of certainty. Analysis of employment market saturation can show if the staffing plan is flexible enough. Another valuable source of information is risk-oriented interviews with project stakeholders, who usually are willing to express their concerns. This information is being categorized into checklists organized by risk source, or "fishbone" diagrams organized by the risk effect. The risk identification activity concludes with documenting three comprehensive lists:

- Sources of risk are categories of risk events and include probability, frequency, and timing of risk. Examples of risk sources include changes of requirements, poor estimates, or lack of necessary skills.

- Potential risk events are isolated random events that can affect project performance.
- Risk symptoms, or triggers, are observations that may signal higher probability of certain risk events.

Risk Quantification

This activity in theory follows the risk identification, although often the two phases can be merged. During the quantification, the identified risk sources and events are measured against the risk tolerances of each project stakeholder. Methods for risk quantification are still poorly understood, mainly because of high uncertainty of both income and outcome of the process. The goal is to identify serious threats (often going in pair with opportunities) that need response actions, and those that will be accepted, usually as a result of the low risk. Risks are quantified using the Expected Monetary Value (EMV), which is a product of the risk event probability, and the expected loss in the case when the event actually occurs. EMV is a single number characterizing the risk, but it would be dangerous to take it as the only risk descriptor. For instance, an unlikely event of significant loss of value (an earthquake) may be characterized by similar EMV as a probable event bringing negligible extra cost (unexpected need of an international phone call). There are a number of elaborate methods to better describe the risk using various levels of mathematical knowledge such as statistical sums or decision trees. However, the quantification often ends with an arbitrary expert judgment.

Risk Response Development

Once the threats have been assessed, the correct strategy needs to be planned. Basically, there are three ways to fight the risk. Risk avoidance means eliminating the threats causing the particular risk. Risk mitigation is a strategy to minimize the EMV of the risk event by either reducing the risk probability or its value (loss). Finally, risk acceptance means focusing on preparation of contingency plan to be launched after the risk event. Risk response planning concludes with a risk management plan, which documents procedures to manage risk throughout the project.

Risk Response Control

Risk response control occurs during the execution of the project and should follow the risk management plan. When changes in project conditions occur, the cycle of risk identifying, quantifying, and response must be repeated to check whether the risk management plan is still relevant. If risk event occurs, corrective action is taken as planned in the risk management plan.

Fighting White Space Risk through Rapid-Result Initiatives

The purpose of the execution risk management, described in the preceding section, is to reduce the risk that the planned actions won't be carried out as planned. As is being recently pointed out by the expert community, these methods are only adequate to the well-known fields of knowledge, where past examples and good practices can be learned from. Real estate businesses and the insurance industry are canonical examples of these kinds of domains. Projects that explore the peripheries of known areas, such as Grid computing, need an alternative approach because of the *white space risk* issue. This term describes the danger that some necessary actions will not have been identified at all in planning phase. White space goes together with *integration risk*, meaning that disparate actions, even if performed according to the plan, will not succeed in completing the common goal. The reason for both white space risk and integration risk is similar. Planning may not be complete. This does not necessarily mean planning errors; it is rather quite natural that plans of entering new technology have holes and omissions, as the best aid in precise planning is past experience.

Traditional risk management is hopeless in this situation, as it focuses on risks prediction, ignoring the fact that the plan may be (and probably is) incomplete. There is a need for another scheme, which instead of assuming accuracy of predictions, accepts errors as natural consequence of the plan. One such methodology focuses on rapid-result initiatives (RRI), injected in the project execution process. A good introduction to the white space risk problem and the RRI scheme (although in nontechnical context) was presented by Nadim F. Matta and Ronald N. Ashkenas in the September 2003 issue of *Harvard Business Review*.

RRIs are aimed at performing the project in a microscale. For instance, if the project implements new customer assistance procedures in a superstore chain, an RRI may do the same thing in two or three stores. If the project improves the quality of the produced software through multidimensional criteria, an associated RRI would pick a limited subset of such criteria (improve communication by engaging developers in virtual interactive environments), and work with small group of developers.

RRIs can be injected in various stages of the project cycle; however, the impact of those initiated at the beginning of the project will be highest. The goal of the initiative is to achieve similar effect to the main project, in a very short time, and with limited resources. Naturally, the expected scale of effect must be proportionally smaller and clearly defined, as in the preceding examples. There are several reasons for RRIs. The microproject, done in compliance with the same guidelines as the main project, will expose deficiencies of the plan. This will reduce (although not eliminate) the white space risk. In the same time, the microprojects positively influence the morale of the executors, by demonstrating positive, clear, and time-constrained relationship between the actions and the results. Successful implementation of rapid-result project boosts the morale of the execution team. These employees can later be assigned for various other tasks in the larger follow-up projects to share their positive experience and influence corrections of the plan. RRIs must adhere to simple characteristics described next.

Result-Oriented

An RRI must be result-oriented rather than process-oriented. The main goal of the initiative is not to produce analysis, documents, or recommendations. These are rather beneficial side effects of the action. The goal is similar to the goal of the main project, in a smaller scale. If the main project aims at an increase in overall productivity by 40 percent, the associated microinitiative might increase productivity by 15 percent in a small section of the enterprise. Also, do not mistake achieving goals with achieving milestones. To quote an example from Grid computing, suppose the new system should double the revenue by increasing connectivity with partners and customers. The RRI cannot focus on deploying a prototype communication system (milestone focus), but should rather aim at increasing connectivity and revenue, for instance by working with two or three well-known partners and a subset of technology (goal focus).

Vertical

RRIs are typically cross-functional. If a macro project involves several simultaneous long-term actions, which can be presented as horizontal bars in a Gantt chart, the microproject should involve a vertical slice of as many of these action lines as possible to minimize the risk of undiscovered issues that will later crop up, and include situations where several such activities interact and affect each other. This gives a realistic view of the project integration risk. The outcome of vertical RRIs can provide information that would otherwise be impossible to discover. For instance, actions related to technical implementations of new systems should go in parallel with change management actions promoting the new solution among the crew. RRIs launched in the past demonstrated that in some cases, the team was not convinced of their personal benefits of switching to the new system. Although the technical integration went as planned, the system did not bring expected results. The RRI approach made it possible to discover the problem and correct the motivation and promotion strategy early on in the game which saved the project from failure.

Fast

The microscale projects need strict time constrains. Typically they last less than 100 days. This is first of all dictated by practical concerns (if the initiatives are to supply early warnings, they must take an order of magnitude less to implement than the macro project). Also, the project done on such a short scale will increase personal involvement of the small executing team. A fast approaching deadline, visible in weeks, creates a sense of personal challenge for the team, and tangible results visible in such a short frame are a reason for personal satisfaction.

Independent

In the rapid results project, the entire microproject responsibility is on the shoulders of the executing team. Management is not directly involved, and it is better if it does not interfere with the chosen strategies. The team becomes a microimage of the entire company. This shift of accountability fosters creativity, independent view of the problems, responsibility, and personal engagement. The personal success of the rapid-result team correlates with the success of the macro project.

White Space in the Grids Sector

The paradigm of RRIs has been designed for project management in general. In the IT sector and Grid computing in particular, adjustments are necessary.

In software business, unlike some other areas of industry, the cost of production of the first specimen of the product is very high, while the cost of generating copies is negligible. This recently became characteristic for all those areas of business whose products can take an electronic and thus virtual form: music industry, software production, book writing, or film making.

If making one copy of the product is comparable in cost and time to producing the complete distribution, then some directions of rapid-results projects are not worth following. For instance, bringing the product to a pilot distribution area can be done only after product development cycle is in an advanced phase, which questions the reason of rapid-result. However, experience shows that modified RRI paradigm can be successfully adapted to the Grid computing projects.

Focus on Selected Elements of SOA

Grid architecture really is an extension of the ideas in a Service-Oriented Architecture (SOA). By nature, the SOA should be easy to integrate because of loose coupling of modules. It follows that the SOA can be built in stages. Some services can be deployed and put to work before the others. If this is not the case, reconsider the architecture. If services are not suitable to work after decomposition, it indicates tight architectural coupling, so the purpose of SOA can be questioned. None of this should be read to imply that you must implement a non-Grid SOA before embarking on a Grid effort. It is merely worth noting that the ideas behind the Grid are a superset of those in SOA literature.

Selected representative service modules can be chosen for an RRI deployment run. The remaining parts of the system can be simulated with "dummy" modules. Such an approach will not only give the first approximation to the expected system problems, but will also be a realistic test as to whether the architecture is indeed modular as assumed. Partial end-to-end solutions with prototyping does not answer the integration risk, but can tell a lot about the white space risk.

Run the Complete System for a Short While

This method aims at standing up the entire system for a short time, months before the final product delivery. When the product is partly in the prototype stage, this is only possible with extra support effort, and for a limited time and range. In NEESgrid, after the second year of the project, the MOST experiment was built. It encompassed all parts of the final system (telecontrol, teleoperation, data acquisition). It was set up with reasonable distribution similar to the expected real conditions (parts of experiment in Boulder, CO and parts in Urbana-Champaign, IL). MOST also operated on 1-to-1 scale structures, two of which were physical models weighing several tons. MOST took six hours to complete and 1500 time steps, and thus was comparable to a production experiment, although in production one would run a series of such experiments. In fact, the MOST experiment produced real data, which was later used for research by the earthquake scientists. But at the same time, MOST was attended and constantly monitored by a team of 50 developers, designers, technicians, and support staff. There was also a burst of activity in the weeks before the experiment, as folks involved with various pieces completed and tested individual machines and Grid services implementations before the big test. This method is costly because it engages a considerable part of the project development team. Also, it focuses their energy, sometimes for weeks, on short-term goal actions, which are often different from or contrary to long-term actions. However, such project brings the benefits characteristic to the RRI initiatives and are most accurate in discovering deficiencies of the system, as well as the transition process. The experience of MOST led to considerable architectural changes of the entire NEESgrid system. The entire NSDS subsystem responsible for data acquisition was eliminated and replaced by a streaming solution based on commercial product, DataTurbine. This solution allowed timely replacement in time for the final software release one year after MOST. These serious deficiencies would not have been noticed without the MOST subproject.

Build Complete Microscale System

Scalability is another important aspect of Grid systems. As we have seen in a Google and Sabre examples, today's large systems must often grow with the Internet, thus obeying Moore's law (microprocessor performance doubles every 18 to 24 months), the Internet growth rate (capacity doubling every two years), and Metcalfe's law (the value of communication is proportional to the square of the nodes in the network).

A scalable system could scale down to a micromodel. A RRI could deploy such a micromodel in a small production environment.

The NEESgrid project has taken a similar approach when building its infrastructure. After the launch and completion of the MOST experiment, a dozen of so-called mini-MOST experiments have been constructed. A mini-MOST was a maximally simplified and scaled down model of the building structure that would be exercised during the real experiment. Mini-MOST hardware consisted of a single three-foot steel bar with a single actuator and sensor. Although its construction cost orders of magnitude less than a typical "real" experiment, it interfaced the other parts of the system in a similar way. Dozens of mini-MOST devices were constructed and shipped to the experiment sites, who were able to install the alpha version of software and construct the full-fledged system. This allowed to try out the system and provide feedback from the entire consortium months before the roll-out of the stable version of the NEESgrid software.

The other parts of the system were also scaled down for the purpose of the miniexperiment. Because the system was aimed at hybrid experiments (mixture of computational simulation and physical simulation), it was decided that the remaining parts of the tested structure would be simulated computationally.

Agile Development

The white space risk can be also fought by deployment of agile software development methodologies. Obviously, the choice of the software engineering method is a severe decision, which cannot be taken without respect to organizational culture, type of project, and the team background. Agile methods have won sympathy with large part of community, but also have enemies who strongly believe in traditional development cycle. We have experienced several styles of software engineering management. Although we recognize that agility is not possible in every project for both social and contractual reasons, we argue that this type of development and elements of Extreme Programming have their particular advantages for the Grid computing projects, and new technologies in general.

Agile methodologies developed and gained popularity as the community reacted to what we all feel the older we get—the world nowadays revolves faster than it used to. In respect to technology, this is true more than it was at any point in the past. To slightly twist the famous Metcalfe's law, the value of the network is exponential to the number of interconnected individuals, and this number is growing fast. People exchange and evaluate ideas more rapidly. Conference organizers who survived several years in this profession know what we speak of: the number of papers submitted each year for review grows systematically. New technologies appear overnight, creating a market niche that could not exist yesterday. Entire new market segments suddenly flourish and attract billion-dollar investments only to collapse after a few months. In this context of new technological and economical dynamics, project management must be adaptive and a change of conditions must be anticipated. In software production, the initial project requirements and assumptions may not hold throughout the product development cycle. Because the IT industry changes so dramatically, each year we're seeing a new, fresh, and immature technology context. In such a poorly understood context, new projects must be started. A separate problem results in the process of collection of user requirements and transforming them to software requirements. This is a difficult task in general, and the nature of human mind implies that the requirements will always be incomplete. Thus the general conclusion is that the project methodology must be designed flexible and change-adaptive. Shifts of requirements must be anticipated. This assumption led to development of so-called agile methodologies of software engineering.

Extreme Programming (XP) is one such method, which gained most popularity in the community and was further popularized by a series of books. Although XP is relatively popular, it remains an ideal difficult to achieve. One has to acknowledge that each methodology must be adjusted to the organization; XP cannot be bought for the same reason the Grid cannot be bought, it must be built, lived in, and customized for each team and business context. Therefore, most people speak of having deployed "elements of XP" that suit the particularities of their institution.

We have successfully deployed elements of agile programming in several projects. The main barrier seems to have been the fact that the consultant is often limited by the methodology of the customer. However, we've also been fortunate to work with such projects as Globus or NEESgrid, which are open to various innovations. Both these projects are in some respect the first of their kind. Globus Tooolkit was the first to implement a number of GGF standards and is indeed the birthplace of the Grid; the NEESgrid suite was the first production application based on SOAP Grid services platform. Thus these projects are useful as case studies of development practices for Grid computing projects in general, which also deal with Grid technologies and move in relatively unknown area. We will now look at specific aspects of agile development and see how they worked for the Globus development team and how they affected the community.

Anticipate Shift of Requirements

Traditional methodologies advise that the complete design, based mainly on thought experiments, is drawn before the production starts. In contrast, XP minimizes the time spent on design phase before launching development. In new technologies, we are moving in unknown, multiple-dimension parameter space. For this reason XP designers maintain that even a poor and sketchy experimental model is better than carefully designed thought model. Development must proceed almost concurrently with design. The customer is also involved in the process. Instead of waiting months or years for the alpha release, in XP the earliest prototype code is delivered to the customer within weeks. This usually involves positive and negative feedback; then the requirements can be adjusted and development proceeds to the next edition of an extended prototype. The main problem this is solving is the imprecision of human communication. Customers are initially unaware of their own intentions or have problems with verbalizing them. The same sentence may be understood differently by people with different backgrounds. Only live demonstrations of how developers understood the needs expose the additional needs that were not articulated during the requirements collection phase.

In Grid computing context, such a shift of requirements is even more likely because grids are interfacing a number of other technologies, and because the technology is relatively unexplored and unstable.

Naturally, such a minimal design model must be applied with moderation. In particular, one cannot mistake the rapid prototyping paradigm with do-before-think attitude. Short design cycle is only justifiable by guarantee of rapid delivery of first testable prototype. If this is impossible, the XP approach must be considered.

We should also observe that recently the graphical developer tools and environments come in handy for those applying the agile process, for they allow seamless, two-way transition between design and development. UML diagrams can transformed into code stubs, and vice versa; the code can be viewed in the form of diagrams. In this approach, the two phases of the process, design and development, become rather two views, or aspects of the product, correlated to each other, so changes in one affect the other.

Refactor Rather than Design in Advance

With XP, the product architecture must not go too far in the future but rather focus on providing the minimal functionality that is required. Unless this is stated in requirements and is obvious, you should not attempt to guess in what way the system would be extended in the future. It seems that such assumptions are often incorrect, while at the same time, they engage energy in producing modules that only contribute to the system's complexity.

A simple, bare-bones production system, when tested by customers, will quickly reveal its deficiencies and point out the direction in which development should proceed. Only at this point should the system be extended to encompass new features.

The code of Globus Toolkit has been refactored several times, as each new version followed new protocol standards, while the features of GRAM, GSI, and GridFTP needed to remain available. Occasionally this resulted in entire modules being rewritten, but it also allowed large chunks of code to be kept in operation for years. This code was gradually perfected by years of community use, which exposed most possible deficiencies and allowed them to be corrected.

Engage Developers in Decision Making

In XP, customers submit slips of paper with "stories", which are an informal way to formulate requirements by describing the future system in various situations. Developers pick each story and estimate the implementation time. What's important is that the time planning decisions are left in the hands of developers, which at first may feel somewhat scary.

Contrary to intuition, experience shows that new developers often take on larger responsibilities than they can handle. However, when their experience in estimation grows, they can usually come up with a better estimate than anyone else, thus reducing the risk of a contract not being delivered on time. Also, the fact of having made the decision strengthens their responsibility and sense of personal challenge.

This shift of accountability can easily be implemented in small time frames. Internal frequent milestones specific to XP can be set up by developers themselves. Unfortunately, the long-term deadlines are usually defined beforehand in the contract. Still, there are various ways to approach impossible deadlines, and here is where the developer's voice should be heard.

Code Is the Documentation

Developers are understandably frustrated by the hours spent on writing documentation. Redundancy is generally considered a bad thing in software engineering, and documentation is a form of redundancy. After all, the well-written code speaks for itself, if the programming-by-intention model is followed. The practical reason for avoiding extra documentation is similar to avoiding code redundancy. In the process of refactoring, it is easy to unintentionally omit the redundant pieces of code and introduce bugs. Similarly, it is even easier to forget to update the documents while updating the associated code, because there are no automatic tools for checking on documentation accuracy. Thus XP recommends that instead of maintaining human readable low-level documentation, developers focus on writing clean code programmed by intention.

However, as long as the lack of internal source code documentation can be justified by XP, the same policy cannot be applied to external application programmer interface (API) documentation, user guides, and other user-centric documentation types. These need to always be available. With the exception to some highly technical communities, users cannot be expected to read the product source code, if it is available at all.

The problem described here used to be painfully present in the Globus project. For many years, clear distinctions between the internal and external documentation policy had not been made. Globus developers internally used minimal or no documentation because they knew the code. Unfortunately, the same rule was transparently projected to the Globus documentation in general, including the external user-oriented documents. This was often lacking, delayed, or incomplete. Because users came from organizations of high technical culture and generally recruited from developers, they were expected to show a similar level of skills in reading the code to the original developers (after all, Globus is open source). Further, significant portions of Globus were meant as a low-level toolkit. Globus users were expected to write higher level tools on top, and only these were to be accessed by the end-users. Unfortunately, for various reasons, including uncertain stability of the toolkit, stable high-level tools rarely got created, while those that got created were niche products that never gained widespread adoption, perhaps with an exception of MPICH-G2. At the same time, while the end-user tools were still not there, the toolkit quickly became popular. As a result, crowds of end-users were seen using bare-bones Globus command line tools and libraries, and wide complaints about the state of documentation were heard. The lesson to remember is that code-as-documentation rule works well only internally, especially in the early stages of the project when refactoring is expected and energy cannot be wasted to polish something that may disappear next week.

Pair Programming

Probably the most frequently ignored XP principle, the somewhat exotic rule of pair programming, says that each line of code must be created by two people sitting at the same screen. Statistics show that visual code scanning is far more effective than automatic testing. Thus two pairs of eyes are better than one. Also, if each section of code is well known by two people, the presence of every single programmer in the team becomes much less critical. This also contributes to the common code "ownership" promoted by XP. Finally, pair programming is more time effective and less tiring.

This theory, however, does not change the usual practice: if something needs to be done quickly, assigning two persons for the same job seems a waste of time. Also, in proof-of-concept prototyping when the code quality is less important than time, typically one person will be more effective. Finally, in a Grid setting one very rarely gets a job that consists solely of coding. What we have mostly seen in our experience is that coding took a rather minor amount of time, when the vast majority of time was spent on developer-level research. This is mainly due to the high number of independent technological areas that Grid systems interface, and immaturity of some of these areas. A Grid programmer is like a Renaissance man who needs to master several seemingly unrelated arts. His eventual Grid code is like a thin layer of intermediate tissue gluing together various protocols and libraries. However, writing these few hundred lines may cost weeks or months of research and trials. For example, we can quote a rather small project that we have recently done, a quite typical task of Grid-enabling a commercial tool. The whole project took six weeks; most of the time was spent researching the technologies needed for integration. Once this was understood, the critical code sections were identified and isolated for refactoring. Then the only surgical modifications of sources resulted in an additional 200 lines of code and took less than a day of work. Eventually an additional few days were needed to complete automatic testing and compilation procedures and to modify the source tree to address the vendor licensing policy.

In such a project where coding itself takes less than 10 percent of the real work, pair programming is impractical, difficult to schedule, and not terribly important to the final results. For the same reason, in Grid computing in general, pair programming can only be applied to some development projects, where coding takes the majority of the time, programmers are comfortable with the base environment, and the number of interfacing technologies is limited. For instance, creating a new Grid product from scratch seems to be an appropriate assignment.

To become effective, pair programming needs to become a policy encouraged by management. If left entirely to the developers, they will more likely each work on their own code to quickly meet the deadlines with individual programming styles. This is a typical social trap, a situation that rewards immediate actions of individuals that, in the long run, will have undesired effects on the entire community. In this case the code eventually may become expensive to maintain.

Test-Driven Programming

Test-driven programming is another principle that is difficult to impose, especially on programmers not familiar with agile methods. The principle is to write the tests before writing the code. This rule is not easy to follow, as it remains in conflict with the desire of making the system prototype ready as quickly as possible. However, note that in the environment of changing requirements, the prototype is at the same time the version 0 of the product. It is hoped that the prototype will not be thrown away but rather refactored several times into a beta version system. During the refactoring, "bugs" will be removed and introduced. The way to minimize the number of bugs is to create a noninteractive unit tests that will be automatically launched after each commit.[4] Sudden failures of tests that used to pass will indicate a recent fault in the refactoring process.

Unfortunately, some failures will appear because of changes of requirements that need refactoring of tests, or even because of bugs in the tests themselves. This introduces an important issue: the size and level of sophistication of testing code cannot exceed the target code being tested. Otherwise developer energy will be spent on test maintenance instead of focusing on the target. Therefore tests must be written in a maximally simple and human-friendly

---

[4] Typically, teams of developers use a version control system to synchronize the code that they all work on in the same time. Each new modification of the code needs to be stored (committed) in the version control system. This is called a 'commit'.

way. Even some redundancy should be allowed if it contributes to the code being clean and easy to read.

Institutionalize the Process

To strengthen the acceptance of agile methods, it is necessary to engage automatic tools for checking on code quality. This does not necessarily involve immediate expenses for license fees; there are enough open-source programmer tools that have been used and polished by generations of developers. A version control system (e.g., CVS, Subversion, SourceSafe) is a must in modern development projects. The Globus project uses CVS along with Bonsai, a Web-based graphical query interface. The Java part of the code is instrumented with automatic Junit tests, as well as human-readable logging statements produced by log4j and Apache commons logging. The tests are used by Tinderbox, another tool from the Mozilla project that on an hourly or nightly basis checks out the repository code, builds the distribution, and tests it. Problems are being automatically reported, and automatic CVS tracking can point out the developer whose activity caused the problem and send him an e-mail.

All these tools make the development process easier but also enhance discipline, as no one would like to be identified as the one breaking the nightly build, and have the entire group waiting and looking over her shoulder next morning when she hurriedly fixes her code.

It is also important not to override the process with the technology. The focus must go to the product; the process should make it easier but not become the goal in itself. Development groups of less than ten people can often happily coexist with a minimal tool set. Advances in the development process must be in step with team readiness. The group itself must feel the need for particular tools.

For example, in the Globus team, some developers expressed the desire to introduce, at a group level, the UML design tools such as ArgoUML, Poseidon, and TogetherSoft. This innovation failed in the early stage, because most team members used an agile approach to design and did not see benefits from investing time in learning UML toolkits.

The Globus Campaign System

The Globus Alliance team in the Distributed Systems Laboratory, part of Argonne National Laboratory, implemented elements of agile programming in the so-called campaign system. At the core of the idea is a notion of a campaign, a self-contained definition of an independent task, usually taking a few weeks and less than a handful of people (often only one person) to implement. Campaigns are defined by management but can also be proposed by the developers. Campaign propositions are evaluated positively if they contribute to the project mission and are realistic within the available resources. For instance, development of a new version of the toolkit consists of a chain of related campaigns. Also, some of the tools mentioned previously were installed and introduced during special campaigns defined by staff. Each campaign has a leader, a designated person responsible for executing the plan and communicating the intermediate status to the management. It often happens naturally that the campaign proponent later becomes the campaign leader. A simple Web interface is available for proposing new campaigns, and browsing the campaign status.

The campaign system encourages incentive and responsibility for the tasks proposed by the team. In this sense it is similar to the RRIs. It also reduces the white space risk because the whole process is decomposed into small semiindependent actions. It certainly is not a flawless system. In particular, the Globus project development cycle is time constrained by important events, such as the Supercomputing conference, as well as community-imposed deadlines, related to implementations of new standards. The voice of important industry partners, such as IBM, must also be heard when scheduling releases. In this context, the long-term schedule for the core campaigns is often the consensus of the political will of project management, customer community, and partners. There is little or no space for adjustments of actions and the intended agility of development must often give room to the rather stiff cycle of milestones and releases.

The agility of the process at large is the decision that must be taken and accepted by developer as well as the customer. With a large and rather differentiated customer base, this is rather difficult. Therefore larger projects constrained by sophisticated relationships with partners and the community must balance between agility and strict major release schedules. There is still a place internally for elements of agile methods.

Treat Customers as Partners

In agile development, users have an important role in the process as the evaluators of the work and the ones who eventually will need to cope with it. The Globus Project was successful in attracting a large community of customers. However, when the number of users grew, more teams started examining the code and the list of complaints grew. The state of user-centered documentation frequently raised concern. Version instability of the toolkit was another reason for community frustration. People developing on top of Globus spoke of "trying to hit a moving target." Some teams stopped the development, watching in amazement how new versions of the toolkit showed up, before they managed to learn the old one. Some parts of the market looked for different solutions such as barebones Web services or Unicore, where limited functionality was compensated by feature stability and a friendly graphical end-user interface.

To address this growing concern, the Globus project chose the toolkit version 2.x for continued support, even long after the revamped version 3 became available. With big vendors issuing support statements to the WSRF standards, many groups refrained from developing on Globus 3, hoping that Globus Toolkit 4 will become another stable platform. Globus Toolkit version 4, indeed based on WSRF, became available in April 2005.

The position of a market leader is definitely difficult as it goes together with support of a large and differentiated user base. It is important to acknowledge that although some forward-thinking users will want improvements and constant change, others will want the stability necessary to build on top.

Treat Developers as Partners

To complete the picture of agile development, we should cite typical errors when introducing these principles. The agile development philosophy shifts the decision-making focus from management to developers. Developers often better understand the low-level problems and like to have their voices heard in decisions that affect them. If this shift of responsibility cannot happen, the entire attempt to deploy the agile process may fail.

The RRI of small evolutionary steps cannot transform into an endless chain of highly demanding goals. The effectiveness of RRI is that it consumes all energy into a single, well-visible goal. If the agile process requires frequent software releases to obtain rapid customer feedback, these releases should not be perceived by the team as energy-consuming milestones, but rather as natural steps in the development process.

Refactoring, as good as it seems in theory, has its limits. The human nature of the passionate programmer requires that he sees new results and new challenges, while the software being developed becomes more intelligent and more powerful. Endless refactoring of same feature set resulting from technology changes is not intellectually stimulating and can have negative effects on morale.

Finally, although the XP promotes collective code ownership, it is natural that people are proud of their own work and like to assume a leader's role with respect to the code they have produced. A programmer who puts all his energy into creating something he is proud of will be discouraged if he is moved to another project while other developers revamps his original code to "improve" it. Certainly, the effort the first programmer will devote to his next project will be rather moderate, since the personal attitude will go away, while the resignation and routine will appear.

No one likes to feel like a replaceable module in the human resources machine, and the agile development should not be a tool for this. People need to see their skills and achievements appreciated. For the project to benefit from personal attitudes of the team, people's emotional attachment to their work, which inevitably follows the completed assignments, must be respected.

Summary

In 1995, Deloitte and Touche surveyed a large numbers of CIOs with regard to why new and innovative projects failed. Most commonly quoted barriers to change were change resistance, lack of sponsorship, unrealistic expectations, poor management, uncompelling business case, lack of skills, project scope uncertainty, lack of change management plan, lack of holistic process view, and nonintegration of IT perspective. Results of this decade-old survey should have educational value for those managing Grid projects today. In this chapter we provided thoughts, supported by examples from our own and community experience, on how these barriers to change could be approached and overcome. In some cases, such as the white space risk and the RRI, we followed theory from outside the Grid community, which matched quite well what was intuitively deployed by many Grid projects and leading vendors.

Creation of a compelling Grid business case should be the first step in the project, followed by definition of its scope and assurance of adequate sponsorship. Change management principles should be used to lower change resistance. White space risk elimination techniques can compensate for inexperience in the global view of the process. Any lack of experience can be quickly repaired by engagement of external resources and initiation of knowledge transfer process. RRI actions injected in the course of the project will allow plan corrections during the execution. Agile programming methodologies will come in handy to correct unrealistic and unstable requirements, at the same time strengthening the code quality, as well as the personal attitude of the development team.

Although this chapter resulted from a collection of the best available community practices, we must acknowledge that the art of managing Grid migration and development projects is far from an organized discipline. The future will certainly bring more research to this subject, and perhaps some uniform theories will emerge.

Afterword

Work on this book has been an adventure for us. We made the best effort to present a comprehensive coverage of a subject that to our knowledge hasn't yet been addressed in a methodical way. Large parts of the material came from our own knowledge and experience of working with grids and the Grid computing community. These sections were easiest to write. Other material resulted from numerous interviews with brave early adopters, Grid visionaries, technologists, managers, vendors, consultants, and market observers. This was difficult but exciting work, during which we met fascinating people, learned a great deal, and in some cases changed the perception of the subject. Finally, there were sections of the material that required us to set out on a quest to a virtually unknown ground, where we had to make our way in the bush through studying related arts, making analogies, putting together pieces of knowledge that had never before been compared, drawing hypotheses and arguing against them, and consulting with our mentors and reviewers.

We acknowledge that an early work like this must be controversial in some circles and has to at least generate discussion. Moreover, we must realize that the network effect is at work and the world of Grid computing that we just described is changing incredibly quickly. Therefore we like to think of this book as an open project which is not complete, but continues to evolve. For this reason we designed the online companion for this project, www.savvy-grid.com to remain as the living counterpart of this "Savvy Manager's Guide" which is now frozen in print.

We live in a fascinating epoch in history. For the first time ever mass communication is becoming bi-directional. The Internet is giving us, as authors, the previously unheard of opportunity to become not solely the speakers, but to hear the voices of our readers. And you, as the readers, can hear what other readers are saying and yourself be heard as well. We do not want to loose this opportunity; we want to transform this monologue into a dialogue heard at savvygrid.com.

Please feel welcome to visit this site to witness the evolution of the subject and contribute to the common knowledge of using Grid computing in business.

Pawel Plaszczak and Richard Wellner, Jr.

Index

National Center for Supercomputing
        Applicatoins (NCSA), 106
National Partnership for Advanced
        Computational Infrastructure,
        98
National Science Foundation (NSF), 102
NEESgrid cyberinfrastructure, 121, 122,
        123, 200, 214–215, 224, 225,
        227
    accomplishments, 109
    case study, 101–103
    data acquisition systems in, 161
    as example of partner grid, 69
    hardware basis, 105–106
    NTCP system, 96
    software, 106
    technical overview, 103–105
    testing and quality management,
        108–109
    user communication problems,
        106–108
Net effect, 2, 26
Netsolve, 30
Network File System (NFS), 29
Network pipes, 33
Network providers, 112, 134
    analogy to Grid infrastructure
        providers, 132
Networking Services, 88
Networks, as resources providing
        transport bandwidths, 33
New product introduction, change driven
        by, 209
NEXTGRID, 85
NICE (Italy), 89, 98
Niche markets, 111
Niche vendors, 86–87
Ninf, 30
NNTP, 38
Noncomputational resources, 33–35
Nontrivial Quality of Service (QoS), as
        requirement of grids, 57
North Carolina BioGrid, 76
North Carolina Research and
        Education Network (NCREN),
        76–77
North Carolina State University, 76

O

OASIS, 39, 83, 188
    Security Assertion Markup Language
        (SAML) authorization server,
        183
    transfer of Grid standards to, 62
Object-oriented programming model, 31
Off-the-shelf services, 166
    assembly by application developers,
        54
OGCE consortium, 97–98
OGSA-DAI interface, 146
Oil and gas research market, 74, 100
On-demand CPU resources, 175–176
On-demand provisioning, 25, 26, 41–42,
        114
    infrastructure cost-cutting through,
        43
    limitations of Web services for, 41
    location-independent, 138
    refactoring applications for, 136–138
    Rolls-Royce case study, 147
    without adding complexity, 36
Online companion book, 5, 65, 90
Open Grid Computing Environments
        collaboration, 97
Open Grid Service Architecture
        Authorization working group
        (GGF), 189
Open Grid Service Architecture (OGSA),
        41, 178
    application contents, 54
    case for, 50–53
    commercial applications of, 199
    composition services in, 53–54
    data services, 56
    databases compliant with, 67
    grouping services in, 53–54
    information and monitoring services
        in, 55
    installation, deployment, and
        provisioning services in, 54
    logging services, 55
    messaging services in, 55
    metering, accounting, and billing
        services in, 54

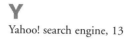